English in Energy and Power Engineering

能源与动力工程专业英语

（第4版）

主　编　吕　薇　李瑞扬
主　审　李九如　王　芳

哈尔滨工业大学出版社

内容提要

本书涵盖了能源与动力工程专业的主要分支学科,以培养能源与动力工程专业学生的专业英语阅读能力为主要目标。全书共分七部分,主要内容为:流体力学与流体机械,热力学与传热,燃料及燃烧,空调与制冷,锅炉,涡轮机,环保与腐蚀,以及参考译文等,书后附录中还给出了常用缩写词和常用英文计量单位换算。本书具有较强的实用性和知识性,高等院校能源与动力工程专业的本科生和研究生可根据其选修方向有针对性地学习相关单元内容。

本书既可作为高校能源与动力工程专业学生的专业英语教材,也可供从事相关专业的工程技术人员学习、参考之用。

图书在版编目(CIP)数据

能源与动力工程专业英语/吕薇,李瑞扬主编. —4 版.

哈尔滨:哈尔滨工业大学出版社,2016.8(2024.1 重印)

ISBN 978-7-5603-5863-5

Ⅰ.①能… Ⅱ.①吕… ②李… Ⅲ.①能源-英语 ②动力工程-英语 Ⅳ.H31

中国版本图书馆 CIP 数据核字(2016)第 032381 号

责任编辑	王桂芝
封面设计	卞秉利
出版发行	哈尔滨工业大学出版社
社　　址	哈尔滨市南岗区复华四道街 10 号　邮编 150006
传　　真	0451-86414749
网　　址	http://hitpress.hit.edu.cn
印　　刷	哈尔滨市工大节能印刷厂
开　　本	880 mm×1 230 mm　1/32　印张 11.875　字数 328 千字
版　　次	2000 年 1 月第 1 版　2016 年 8 月第 4 版 2024 年 1 月第 4 次印刷
书　　号	ISBN 978-7-5603-5863-5
定　　价	35.00 元

(如因印装质量问题影响阅读,我社负责调换)

第4版前言

《能源与动力工程专业英语》(原书名:《热能与动力工程专业英语》)一书自2000年1月出版以来,受到广大高校师生和相关专业技术人员的欢迎。目前国内已有多所高校将此书作为能源与动力工程的专业英语教材,并在教学中收到良好效果。本书已修订4次,重印7次,读者反馈意见较好,为了进一步满足教学要求和读者需要,增强本书的科学性和实用性,综合各校使用的情况,在保证本书基本体系和主要内容不变的前提下,此版做了如下修改:

(1) 第一、四、五部分内容做了替换;

(2) 为了突出内容的完整性,在内容编排上进行了适当增减和调整,充实了更能突出反映本学科发展的相关内容;

(3) 对各课生词及译文进行了核准和调整。

由于参与修订本书的人员及分工有变,书中各部分的负责人员、主编、主审等都发生了变化。全书由英文原文、参考译文及附录组成,英文部分共分七部分,其中第一部分由陈伟锋编写,第四部分由苏宝焕编写,第五部分由姜姗、李瑞扬编写,第二、三、六部分及参考译文部分由吕薇编写,第七部分、附录等由李瑞扬编写。全书由吕薇、李瑞扬主编,由李九如、王芳主审。

由于编者水平有限,对书中的不足之处,请广大读者批评指正。

编　者
2016年6月

CONTENTS

1 Fluid Mechanics and Fluid Machines
   1.1 The Viscosity of Fluids .... (1)
   1.2 The Continuum Hypothesis, Density and Specific Volume of Fluid .... (5)
   1.3 Perfect Gas .... (7)
   1.4 Fluid Flow .... (10)
   1.5 Fluid Machinery .... (14)
   1.6 The Surface Tension of Fluid .... (22)

2 Thermodynamics and Heat Transfer
   2.1 Basic Concepts of Thermodynamics .... (28)
   2.2 Thermodynamic Systems .... (32)
   2.3 General Characteristics of Heat Transfer .... (34)
   2.4 Conduction .... (37)
   2.5 Natural Convection .... (41)
   2.6 Radiation .... (44)

3 Fuels and Combustion
   3.1 Heat of Combustion .... (48)
   3.2 Combustion Equipment .... (52)
   3.3 Fuel-ash .... (55)
   3.4 The Mechanisms of Gaseous Fuels Combustion .... (59)
   3.5 The Combustion of Liquid Fuels and Solid Fuels ..... (63)
   3.6 Nuclear Fuels .... (69)
   3.7 Liquid By-product Fuels .... (73)

4 Air-conditioning and Refrigeration
   4.1 Air-conditioning .... (76)
   4.2 Air-Conditioning Cycle .... (80)

- 4.3 Refrigeration ………………………………………………… (82)
- 4.4 Ideal Single-stage Vapor Compression Cycle ……………… (85)
- 4.5 Refrigeration Compressors ………………………………… (90)
- 4.6 Refrigeration Systems ……………………………………… (97)
- 4.7 Absorption System ………………………………………… (107)
- 4.8 Air-Conditioning Systems ………………………………… (116)

5 Boiler
- 5.1 Fossil-fuel Boilers for Electric Utilities …………………… (125)
- 5.2 Selection of Coal-burning Equipment …………………… (129)
- 5.3 Superheaters and Reheaters ……………………………… (136)
- 5.4 Boiler and Its Role Playing in National Economy ………… (145)
- 5.5 Technical Economic Indices of Boiler …………………… (151)
- 5.6 Brief History of Boiler …………………………………… (158)
- 5.7 Basic Components and General Working Processes of a Boiler … (165)
- 5.8 Classifications and Types of Boilers ……………………… (171)
- 5.9 Basic Operating Principles ………………………………… (175)

6 Turbine
- 6.1 Steam Turbine ……………………………………………… (180)
- 6.2 Gas Turbine ………………………………………………… (186)
- 6.3 Compressor ………………………………………………… (193)
- 6.4 Gas Turbine Plants ………………………………………… (196)
- 6.5 Classification of Steam Turbines …………………………… (200)
- 6.6 Current Practice and Trends of Turbine …………………… (204)
- 6.7 The Modern Steam Power Plant …………………………… (207)
- 6.8 Wind Turbines ……………………………………………… (215)
- 6.9 The Principle of Steam Turbine …………………………… (221)

7 Environmental Protection, Corrosion and Others
- 7.1 Ash Removal and Disposal ………………………………… (228)
- 7.2 Oil-ash Corrosion ………………………………………… (233)
- 7.3 Control of Pollutant Gases ………………………………… (240)
- 7.4 Fans ………………………………………………………… (246)
- 7.5 Stokers ……………………………………………………… (250)
- 7.6 Flue Gas Desulfunzation …………………………………… (255)

7.7	Steam Separation	(260)
7.8	Pulverizers	(265)
7.9	Prevention of Scaling in Boilers	(271)
7.10	Air Pollution	(275)
7.11	Pressure Measurement	(278)
7.12	Clean Coal Teachnologies	(286)

参考译文

流体黏度(1.1)	(291)
流体的连续性假设、密度和比体积(1.2)	(293)
热力学的基本概念(2.1)	(294)
导热(2.4)	(296)
液体燃料和固体燃料的燃烧(3.5)	(297)
核燃料(3.6)	(299)
液态副产品燃料(3.7)	(302)
空气调节(4.1)	(303)
空调循环(4.2)	(305)
制冷(4.3)	(306)
电力公用事业电站燃用矿物燃料的锅炉(5.1)	(308)
过热器和再热器(5.3)	(310)
锅炉的技术经济指标(5.5)	(316)
锅炉的发展历史(5.6)	(318)
汽轮机(6.1)	(320)
燃气轮机(6.2)	(323)
除灰及灰的处理(7.1)	(327)
油灰腐蚀(7.2)	(329)
压力测量(7.11)	(333)
洁净煤技术(7.12)	(335)

附录Ⅰ	常用缩写词	(338)
附录Ⅱ	常用计量单位换算	(367)

1

Fluid Mechanics and Fluid Machines

1.1 The Viscosity of Fluids

Of all the fluid properties, viscosity requires the greatest consideration in the study of fluid flow. The nature and characteristics of viscosity are discussed in this section, as well as dimensions and conversion factors for both absolute and kinematic viscosity. Viscosity is that property of a fluid by virtue of which it offers resistance to shear. Newton's law of viscosity states that for a given rate of angular deformation of fluid the shear stress is directly proportional to the viscosity. Molasses and tar are examples of highly viscous liquids; water and air have very small viscosities.

The viscosity of a gas increases with temperature, but the viscosity of a liquid decreases with temperature. The variation in temperature trends can be explained by examining the causes of viscosity. The resistance of a fluid to shear depends upon its cohesion and upon its rate of transfer of molecular momentum. A liquid, with molecules much more closely spaced than a gas, has cohesive forces much larger than a gas.

Cohesion appears to be the predominant cause of viscosity in a liquid; and since cohesion decreases with temperature, the viscosity does likewise. A gas, on the other hand, has very small cohesive forces. Most of its resistance to shear stress is the result of transfer of molecular momentum.

As a rough model of the way in which momentum transfer gives rise to an apparent shear stress, consider two idealized railroad cars loaded with sponges and on parallel tracks, as in Fig. 1.1. Assume each car has a water tank and pump so arranged that the water is directed by nozzles at right angles to the track. First, consider A stationary and B moving to the right, with the water from its nozzles striking A and being absorbed by the sponges. Car A will be set in motion owing to the component of the momentum of the jets which is parallel to the tracks, giving rise to an apparent shear stress between A and B. Now if A is pumping water back into B at the same rate, its action tends to slow down B and equal and opposite apparent shear forces result. When both A and B are stationary or have the same velocity, the pumping does not exert an apparent shear stress on either car.

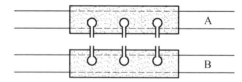

Fig. 1.1 Model illustrating transfer of momentum

Within fluid there is always a transfer of molecules back and forth across any fictitious surface drawn in it. When one layer moves relative to an adjacent layer, the molecular transfer of momentum brings momentum from one side to the other so that an apparent shear stress is set up that resists the relative motion and tends to equalize the velocities of adjacent layers in a manner analogous to that of Fig. 1.1. The measure of the motion of one layer relative to an adjacent layer is $\dfrac{du}{dy}$.

Molecular activity givesthe rise to an apparent shear stress in gases which is more important than the cohesive forces and since molecular activity increases with temperature, the viscosity of a gas also increases with temperature.

For ordinary pressures viscosity is independent of pressure and depends upon temperature only. For very great pressures, gases and most liquids have shown erratic variations of viscosity with pressure.

A fluid at rest or in motion so that no layer moves relative to an adjacent layer will not have apparent shear forces set up, regardless of the viscosity, because du/dy is zero throughout the fluid. Hence, in the study fluid static, no shear forces can be considered because they do not occur in a static fluid, and the only stresses remaining are normal stresses, or pressures. This greatly simplifies the study of fluid static, since any free body of fluid can have only gravity forces and normal surface forces acting on it.

The dimensions of viscosity are determined from Newton's law of viscosity. Solving for the viscosity μ, and inserting dimensions F, L, T for force, length, and time, shows that μ has the dimensions $FL^{-2}T$. With the force dimension expressed in terms of mass by use of Newton's second law of motion, $F = M \cdot LT^{-2}$, the dimensions of viscosity may be expressed as $ML^{-1}T^{-1}$.

The SI unit of viscosity, the Newton-second per square meter $((N \cdot s)/m^2)$ or the kilogram per meter per second $(kg/(m \cdot s))$, has no name. The U.S. customary unit of viscosity (which has no name) is

1(lb · s)/ft² or 1 slug/(ft · s)(these are identical). A common unit of viscosity is the cgs unit, called the poise; it is 1 (dyne · s)/cm² or 1 g/(cm · s). The SI unit is 10 times larger than the poise unit.

The viscosity μ is frequently referred to as the absolute viscosity or the dynamic viscosity to avoid confusing it with the kinematic viscosity v which is the ratio of viscosity to mass density:

$$v = \frac{\mu}{\rho} \quad (1.1)$$

The kinematic viscosity occurs in many applications, e. g. in the dimensionless Reynolds number for motion of a body through fluid, VL/v, in which V is the body velocity and L is a representative linear measure of the body size. The dimensions of v are $L^2 T^{-1}$. The SI unit of kinematic viscosity is 1 m²/s, and the U. S. customary unit is 1 ft²/s. The cgs unit, called the Stoke, is 1 cm²/s.

In SI units, to convert from v to μ it is necessary to multiply v by ρ, the mass density in kilograms per cubic meter. In U. S. customary units μ is obtained from v by multiplying by the mass density in slugs per cubic foot. To change from the Stokes to the poise, one multiplies by mass density in grams per cubic centimeter, which is numerically equal to specific gravity.

Viscosity is practically independent of pressure and depends upon temperature only. The kinematic viscosity of liquids, and of gases at a given pressure is substantially a function of temperature.

Words and Expressions

viscosity　　[vɪˈkɑsətɪ]　　n. 黏性
characteristic　　[ˌkærɪktəˈrɪstɪk]　　n/adj. 典型的,特有的
dimension　　[dɪˈmenʃn]　　n/v. 规模,尺寸,在……上标尺寸
resistance　　[rɪˈzɪstəns]　　n. 电阻,阻力,抵抗,抗力
shear　　[ʃɪə(r)]　　v/n. 剪切,穿越,大剪刀

angular ['æŋgjələ(r)] *adj.* 有角的,用角测量的,角度的
deformation [ˌdiːfɔːˈmeɪʃn] *n.* 变形,形态损伤
proportional [prəˈpɔːʃənl] *n/adj.* 比例的,比例项,比例量
cohesion [kəʊˈhiːʒn] *n.* 凝聚,内聚,(各部的)结合
molecular [məˈlekjələ(r)] *adj.* 分子的,由分子组成的
stationary [ˈsteɪʃənri] *n/adj.* 固定物,不动的,静止的,不变的
momentum [məˈmentəm] *n.* 动量,要素
velocity [vəˈlɑsəti] *n.* 速率,速度,周转率
apparent [əˈpærənt] *adj.* 易看见的,可看见的,显然
kinematic [ˌkɪnɪˈmætɪk] *adj.* 运动的,运动学的
dimensionless [dəˈmenʃənləs] *adj.* 无量纲的,无因次的

1.2 The Continuum Hypothesis, Density and Specific Volume of Fluid

Obviously there are gaps between the fluid and all substances molecules. In fluid mechanics, the macrofluid is consisted of a large number of molecules, the physical quantities of macrofluid (such as pressure, velocity and density) is the statistical average of the action and the behavior of most fluid molecules. In 1753, the continuous media was first proposed as macrofluid model by Euler. The real fluid is considered as no-gap continuous media, called the basic assumption of continuity fluid of fluid or the continuum of fluid.

In dealing with fluid-flow relations on a mathematical or analytical basis, it is necessary to consider that the actual molecular structure is replaced by a hypothetical continuous medium, called the continuum, for example, velocity at a point in space is indefinite in a molecular medium, as it would be zero at all times except when a molecule occupied this exact point, and then it would be the velocity of the molecule and not the mean mass velocity of the particles in the neighborhood. This dilemma is avoided if one considers velocity at a point to be the average or mass velocity of all molecules surrounding the point, say, within a small sphere with radius large compared with the mean distance between molecules. With n molecules per cubic centimeter, the mean distance between molecules is of the order $n^{-1/3}$ cm. Molecular theory, however, must be used to calculate fluid properties (e. g. viscosity) which are associated with molecular motions, but continuum equations can be employed with the results of molecular calculations.

In rarefied gases such as the atmosphere at 50 mi above sea level the ratio of the mean free path or the gas to a characteristic length for a body or conduit is used to distinguish the type of flow, The flow regime is called gas dynamics for very small values of the ratio; the next regime is called slip flow; and for large values of the ratio it is free molecule flow. In this text only the gas-dynamics regime is studied.

The quantities density, specific volume, pressure, velocity and acceleration are assumed to vary continuously throughout a fluid (or be constant).

The density ρ of a fluid is defined as its mass per unit volume.

Density $\rho = \dfrac{\text{mass}}{\text{volume}}$, that is Eq. (1.2).

$$\rho = \frac{m}{V} \tag{1.2}$$

To define density at a point, the mass $\triangle m$ of fluid in a small volume $\triangle V$ surrounding the point is divided by $\triangle V$ and the limit is becomes a value ε^3 in which ε is still large compared with the mean distance between molecules. For water at standard pressure (760 mmHg) and 4 ℃ (39.2 ℉), $\rho = 1.94$ (slug · s)/ft^3, or 1 000 kg/m^3.

The specific volume v_s is the reciprocal of the density ρ ; it is the volume occupied by unit mass of fluid. Hence

$$v_s = \frac{1}{\rho} \tag{1.3}$$

Words and Expressions

hypothesis [haɪ'pɑθəsɪs] n. 假设,假说
gap [gæp] n. 间隙
macrofluid ['mækrə'flʊ(:)ɪd] n. 宏观流体
continuity [ˌkɒntɪ'njuːəti] n. 连续性,继续
analytical [ˌænə'lɪtɪkl] adj. 分析的,分析法的,善于分析的
structure ['strʌktʃə(r)] n. 结构,构造
radius ['reɪdiəs] n. 半径范围,半径
continuum [kən'tɪnjuəm] n. 连续统一体
rarefied ['reərɪfaɪd] adj. 纯净的,稀薄的

1.3 Prefect Gas

In this treatment, thermodynamic relations and compressible-fluid-flow cases have been limited generally to perfect gases. The perfect gas is defined in this section.

The perfect gas, as used herein, is defined as a substance that satisfied the perfect-gas law. And that has constant specific heats p is the absolute pressure; v_s is the specific volume; R is the gas constant; and T is the absolute temperature.

$$pv_s = RT \tag{1.4}$$

The perfect gas must be distinguished from the ideal fluid. An ideal fluid is frictionless and incompressible. The perfect gas has viscosity and can therefore develop shear stresses, and it is compressible according to Eq. (1.4).

Equation (1.4) is the equation of state for a perfect gas. It may be written Eq. (1.5).

$$p = \rho RT \qquad (1.5)$$

The units of R can be determined from the equation when the other units are known. For p in pascals, ρ in kilograms per cubic meter, and T in degrees Kelvin(K) (℃+273).

Real gases below critical pressure and above the critical temperature tend to obey the perfect-gas law.

As the pressure increase, the discrepancy increases and becomes serious near the critical point.

The perfect-gas law encompasses both Charles' law and Boyle's law states that for constant pressure the volume of a given mass of gas varies as its absolute temperature. Boyle's law (Isothermal law) states that for constant temperature the density varies directly as the absolute pressure. The volume V of m mass units of gas is mv_s; hence

$$pV = mRT \qquad (1.6)$$

Certain simplications result from writing the perfect-gas law on a mole basis. A kilogram mole of gas is the number of kilograms mass of gas equal to the molecular weight. e.g, a kilogram mole of oxygen O_2 is 32 kg. With $\overline{v}_s$ being the volume per mole, the perfect-gas law becomes

$$p\overline{v}_s = MRT \qquad (1.7)$$

If m is the molecular weight. In general, if n is the number of moles of the gas in volume V.

$$pV = nMRT \qquad (1.8)$$

Since $nM = m$ Now, from Avogadro's law, equal volumes of gases at the same absolute temperature and pressure have the same number of molecules; hence their masses are proportional to the molecular weights. From Eq. (1.8) it is seen that MR must be constant, since pV/nT is the same for any perfect gas. The product MR, called the universal gas constant, has a value depending only upon the units employed.

The specific heat C_V of a gas is the number of units of heat added per unit mass to raise the temperature of the gas one degree when the volume is held constant. The specific heat C_P is the number of heat units added per unit mass to raise the temperature one degree when the temperature is hold constant. The specific heat ratio k is $\dfrac{C_P}{C_V}$. The intrinsic energy U(dependent upon p, ρ, and T) is the energy per unit mass due to molecular spacing and forces. The enthalpy (h) h is an important property of a gas given by Eq. (1.9).

$$h = U + pV \qquad (1.9)$$

C_P and C_V have the units kilocalorie per kilogram per Kelvin (kcal/(kg · K)) or Btu per pound mass per degree Rankine. One kilocalorie of heat added raises the temperature of one kilogram of water one degree Celsius at standard conditions. One Btu of heat added raises the temperature of one pound mass of water one degree Fahrenheit. Because of these definitions of kilocalorie and Btu, the numerical values of C_V and C_P are the same in both systems of units. R is related to C_V and C_P by Eq. (1.10).

$$C_P = C_V + R \qquad (1.10)$$

In which all quantities must be in either mechanical or thermal units. If the slug unit is used, C_P, C_V, and R are 32.174 times greater than with the pound mass unit.

Words and Expressions

thermodynamic　[θɛːməudaɪ'næmɪk]　*adj.* 热力学的,使用热动力的
substance　['sʌbstəns]　*n.* 物质,材料,实质,内容
frictionless　[f'rɪkʃnles]　*adj.* 无摩擦的,光滑的
incompressible　[ˌɪnkəm'presəbl]　*adj.* 不可压缩的

Kelvin ['kelvɪn] n. 绝对温标,开氏温标
discrepancy ['dis‚krepənsi] n. 矛盾,差异,不符合之处
kilocalorie ['kɪləʊ‚kælərɪ] n. 千卡,大卡(热量单位)
prefect gas 理想气体

1.4　Fluid Flow

Fluid mechanics deals with the behaviour of liquids and gases. The liquid is either at rest or in motion. Fluid at rest is fluid statics; examples such as water in a container or reservoir of water behind a dam. Fluid at rest has weight and exerts pressure. Fluid in motion is fluid dynamics. Examples are rivers, flow in pipes, flow in pumps and turbines. The fluids that are commonly studied are air and water. External flow is study of fluid flow over car, aeroplane, ships and rockets. Flow in pipes, impellers of pumps are referred to as internal flow. Compressible flow is when density does not remain constant with application of pressure. Incompressible flow is the density remains constant with application of pressure. Water is incompressible whereas air is compressible. Compressibility criteria is Mach number.

The chapter deals with the concept of momentum and Newton's second and third law of motion. With the knowledge of continuity equation and momentum equation, Bernoullis and Eulers equations are derived. With the help of second law of Newton force acting by a jet on stationary and moving plate is obtained. The impact of jet on vanes has direct application on hydraulic turbines.

Scope of Fluid Mechanics

The dimensional analysis deals with the units of measurement in SI units both fundamental and derived units, and non-dimentional quatities.

The properties of fluids deal with measurement of mass, density, specific weight, specific gravity, compressibility of fluids, surface tension, capillary action.

The fluid statics deals with fluid pressure, fluid at rest, manometry, hydrostatic forces, buoyancy floation and stability.

The fluid kinematics deals with one, two and three-dimensional flows, steady and unsteady flows, Reynold's number, streamlines, streaklines and pathlines.

The internal flowsdeal with now in pipes, pumps, laminar and turbulent flows in pipes, single and multipipe system, Moody chart, minor losses, velocity profiles for laminar and turbulent flows.

The external flow deals with flow over immersed bodies, lift and drag concepts, boundary layer laminar and turbulent, friction drag, pressure drag and drag coefficients.

The flow in turbomachines deals with energy considerations, angular momentum considerations, centrifugal pump and their characteristics, similarity laws, turbines, axial and rapid flow, impulse and reaction.

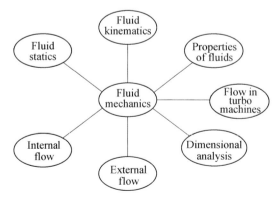

Fig. 1.2 Scope of Fluid Mechanics

Laminar and turbulent flow

The transport of fluid is done in closed conduit commonly called a pipe usually of round cross-section. The flow in pipes is laminar or turbulent; Osborne Reynolds has done experiment in pipe flow. Laminar flow is one where the streamline moves in parallel lines and turbulent flow when streamlines cross each other and the flow is diffused. Example: Flow of highly viscous syrup onto a pan cake, flow of honey is laminar whereas splashing water is from a faucet into a sink below it or irregular gustiness of wind represents turbulent flow. Reynold's number is to distinguish the two types of flow.

Reynolds number for the pipe flow is given by Eq. (1.11)

$$Re = \frac{\rho D v}{\mu} \quad (1.11)$$

where D diameter of pipe, ρ density, v velocity and μ viscosity of fluid.

If the flow is laminar Reynolds no. is less than 2 100 and if the flow is turbulent Reynolds no. is more than 4 000. The hydraulic losses depend on whether the flow is laminar or turbulent.

Momentum Equation for One-Dimensional Flow

The momentum of a particle of fluid is defined as the product of mass m and velocity v.

$$\text{Momentum} = mv$$

If there is a change in the velocity of the fluid there will be corresponding change in the momentum of the fluid. According to Newton's second law of motion, rate of change of momentum is proportional to the applied force.

In order to determine the rate of change of momentum, consider a control volume of the fluid ABCD as shown in Fig. 1.3.

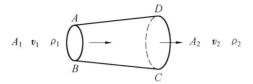

Fig. 1.3 Control volume for one-dimensional flow

Assuming the flow to be steady and also assuming there is no storage within the control volume, we may write the continuity equation for mass flow rate

$$m = \rho_2 A_2 v_2 = \rho_1 A_1 v_1 \qquad (1.12)$$

Rate of momentum across the boundary CD is mass flow rate times the velocity

$$\rho_2 A_2 v_2 \cdot v_2$$

Rate of momentum across the boundary AB is mass flow rate times the velocity

$$\rho_1 A_1 v_1 \cdot v_1$$

Rate of change of momentum across the control volume $ABCD$

$$\rho_2 A_2 v_2 \cdot v_2 - \rho_1 A_1 v_1 \cdot v_1$$

From the continuity of mass flow equation

$$\rho_1 A_1 v_1 \cdot (v_2 - v_1) = m(v_2 - v_1)$$

Thus rate of change of momentum is

$$m(v_2 - v_1)$$

According to Newton's law it is caused by a force, such as

$$F = m(v_2 - v_1) \qquad (1.13)$$

Note: Here the velocities have been assumed to be in straight line. One must remember that this is the force acting on the fluid and according to Newton's third law of motion, force exerted by the fluid will be opposite to this force.

Words and Expressions

external [ɪkˈstɜːnl] *adj.* 外部的,表面的
impeller [ɪmˈpelə] *n.* 叶轮,推进器
internal [ɪnˈtɜːnl] *adj.* 内部的,国内的,体内的
compressible [kəmˈpresɪbl] *adj.* 可压缩的
Bernoulli [bəːˈnuːli] *n.* 伯努利
Euler [ˈɔilə] *n.* 欧拉
scope [skəʊp] *n./v.* 范围,见识,审视,仔细研究
manometry [məˈnɒmɪtrɪ] *n.* 测压方法,压力测量法
hydrostatic [ˌhaɪdrəˈstætɪk] *adj.* 静水力学的,流体静力学的
streakline [stˈriːklaɪn] *n.* 纹线
laminar [ˈlæmɪnə] *n./adj.* 层流,层流的,薄片状的,薄层的
turbulent [ˈtɜːbjələnt] *adj.* 湍流的,激流的
coefficient [ˌkəʊɪˈfɪʃnt] *n./adj.* 系数,率,共同作用的,合作的
turbomachine [tɜːbəʊmæˈʃiːn] *n.* 涡轮机,叶轮机械
pump [ˈpʌmp] *n.* 泵,打气筒
capillary action 毛细作用
surface tension 表面张力
hydraulic turbines 水轮机
momentum equation for one-dimensional flow 一维流动动量方程

1.5 Fluid Machinery

Fluid machines can be classified as:
· Positive displacement machines.
· Rotodynamic machines.

In positive displacement machines fluid is drawn into a finite space bounded by mechanical parts, then sealed in it, and then forced out from space and the cycle is repeated. The flow is intermittent and depends on the dimensions of the space (chamber), and speed of the pump. Gear pumps, vane pumps are all positive displacement pumps.

In rotodynamic machines there is free passage between inlet and outlet of the machine without intermittent sealing taking place. In these machines there is a rotor which is able to rotate continuously and freely in the fluid. The transfer of energy is continuous which results in change of pressure or momentum of the fluid. Centrifugal blower, centrifugal pumps and hydraulic turbines are some examples of rotodynamic machines.

Fluid machines are dynamic fluid machines that add (for pump) or extract (for turbines) flow energy. The term pump is used when the working fluid is water or oil. The term compressor is used when the working fluid is air/gas. Fluid machines do a variety of jobs and are applied in hydro and thermal power stations, in aircraft as propulsive devices, in ships as propellers, in automobiles, and earth moving machinery.

Fluid machines serve in enormous array of applications in our daily lives, and they play an important role in modern world. The machines have a high power density (large power output per size of the machine) relatively few moving parts and high efficiency.

The two criteria, namely, the energy transfer and type of action, form the basis of classification of hydraulic machines, as shown in Fig. 1.4. From the chart it can be seen that pumps and compressors increase the energy of the fluid and may be positive displacement or rotodynamic. Fans are always rotodynamic. Turbine does work and is rotodynamic.

Further classification is based on flow and energy transfer. Fluid used as means of energy transfer.

(a) Classification based on the geometry of flow path:
· Radial flow;

- Axial flow;
- Mixed flow.

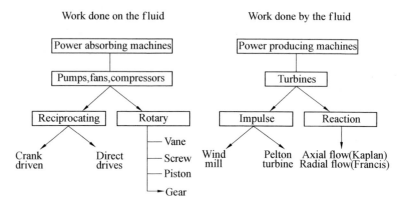

Fig. 1.4   Classification of fluid machines

In radial flow the flow path is essentially radial with significant changes in radius.

In axial flow machines the flow path is nearly parallel to the machine centre line and the path does not change.

In mixed flow it is partly axial and partly radial.

(b) Fluid machines can use any of the following forms of energy
- Heat energy(steam and gas turbines)
- Potential energy(hydraulic turbines)
- Kinetic energy(wind mills)

In power producing machines work is done by the fluid flow and in power absorbing machines work is done on the fluid to raise potential energy.

Fig. 1.5 shows power producing machine.

Fig. 1.6 shows power absorbing machine.

A pump is a turbo machine wherein the fluid is liquid and power is given by an electric motor to raise pressure of the fluid.

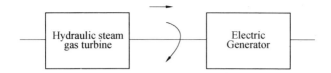

Fig. 1.5 Power producing machine

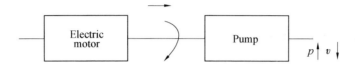

Fig. 1.6 Power absorbing machine

A compressor transmits power to a gas to raise pressure but with small increase in velocity (Fig. 1.7).

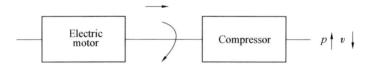

Fig. 1.7 Compressor transmits power

A fan imparts motion to gas with small change in pressure (Fig. 1.8).

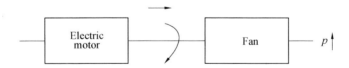

Fig. 1.8 Fan imparts motion

A fan blower increases the velocity of gas with small pressure Fig. 1.9. The steam and gas turbines, hydraulic machines come under first category, and pumps, fans, compressors come under second category. In power absorbing machines the driver is usually an electric motor but it can be also an I. C. engine or a gas turbine.

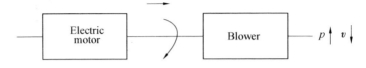

Fig. 1.9 Fan blower

Pumps(Axial and Radial)

A single-stage centrifugal pump is shown in Fig. 1.10. The rotating element is called the impeller which is contained within the pump housing or casing. The shaft transfers mechanical energy to impeller which must penetrate the casing, a system of bearings. Seals are required against the leakage of the fluid.

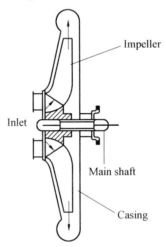

Fig. 1.10 Single-stage centrifugal pump

Fluid enters the machine nearly in axial direction at inlet through the eye of the impeller and leaves the impeller radially out. Flow leaving the impeller is collected in a scroll or volute, which gradually increases in area as fluid moves out through exit. The impeller has vanes to convey the fluid. A multi-stage pump is shown in Fig. 1.11.

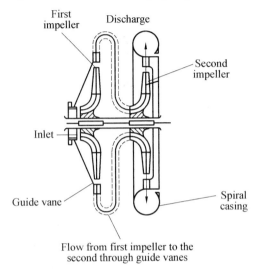

Fig. 1.11   Multi-stage centrifugal pump

In this pump exit of first impeller is connected to inlet of second impeller and pressure builds up.

An axial pump is shown in Fig. 1.12. The shaft is vertical and propeller type blades are fixed to it to form the impeller. The guide blades increase the pressure of the fluid.

Compressors (Axial and Radial)

A centrifugal compressor is shown in Fig. 1.13. Air enters the unit near axial through the eye of the impeller and flows radially outwards. There are diffuser vanes which increase the static pressure and guide air to the volute. The air leaves the volute at higher pressure. The impeller is mounted on a shaft supported by bearings.

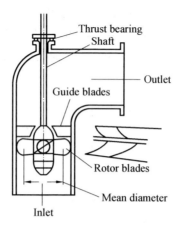

Fig. 1.12 Schematic diagram of an axial flow pump

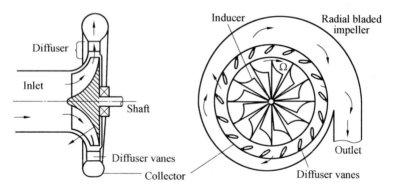

Fig. 1.13 Schematic diagram of a section of a centrifugal compressor

A typical blower is shown in Fig. 1.14. The impeller has vanes and air is discharged into volute which increases the pressure. An axial flow compressor is shown in Fig. 1.15. Flow enters nearly parallel to rotor axis and maintains nearly the same radius through the stage. A typical stage consists of a row of stationary vanes (S) and a row of rotating vanes (R) and pressure increases from stage to stage. Axial flow compressors are typically used in turbo-jet engines and are multistage compressors.

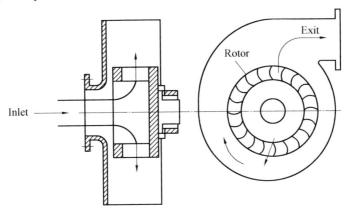

Fig. 1.14　Centrifugal blower

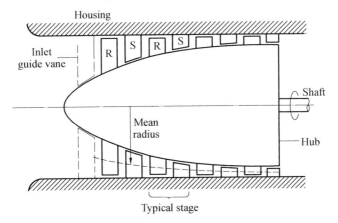

Fig. 1.15　Schematic diagram of an axial flow compressor

Turbines

Here is a brief introduction of turbine.

Machines that extract energy from fluid stream are called turbines. They are classified as:

- Hydraulic turbines (Pelton, Francis, Kaplan)
- Steam turbines
- Gas turbines

In hydraulic turbines the working fluid is water and is incompressible. More general classification of hydraulic turbines are:
- impulse
- reaction

Words and Expressions

intermittent [ˌɪntəˈmɪtənt] adj. 间歇性, 间歇的, 断断续续的
centrifugal [ˌsentrɪˈfjuːgl] adj. 离心的
hydraulic [haɪˈdrɔːlɪk] adj. 水利的, 液压的
enormous [ɪˈnɔːməs] adj. 巨大的, 庞大的
radial [ˈreɪdiəl] adj. 径向的, 辐射状的
axial [ˈæksiəl] adj. 轴的, 成轴的, 轴向的
compressor [kəmˈpresə(r)] n. 压缩机
vane [veɪn] n/adj. 叶, 风向标; 变化不定的, 反复无常的
turbine [ˈtɜːbaɪn] n. 涡轮机, 汽轮机

1.6　The Surface Tension of Fluid

Surface tension is a force which manifests itself only in liquids at an interface, usually a liquid-gas interface. And Surface tension is also the elastic tendency of a fluid surface which makes it acquire the least surface area possible. Surface tension allows insects (e.g. water striders), usually denser than water, to float and stride on a water surface.

At liquid-air interfaces, surface tension results from the greater attraction of liquid molecules to each other (due tocohesion) than to the molecules in the air (due to adhesion). The net effect is an inward force at its surface that causes the liquid to behave as if its surface were covered with a stretched elastic membrane. Thus, the surface becomes under tension from the imbalanced forces, which is probably where the term "surface tension" came from. Because of the relatively high attraction of water molecules for each other, water has a higher surface tension (72. 8 millinewtons per meter at 20 ℃) compared to that of most other liquids. Surface tension is an important factor in the phenomenon of capillarity.

Surface tension has units of force per unit length, is N/m. The force due to surface tension is the surface tension multiplied by the length or the circumference in case of a bubble or droplet of water. A surface tension effect can be illustrated by analysing a free-body diagram of half a droplet as shown in Fig. 1. 16.

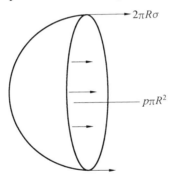

Fig. 1. 16   Internal force in a droplet

The pressure force exerted in the droplet is given by

$$F = p\pi R^2$$

The force due to surface tension is surface tension multiplied by the circumference and is

$$F = 2\pi R\sigma$$

The pressure force and tension force must balance each other

$$p\pi r^2 = 2\pi R\sigma$$

$$p = \frac{2\sigma}{R} \qquad (1.14)$$

In materials science, surface tension is used for either surface stress or surface free energy.

Causes

The cohesive forces among liquid molecules are responsible for the phenomenon of surface tension. In the bulk of the liquid, each molecule is pulled equally in every direction by neighboring liquid molecules, resulting in a net force of zero. The molecules at the surface do not have the same molecules on all sides of them and therefore are pulled inwards. This creates some internal pressure and forces liquid surfaces to contract to the minimal area.

Surface tension is responsible for the shape of liquid droplets. Although easily deformed, droplets of water tend to be pulled into a spherical shape by the imbalance in cohesive forces of the surface layer. In the absence of other forces, including gravity, drops of virtually all liquids would be approximately spherical. The spherical shape minimizes the necessary "wall tension" of the surface layer according to Laplace's law.

Another way to view surface tension is in terms of energy. A molecule in contact with a neighbor is in a lower state of energy than if it were alone (not in contact with a neighbor). The interior molecules have as many neighbors as they can possibly have, but the boundary molecules are missing neighbors (compared to interior molecules) and therefore have a higher energy. For the liquid to minimize its energy state, the number of higher energy boundary molecules must be minimized. The minimized quantity of boundary molecules results in a minimal surface area. As a result of surface area minimization, a surface will assume the smoothest shape it can (mathematical proof that "smooth" shapes minimize surface area relies on use of the Euler-Lagrange equation). Since any curvature in the surface shape results in greater area, a higher energy will also result. Consequently, the surface will push back against any curvature in much the same way as a ball pushed uphill will push back to minimize its gravitational potential energy.

Effects of surface tension

water

Several effects of surface tension can be seen with ordinary water:

(1) Beading of rain water on a waxy surface, such as a leaf. Wateradheres weakly to wax and strongly to itself, so water clusters into drops. Surface tension gives them their near-spherical shape, because a sphere has the smallest possible surface area to volume ratio.

(2) Formation ofdrops occurs when a mass of liquid is stretched. The animation shows water adhering to the faucet gaining mass until it is stretched to a point where the surface tension can no longer keep the drop linked to the faucet. It then separates and surface tension forms the drop into a sphere. If a stream of water was running from the faucet, the stream would break up into drops during its fall. Gravity stretches the stream, then surface tension pinches it into spheres.

(3) Flotation of objects denser than water occurs when the object is nonwettable and its weight is small enough to be borne by the forces arising from surface tension. For example, water striders use surface tension to walk on the surface of a pond. The surface of the water behaves like an elastic film: the insect's feet cause indentations in the

water's surface, increasing its surface area.

(4) Separation of oil and water (in thiscase, water and liquid wax) is caused by a tension in the surface between dissimilar liquids. This type of surface tension is called "interface tension", but its chemistry is the same.

(5) Tears of wine is the formation of drops and rivulets on the side of a glass containing an alcoholic beverage. Its cause is a complex interaction between the differing surface tensions of water and ethanol; it is induced by a combination of surface tension modification of water by ethanol together with ethanolevaporating faster than water.

Surfactants

Surface tension is visible in other common phenomena, especially when surfactants are used to decrease it:

- Soap bubbles have very large surface areas with very little mass. Bubbles in pure water are unstable. The addition of surfactants, however, can have a stabilizing effect on the bubbles (see Marangoni effect). Notice that surfactants actually reduce the surface tension of water by a factor of three or more.

- Emulsions are a type of solution in which surface tension plays a role. Tiny fragments of oil suspended in pure water will spontaneously assemble themselves into much larger masses. But the presence of a surfactant provides a decrease in surface tension, which permits stability of minute droplets of oil in the bulk of water (or vice versa).

Words and Expressions

manifest ['mænɪfest] v/adj. 显示,表明;明白的,明显的
interface ['ɪntəfeɪs] n. 界面,交界面
adhesion [əd'hi:ʒ(ə)n] n. 粘合,支持,粘连,黏附力
membrane ['membreɪn] n. 隔膜,薄膜

tension　　　　　['tenʃn]　　n. 张力,拉力
imbalance　　　[ɪm'bæləns]　　n. 不平衡,失调,不安定
capillarity　　　[ˌkæpɪ'lærɪtɪ]　　n. 毛细管作用,毛细管现象
multiplied　　　['mʌltɪplaɪd]　　v. (使)相乘,(使)增加,(使)繁殖
circumference　[sə'kʌmfərəns]　n. 胸围,周围,圆周
bubble　　　　['bʌbl]　　n/adj. 泡,水泡;起泡,使冒气泡
droplet　　　　['drɑplət]　　n. 滴,微滴,小水珠
minimal　　　　['mɪnɪməl]　　adj. 极小的,最小的,极少的
spherical　　　['sferɪkl]　　adj. 球形的,球面的,天体的,天空的
formation　　　[fɔː'meɪʃn]　　n. 形成,构成,结构,形成物
flotation　　　　[fləʊ'teɪʃn]　　n. 浮选,漂浮
separation　　　[ˌsepə'reɪʃn]　　n. 分离,分开,间隔
emulsion　　　　[ɪ'mʌlʃn]　　n. 乳剂,乳胶
surface tension　表面张力

2

Thermodynamics and Heat Transfer

2.1 Basic Concepts of Thermodynamics

Most applications of thermodynamics require that the system and its surroundings be defined. A thermodynamic system is defined as a region in space or a quantity of matter bounded by a closed surface. The surroundings include everything external to the system, and the system is separated from the surroundings by the system boundaries. These boundaries can be either movable or fixed; either real or imaginary.

Two master concepts operate in any thermodynamic system, energy and entropy. Entropy(s) measures the molecular disorder of a given system. The more shuffled a system is, the greater its entropy; conversely, an orderly or unmixed configuration is one of low entropy.

Energy is the capacity for producing an effect, and can be categorized into either stored or transient forms. Stored forms of energy include:

thermal(internal) energy, u—the energy(possessed by a system) caused by the motion of the molecules and/or intermolecular forces;

potential energy, $P.\ E.$ —the energy possessed by a system caused by the attractive forces existing between molecules, or the elevation of the system:

$$P.\ E. = mgz \tag{2.1}$$

where m = mass

g = local acceleration of gravity

z = elevation above a horizontal reference plane

kinetic energy, $K.\ E.$ —the energy possessed by a system caused by the velocity of the molecules:

$$K.\ E. = mv^2/2 \tag{2.2}$$

where m = mass

v = velocity of the fluid streams crossing system boundaries

chemical energy, E_c —energy possessed by the system caused by the arrangement of atoms composing the molecules.

nuclear (atomic) energy, E_a —energy possessed by the system from the cohesive forces holding protons and neutrons together as the atom's nucleus.

Transient energy forms include:

heat, Q —the mechanism (that transfers energy across the boundary of systems with differing temperatures), always in the direction of the lower temperature.

work—the mechanism that transfers energy across the boundary of systems with differing pressures (or force of any kind), always in the direction of the lower pressure; if the total effect produced in the system can be reduced to the raising of a weight, then nothing but work has crossed the boundary. Mechanical or shaft work, W, is the energy delivered or absorbed by a mechanism, such as a turbine, air compressor or internal combustion engine.

Flow work is energy carried into or transmitted across the system boundary because a pumping process occurs somewhere outside the system, causing fluid to enter the system. It can be more easily understood as the work done by the fluid just outside the system on the adjacent fluid entering the system to force or push it into the system. Flow work also occurs as fluid leaves the system.

$$\text{Flow Work (per unit mass)} = pV \qquad (2.3)$$

where p is the pressure and V is the specific volume, or the volume displaced per unit mass.

A property of a system is any observable characteristic of the system. The state of a system is defined by listing its properties. The most common thermodynamic properties are: temperature (T), pressure (p) and specific volume (V) or density (ρ). Additional thermodynamic properties include entropy, stored forms of energy and enthalpy.

Frequently, thermodynamic properties combine to form new properties. Enthalpy (h), a result of combining properties, is defined as:

$$h = u + pV \qquad (2.4)$$

where u = internal energy
p = pressure
V = specific volume

Each property in a given state has only one definite value, and any property always has the same value for a given state, regardless of how the substance arrived at that state.

A process is a change in state that can be defined as any change in the properties of a system. A process is described by specifying the initial and final equilibrium states, the path (if identifiable) and the interactions that take place across system boundaries during the process. A cycle is a process, or more frequently, a series of processes wherein the initial and final states of the system are identical. Therefore, at the conclusion of a cycle all the properties have the same value they had at the beginning.

A pure substance has a homogeneous and invariable chemical composition. It can exist in more than one phase, but the chemical composition is the same in all phases.

If a substance exists as vapor at the saturation temperature, it is called saturated vapor. (Sometimes the term dry saturated vapor is used to emphasize that the quality is 100%.) When the vapor is at a temperature greater than the saturation temperature, it is superheated vapor. The pressure and temperature of superheated vapor are independent properties, since the temperature can increase while the pressure remains constant. Gases are highly superheated vapors.

Words and Expression

thermodynamics　['θəməudai'næmiks]　n. 热力学
entropy　['entrəpi]　n. 熵(热力学函数)
shuffle　['ʃʌfl]　vt. 搅乱,弄混
configuration　[kən'figju'reiʃən]　n. 构造,结构
categorize　['kætigəraiz]　v. 把……分类
transient　['trænziənt]　a. (物)瞬变的
thermal　[θə:məl]　a. 热的
elevation　[,eli'veiʃən]　n. 高度
acceleration　[æk,selə'reiʃən]　n. (物)加速,加速度
kinetic　[kai'netik]　a. 动力(学)的,动力的
cohesive　[kəu'hi:siv]　a. 内聚的
proton　['prəutɔn]　n. 质子
neutron　['nju:trɔn]　n. 中子
mechanism　['mekənizəm]　n. 机械装置,机械结构
shaft　[ʃa:ft]　n. 轴

compressor [kəːmˈpresə] n. 压缩机,压气机
combustion [kəmˈbʌstʃən] n. 燃烧
adjacent [əˈdʒeisənt] a. 邻近的,因此相连的
specific volume 比容
displace [disˈpleis] vt. 排(水)
enthalpy [enˈθælpi] n. 给
equilibrium [iːkwiˈlibriəm] n. 平衡,均衡
homogeneous [hɔˈmɔdʒinəs] a. 均匀的
saturation [ˌsætʃəˈreiʃən] n. 饱和(状态)
saturated [ˈsætʃəreitid] a. 饱和的

2.2 Thermodynamic Systems

In the engineering world, objects normally are not isolated from one another. In most engineering problems many objects enter into a given problem. Some of these objects, all of these objects, or even additional ones may enter into a second problem. The nature of a problem and its solution are dependent on which objects are under consideration. Thus, it is necessary to specify which objects are under consideration in a particular situation. In thermodynamics this is done either by placing an imaginary envelope around the objects under consideration or by using an actual envelope if such exists. The term system refers to everything lying inside the envelope. The envelope, real or imaginary, is referred to as the boundaries of the system. It is essential that the boundaries of the system be specified very carefully. For example, when one is dealing with a gas in a cylinder where the boundaries are located on the outside of the cylinder, the system includes both the cylinder and its contained gas. On the other hand, when the boundaries are placed at the inner face of the cylinder, the system consists solely of the gas itself.

When the boundaries of a system are such that it cannot exchange matter with the surroundings, the system is said to be a closed system (see Fig. 2.1(a)). The system, however, may exchange energy in the form of heat or work with the surroundings. The boundaries of a closed system may be rigid or may expand or contract, but the mass of a closed system cannot change. Hence, the term control mass sometimes is used for this type of system. When the energy crossing the boundaries of a closed system is zero or substantially so, the system may be treated as an isolated system (Fig. 2.1(b)).

In most engineering problems, matter, generally a fluid, crosses the boundaries of a system in one or more places. Such a system is known as an open system (see Fig. 2.1(c)). The boundaries of an open system are so placed that their location does not change with time. Thus, the boundaries enclose a fixed volume, commonly known as the control volume.

Sometimes a system may be a closed system at one moment and an open one the next. For example, consider the cylinder of an internal combustion engine with the boundaries at the inner walls. With the valves closed, the system is a closed one. However, with either or both of the valves open, the system becomes an open system.

Frequently the total system to be considered may be large and complicated. The system may be broken down into component parts and an analysis of the component parts made. Then the performance of the entire system can be determined by the summation of the performance of the individual component systems. For example, consider the liquid-vapor part of a steam power plant as an entire system. This system, which is closed, contains the steam generator, the steam turbine, the steam condenser, the feed-water pumps, and the feed-water heaters. Any or all of these units may be considered

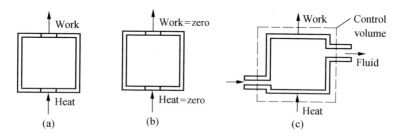

Fig. 2.1 Types of systems
(a) Closed system (b) Isolated system (c) Open system

separately by throwing a boundary around them. Since a fluid enters and leaves each of these smaller systems, each one is an open system and must be analyzed as such.

Words and Expression

isolate   ['aisəleit]   v. 使隔离,使独立
additional   [ə'diʃənəl]   a. 额外的,附加的,补充的
imaginary   [i'mædʒinəri]   a. 虚构的,想像的
envelope   ['enviləup]   n. 壳层,外壳,包裹物
cylinder   ['silində]   n. 圆筒,圆柱体,汽缸
boundary   ['baundəri]   n. 界线,分界,边界
location   [ləu'keiʃən]   n. 地点,位置,场地
individual   [ˌindi'vidjuəl]   a. 个别的,单独的,一个人的

2.3 General Characteristics of Heat Transfer

Heat or thermal energy is transferred from one region to another by three modes: conduction, convection and radiation. Each is important in the design or application of heating, air-conditioning or refrigeration equipment. Heat transfer is among the transport phenomena that include mass transfer, momentum transfer or fluid friction and electrical conduction. Transport phenomena have similar rate equations and flux is proportional to a potential difference. In heat transfer by conduction and convection, the potential difference is the temperature difference. Heat, mass and momentum transfer, because of their similarities and interrelationship in many common physical processes, receive unified treatment in some textbooks.

Thermal conduction is the mechanism of heat transfer whereby energy is transported between parts of a continuum from the transfer of kinetic energy between particles or groups of particles at the atomic level. In gases, conduction is a result of elastic collision of molecules; in liquids and electrically nonconducting solids, it is believed to be caused by longitudinal oscillations of the lattice structure. Thermal conduction in metals occurs like electrical conduction, through motions of free electrons. The second Law of Thermodynamics states that thermal transfer occurs in the direction of decreasing temperature. In solid opaque bodies, the significant heat transfer mechanism is thermal conduction, since there is no net material flow in the process. With flowing fluids, thermal conduction dominates in the region very close to a solid boundary where the flow is laminar and parallel to the surface, and there is no eddy motion.

Thermal convection may involve energy transfer by eddy mixing and diffusion in addition to conduction. Consider heat transfer to a fluid flowing inside a pipe. If the Reynolds number is sufficiently great, three different flow regions will exist. Immediately adjacent to the wall is a laminar sublayer where heat transfer occurs by thermal conduction; outside the laminar sublayer is a transition region called the buffer layer, where both eddy mixing and conduction effects are significant; beyond the buffer layer and extending to the center of the pipe is the turbulent region, where the dominant mechanism of transfer is eddy mixing.

In most equipment, the main body of fluid is in turbulent flow, and the laminar layer exists at the solid walls only. In cases of low velocity flow in small tubes, or with viscous liquids such as oil (i. e. , at low Reynolds numbers), the entire flow may be laminar with no transition or eddy region.

When fluid currents are produced by sources external to the heat transfer region, for example, a blower or pump, the solid-to-fluid heat transfer is termed forced convection. If the fluid flow is generated internally by nonhomogeneous densities caused by temperature variation, the heat transfer is termed free or natural convection.

In conduction and convection, heat transfer takes place through matter. For radiant heat transfer, there is a change in energy form; from internal energy at the source to electromagnetic energy for transmission, then back to internal energy at the receiver. Whereas conduction and convection are affected primarily by temperature difference and somewhat by temperature level, the heat transferred by radiation increases rapidly as the temperature increases.

Although some generalized heat transfer equations have been mathematically derived from fundamentals, usually they are obtained from correlations of experimental data. Normally, the correlations employ certain dimensionless numbers from analyses such as dimensional analysis or analogy.

Words and Expression

momentum [məu'mentəm] n. 动量,运动量
friction ['frikʃən] n. 摩擦(力),阻力
collision [kə'liʒən] n. 猛烈相撞,抵触(意见)冲突
lattice ['lætis] n. 格子,晶格
laminar ['læminə] a. 成薄层的,薄层状的
diffusion [di'fju:ʒən] n. 扩散,散布

nonhomogeneous ['nɔnhɔmə'dʒi:niəs] a. 非均匀的
correlation [ˌkɔri'leiʃən] n. 相互关联,交互作用,关联式
analogy [ə'nælədʒi] n. 类比,类推

2.4 Conduction

Heat transferred by conduction may be thought of as the heat transferred through a substance (or combination of substances) from a region of high temperature to a region of low temperature by the progressive exchange of energy between the molecules of the substance. In the process of transferring heat by conduction, no bodily displacement of the molecules occurs. In the case of metals, however, electron movement greatly assists in heat transfer by conduction.

The fundamental law of conduction is credited to Fourier. This law may be illustrated as follows. Consider steady-state, unidirectional heat flow through a solid, as is indicated in Fig. 2.2. Take a slab of the solid having a cross-sectional area A normal to the path of heat flow. Let the thickness of the slab be dx, and let the temperature difference across the slab be dt. From his experimental work Fourier developed the following relationship:

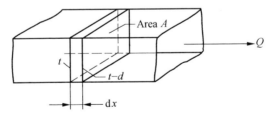

Fig. 2.2 Fourier's law of heat conduction

$$Q = -kA \frac{dt}{dx} \qquad (2.5)$$

where Q = heat flow per unit of time

k = proportionality factor, called the thermal conductivity

dt/dx = rate of change in temperature with distance in the direction of heat flow.

In the SI system of units, thermal conductivity may be expressed as

$$W/m^2 \div K/m = W/mK$$

Extensive experimental investigations have established the values of thermal conductivities of many substances and the effect of temperature on these conductivities. Note that the thermal conductivity of any metal is very high in comparison with that of any gas. The reported values of thermal conductivities of metals are valid only for metals of a given degree of purity. Particularly for those metals with the highest values of thermal conductivity, the introduction of a slight amount of another metal will cause a significant change in the thermal conductivity.

The best heat-insulating solids owe their insulating properties to the air or to other gases contained in cells within the material. These cells cause the heat to flow through the solid material through a long tortuous passage. In addition, the available cross-sectional area of the solid material is much less than the projected area. Experimental evidence shows that many small unicellular pockets of gas are much more effective than a series of connected cells having the same total volume in giving insulating value to a substance. There may be considerable variation in the thermal conductivity of any given insulating material because the conductivity depends on its density, the size and number of its air cells, and its absorbed moisture.

There are several accepted methods of experimentally determining the thermal conductivity of solids. When proper care is used, fairly accurate values can be obtained for the thermal conductivity of a given solid of specified composition. It is much more difficult, however, to determine the thermal conductivity of a gas, a vapor, or a liquid, since it is almost impossible to eliminate the heat transferred by convection, which occurs simultaneously with that transferred by conduction, without introducing difficulties in the accurate measurement of other factors. For these reasons there are differences of perhaps 10 to 25 percent in reported values of the thermal conductivities of fluids.

Fig. 2.3 shows the heat conduction in a simple wall. It is assumed that the width and height of the wall are so large in comparison with the thickness of the wall that the heat flow may be considered to be unidirectional. One face of the wall is maintained at a uniform temperature t_1, and the other face is kept at temperature t_2. The heat flow through the wall may be obtained by integration of Eq. 2.5.

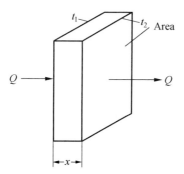

Fig. 2.3 Conduction through a single wall

An examination of the thermal conductivities of the various materials shows that, for many materials, the thermal conductivity may be taken as constant over an appreciable range in temperature. Furthermore, for most materials, the thermal conductivity is a straight-line function of temperature within the range of temperature for which information is available. Thus, the arithmetic mean thermal conductivity k_m may be used as the true thermal conductivity. For the simple wall, Eq. 2.5 may be integrated as follows:

$$Q = \frac{k_m A}{x}(T_1 - T_2) \quad (2.6)$$

According to Eq. 2.6, the rate of heat flow is proportional to the heat-flow area, the temperature difference causing heat flow, and the term k_m/x. This term is known as the thermal conductance.

When the thermal conductivity does not vary linearly with temperature, the mean thermal conductivity k_m cannot be determined readily. In such a case it becomes desirable to express the thermal conductivity as a function of temperature in Eq. 2.5 and then to perform the integration.

Words and Expression

progressive ['prə'gresiv] a. 进行的
bodily ['bɔdili] a. 具体的,有形的
credit(to) v. 把……归于,认为……
Fourier's law 傅里叶定律
unidirectional ['ju:nidi'rekʃənl] a. 单向的
slab [slæb] n. 厚片,平板
cross-sectional area 横截面积
proportionality [prə'pɔ:ʃə'næliti] n. 比例
conductivity [,kɔndʌk'tiviti] n. 导热系数
purity ['pjuəriti] n. 纯度
insulating ['insjuleitiŋ] a. 绝热的
tortuous ['tɔ:tjuəs] a. 弯曲的
projected area 投影面积
unicellular ['ju:ni'seljulə] a. 单细胞的,单孔的
convection [kən'vekʃən] n. 对流

integration [ˌinti'greiʃən] n. 积分
appreciable [ə'priːʃiəbl] a. 相当大的
conductance [kən'dʌktəns] n. 导热率
linearly ['liniəli] ad. 线性地

2.5 Natural Convection

Heat transfer involving motion in a fluid caused by the difference in density and the action of gravity is called natural or free convection. Heat transfer coefficients for natural convection are generally much lower than for forced convection, and it is therefore important not to ignore radiation in calculating the total heat loss or gain. Radiant transfer may be of the same order of magnitude as natural convection, even at room temperatures, since wall temperatures in a room can affect human comfort.

Natural convection is important in a variety of heating and refrigeration equipment: (1) gravity coils used in high humidity cold storage rooms and in roof-mounted refrigerant condensers, (2) the evaporator and condenser of household refrigerators, (3) baseboard radiators and convectors for space heating and (4) cooling panels for air conditioning. Natural convection is also involved in heat loss or gain to equipment casings and interconnecting ducts and pipes.

Consider heat transfer by natural convection between a cold fluid and a hot surface. The fluid in immediate contact with the surface is heated by conduction, becomes lighter and rises because of the difference in density of the adjacent fluid. The motion is resisted by the viscosity of the fluid. The heat transfer is influenced by: (1) gravitational force due to thermal expansion, (2) viscous drag and (3) thermal diffusion. It may be expected to depend on the gravitational acceleration g, the coefficient of thermal expansion β, the kinematic viscosity $v\ (=\mu/\rho)$, and the thermal diffusivity $\alpha = (k/\rho c_p)$. These variables can be expressed in terms of dimensionless numbers: the Nusselt number, Nu, is a function of the product of the Prandtl number, Pr, and Grashof number, Gr, which, when combined, depend on the fluid properties, the temperature difference between the surface and the fluid, Δt, and the characteristic length of the surface, L. The constant c and exponent n depend on the physical configuration and nature of flow.

The entire process of natural convection cannot be represented by a single value of exponent n, but can be divided into three regions: (1) turbulent natural convection for which n equals 0.33, (2) laminar natural convection, for which n equals 0.25 and (3) a region that has ($Gr \cdot Pr$) less than for laminar natural convection, for which the exponent n gradually diminishes from 0.25 to lower values. Note that, for wires, the ($Gr \cdot Pr$) is likely to be very small, so that the exponent n is 0.1.

To calculate the natural convection heat transfer coefficient, determine ($Gr \cdot Pr$) to find whether the boundary layer is laminar or turbulent, then apply the appropriate equation. The correct characteristic length indicated must be used. Since the exponent n is 0.33 for a turbulent boundary layer, the characteristic length cancels out, and the heat transfer coefficient is independent of the characteristic length. Turbulence occurs when length or temperature difference is large. Since the length of a pipe is generally greater than its diameter, the heat transfer coefficient for vertical pipes is larger than for horizontal pipes.

Convection from horizontal plates facing downward when heated (or upward when cooled) is a special case. Since the hot air is above the colder air, there is no theoretical reason for convection. Some convection is caused, however, by secondary influences such as temperature differences on the edges of the plate. As an approximation, a coefficient of somewhat less than half of the coefficient for a heated horizontal plate facing upward can be used.

Since air is often the heat transport fluid, simplified equations for air are given. Other information on natural convection is available in the general heat transfer references.

Observed differences in the comparisons of recent experimental and numerical results with existing correlations for natural convective heat transfer coefficients indicate that caution should be taken when applying coefficients for (isolated) vertical plates recommended by ASHRAE for situations with vertical surfaces in enclosed spaces (buildings). Improved correlations for calculating natural convective heat transfer from vertical surfaces in rooms under certain temperature boundary conditions have been developed.

Natural convection can affect the heat transfer coefficient in the presence of weak forced convection. As the forced convection effect, i. e. , the Reynolds number, increases, the " mixed convection " (superimposed forced-on-free convection) gives way to the pure forced convection regime. Since the heat transfer coefficient in the mixed convection region is often larger than that calculated based on the natural or forced convection calculation alone, attention is called to references on combined free and forced convection heat transfer. The reference given before summarizes natural, mixed, and forced convection regimes for vertical and horizontal tubes. Local conditions influence the values of the convection coefficient in a mixed convection regime, but the references permit locating the pertinent regime and approximating the convection coefficient.

Words and Expression

humidity [hju(ː)'miditi] n. 湿度
roof-mounted 屋顶安装的
baseboard n. 踢脚板
casings ['keisiŋz] n. 壳
ducts [dʌkts] n. 风管,管道
viscous ['viskəs] a. 黏性的,黏滞的
diffusivity [ˌdifjuː'siviti] n. 扩散性,扩散系数
Nusselt number 努谢尔特数
Prandtl number 普朗特数
Grashof number 格拉晓夫数
diminish [di'miniʃ] vt. 减小,减少
turbulence ['təːbjuləns] n. 紊流,扰动
correlation [ˌkɔri'leiʃən] n. 关系式
ASHRAE = American Society of Heating Refrigerating and Air-conditioning Engineers 美国供热制冷和空调工程师协会
superimpose ['sjuːpərim'pəuz] vt. 加上,附加,叠加
forced-on-free convection 加上自然对流影响的受迫对流
regime [rei'ʒiːm] n. 区域,状态
pertinent ['pəːtinənt] a. 恰当的,相关的

2.6 Radiation

Every free surface emits energy in the form of electromagnetic waves; the amount of energy is a function of the surface temperature. This emitted energy is known as radiant thermal energy. The nature of this radiant energy is not completely understood, but laws have been formulated that describe its behavior. It is recognized that, as with other forms of radiant energy, radiant heat energy is transmitted in the form of electromagnetic waves. The complete formulation of the laws governing radiant heat energy must consider that this energy is quantized, that is, the energy is transferred in quanta. In contrast with other modes of heat transfer, no medium is required to transmit radiant energy. In fact some gases, for instance, carbon dioxide and water vapor, absorb some of the radiant energy passing through them.

For a fixed set of conditions, any free surface emits radiant energy of varying wavelengths. The frequency of vibration (ν) of radiant waves is dependent solely on the source of radiation and is independent of the medium through which they pass. The velocity of radiant waves (V) is a function solely of the medium through which they pass. Thus, the wavelength ($\lambda = V\nu$) is a function of both the source and the medium.

All free surfaces receive radiant energy from all other surfaces that they can "see," that is, surfaces in direct line of sight. Most problems in radiation deal with the net radiant energy exchanged between a given surface and those that surround it. In common parlance, the term "heat exchanged by radiation" is used. It must be emphasized, however, that radiation is not heat. Heat is conducted to a surface. By virtue of the temperature of a surface, electromagnetic waves transmit energy from the surface. When these strike another surface, part of the energy will be absorbed, tending to increase the temperature of the surface struck by them, and part will be reflected. When the object is transparent, or partially so, to radiant waves, some or all of the radiant energy received by the surface will pass into the object. The transparency of an object to radiant energy is a function of the wavelength of the radiant waves. These statements relating to the radiant energy received by a surface may be put in equation form as follows:

$$\alpha + \rho + \tau = 1 \qquad (2.7)$$

where α = absorptivity, or the portion of the radiant energy that is absorbed;

ρ = reflectivity, or the portion of the radiant energy that is reflected;

τ = transmissivity, or the portion of the radiant energy that is transmitted.

A black surface has an absorptivity close to unity. For this reason the term blackbody has been used to designate an imaginary object whose surface has an absorptivity of unity. Since no known surface completely absorbs radiant energy, the term blackbody refers to an ideal surface. kirchhoff conceived a method of completely absorbing radiant energy. Assume that a hollow sphere contains a very small opening, as is indicated in Fig. 2.4 Radiation entering this opening will be received by the back wall of the sphere. Here it will be partially absorbed and partially reflected to other parts of the walls of the sphere. The reflected waves are, in turn, partially reflected, so that each reflected portion is a progressively smaller portion of the energy entering the sphere until ultimately all of it is absorbed. Strictly speaking, some of the reflected radiant energy will pass out through the hole. However, the surface area of the sphere is πD^2. Hence, when the diameter of the sphere is chosen to be 50 times that of the opening, the inside surface area is 10 000 times that of the opening, and it may be assumed that the hollow sphere absorbs all of the radiant energy.

The amount of radiant energy emitted by a surface is a function of the nature of the surface and its temperature. The term blackbody is also used to denote a surface that emits the maximum conceivable amount of radiant energy at any given temperature. There is no actual surface that is a perfect emitter, but the hollow-sphere concept may be used to establish a standard. The process of emission from the inner surface of the sphere is the reverse of that of absorption.

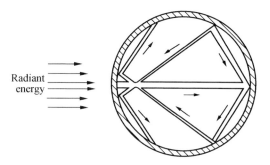

Fig. 2.4 Radiant energy absorbed in a hollow sphere

The total radiant energy emitted in a unit time by a unit area is known as the total emissive power and is designated by E. Since radiant energy is emitted over a range of wavelengths,

$$E = \int_{\lambda=0}^{\lambda=\infty} E_\lambda d\lambda \tag{2.8}$$

where E_λ is the monochromatic emissive power. It is assumed that E_λ in Eq. 2.8 is a continuous function of λ.

Words and Expression

emit [i′mit] v. 放射,发出
frequency [′fri:kwənsi] n. 频繁,频率
vibration [vai′breiʃən] n. 振动,动摇,共鸣,感应
transparency [træns′pɛərənsi] n. 透明,透明物,透明性,透明度
reflectivity [riflek′tiviti] n. 反射率
transmissivity [træzmi′siviti] n. 透射系数,透射率
assumed [ə′sju:md] a. 假装的,虚构的,假想的
emissive power   辐射力
monochromatic emissive power   单色辐射力

3

Fuels and Combustion

3.1 Heat of Combustion

In a boiler furnace (where no mechanical work is done) the heat energy evolved from the union of combustible elements with oxygen depends on the ultimate products of combustion and not on any intermediate combinations that may occur in reaching the final result.

A simple demonstration of this law is the union of 1 lb of carbon with oxygen to produce a specific amount of heat. The union may be in one step to form the gaseous product of combustion, CO_2, or under certain conditions the union may be in two steps, first to form CO, producing a much smaller amount of heat and, second the union of the CO so obtained to form CO_2, releasing 9 755 Btu. However, the sum of the heats released in the two steps equals the 14 100 Btu evolved when carbon is burned in one step to form CO_2 as the final product.

That carbon may enter into these two combinations with oxygen is of utmost importance in the design of combustion equipment. Firing methods must assure complete mixture of fuel and oxygen to be certain that all of the carbon burns to CO_2 and not to CO. Failure to meet this requirement will result in appreciable losses in combustion efficiency and in the amount of heat released by the fuel, since only about 28% of the available heat in the carbon is released if CO is formed instead of CO_2.

Measurement of heat of combustion

In boiler practice the heat of combustion of a fuel is the amount of heat, expressed in Btu, generated by the complete combustion, or oxidation, of a unit weight (1 lb in the United States) of fuel. Calorific value or "fuel Btu value" are terms also used.

The amount of heat generated by complete combustion is a constant for any given combination of combustible elements and compounds and is not affected by the manner in which the combustion takes place, provided it is complete.

The heat of combustion of a fuel is usually determined by direct measurement in a calorimeter of the heat evolved during combustion. Combustion products within a calorimeter are cooled to the initial temperature and the heat absorbed by the cooling medium is measured to determine the higher or gross heat of combustion.

For solid fuels and most liquid fuels, calorimeters of the "bomb" type, in which combustible substances are burned in a constant volume of oxygen, give the most satisfactory results. With bomb calorimeters properly operated, combustion is complete, all of the heat generated is absorbed and measured, and heat from external sources either can be excluded or proper corrections can be applied.

For gaseous fuels, calorimeters of the continuous or constant-Flow type are usually accepted as standard. The principle of operation is the same as for the bomb calorimeter except that the heat content is determined at constant pressure rather than at constant volume. For most fuels, the difference in the heating values from the constant-pressure and constant-volume determinations is small and is usually neglected.

For accurate heat values of solid and liquid fuels calorimeter determinations are required. However, approximate heat values may be determined for most coals if the ultimate chemical analysis is known. Dulong's formula gives reasonably accurate results (within 2 to 3%) for most coals and is often used as routine check of values determined by calorimeter:

$$\text{Btu/lb} = 14\,544\,C + 62\,028\,(H_2 - O_2/8) + 4\,050\,S \qquad (3.1)$$

In this formula, the symbols represent the proportionate parts by weight of the constituents of the fuel—carbon, hydrogen, oxygen and sulfur—as determined by an ultimate analysis; the coefficients represent the approximate heating values of the constituents in Btu per lb. The term $O_2/8$ is a correction applied to the hydrogen in the fuel to account for the hydrogen already combined with the oxygen in the form of moisture. This formula is not generally suitable for calculating the Btu values of gaseous fuels.

High and low heat values

Water vapor is one of the products of combustion for all fuels which contain hydrogen. The heat content of a fuel depends on whether this water vapor is allowed to remain in the vapor state or is condensed to liquid. In the bomb calorimeter the products of combustion are cooled to the initial temperature and all of the water vapor formed during combustion is condensed to liquid. This gives the high, or gross, heat content of the fuel with the heat of vaporization included in the reported value. For the low, or net heat of combustion, it is assumed that all products of combustion remain in the gaseous state.

While the high, or gross, heat of combustion can be accurately determined by established (ASTM) procedures, direct determination of the low heat of combustion is difficult. Therefore, it is usually calculated using the following formula:

$$Q_L = Q_H - 1\ 040\ W \tag{3.2}$$

where:

Q_L = low heat of combustion of fuel, Btu/lb

Q_H = high heat of combustion of fuel, Btu/lb

W = lb water formed per lb of fuel

1 040 = factor to reduce high heat of combustion at constant volume to low heat of combustion at constant pressure

In the United States the practice is to use the high heat of combustion in boiler combustion calculations. In Europe the low heat value is used.

Words and Expressions

boiler ['bɔilə] n. 锅炉,煮器
furnace ['fə:nis] n. 火炉,炉膛
oxygen ['ɔksidʒən] n. 氧,氧气
ultimate ['ʌltimit] a. 最后的,最终的
failure ['feiljə] n. 失败,忽略
carbon ['ka:bən] n. 碳
calorimeter [ˌkælə'rimitə] n. 热量计,量热器
gross [grəus] a. 总体的,总的
bomb [bɔm] n. 高压弹,炸弹
approximate [ə'prɔksimit] a. 近似的,大概的
routine [ru:'ti:n] a. 日常的,例行的
hydrogen ['haidrədʒən] n. 氢,氢气

3.2 Combustion Equipment

A steam generating system is large and complex. It consists of combustion equipment, furnace, and various heat transfer surfaces. In addition, the steam generating system has some auxiliary equipment needed for efficient operation. These auxiliaries include at least the boiler fans (forced-draft and induced-draft), stack, precipitatoer, and SO_2 removal system.

The selection of combustion equipment depends on the type of the fuel used. For solid fuels such as coal, three combustion systems (mechanical stoker, pulverizer burner and cyclone-furnace) are generally suitable. Mechanical stokers were first developed in the history of the boiler. Almost any coal can be burned on some type of stoker. Other advantages of stokers include low power requirements and large operating range. Because of the small capacity, they are seldom used for today's central electric power station.

The pulverizer-burner system was introduced in the third decade of last century. This system overcomes the size limitation of the mechanical stoker. Modern pulverizing systems are so well developed that they can burn almost any type of coal, particularly those in the higher grades and ranks. In addition, the system has improved response to the load change, higher combustion efficiency, and less manpower required in operation.

Fig. 3.1 shows a typical firing system for pulverized coal. The function of this system is to pulverize the coal, deliver the coal powder to the burners, and accomplish complete combustion in the furnace. The system must operate in continuous process and can adjust itself to the load demand in a reasonable time. There are two major equipment components, pulverizer and burner, in the system. The pulverizer receives coal from the coal bunker through the coal feeder, and produces the coal powder according to the fitness requirement. At the same time the pulverizer receives the hot air from the primary-air fan for drying and transporting the coal powder to the burners. Each pulverizer is usually connected with several burners. In operation, the coal feed is proportioned to the load demand, and the primary air supply is adjusted to the rate of coal feed. The air-coal ratio is so determined that the air-coal mixture leaving the pulverizer should have a proper temperature and moisture. Generally, the temperature and moisture are, respectfully, 65 ℃ and 1% to 2% for bituminous coals.

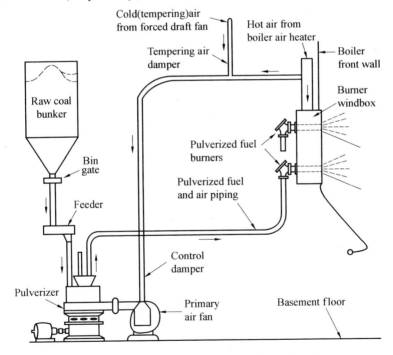

Fig. 3.1 Typical firing system for pulverized coal

In addition to delivering a sufficient amount of air, the primary air fan is designed to maintain a high velocity of the air-coal mixture in pulverizer discharge lines. The velocity must be such that there is no settling and drifting of coal in the piping. At the burner the air-coal mixture is combined with secondary air and both injected into furnace. As indicated in Fig. 3.1, both primary air and secondary air are from the boiler air preheater. When the moisture of coal is below the maximum level, or the boiler is in a low load condition, cold air is used to temper the primary air.

Combustion equipment for oil and natural gas is relatively simple. There is no need for a coal pulverizer, coal crusher, or other fuel preparation facilities. Because of the high viscosity of the fuel oil, some types of heaters are usually needed in the oil storage tank to warm the oil and to facilitate pumping. Oil pumps receive the oil from the strainers and discharge it to the burners through heaters. To maintain a good combustion, the temperature of the fuel oil entering the burners should be around 65 ℃. The recirculation lines are provided in the fuel oil system. The recirculation lines are used to prevent stagnant oil from collecting in the piping system and cooling to the point of solidification. The burners for the fuel oil are similar to those for the pulverized coal.

Words and Expressions

forced-draft 送风机
induced-draft 引风机
stoker ['stəukə] n. 层燃炉
capacity [kə'pæsiti] n. 容量,生产力,功率
powder ['paudə] n. 煤粉
bunker ['bʌŋkə] n. 容器,仓
feeder ['fi:də] n. 给煤机
fitness ['fitnis] n. 适合,恰当

discharge [dis'tʃɑːdʒ] vt. 排出,离开
settling ['setliŋ] n. 沉淀,沉降
drifting ['driftiŋ] adj. 漂移,偏差
crusher ['krʌʃə] n. 破碎机
facilitate [fə'siliteit] vt. 使方便
strainer ['streinə] n. 过滤器,滤网
stagnant ['stægnənt] adj. 停滞的,不流动的
solidification [ˌsɔlidifi'keiʃən] n. 凝固,浓缩

3.3 Fuel-ash

Ash content of coal

The ash content of coals varies over a wide range. This variation occurs not only in coal from different parts of the world or from different seams in the same region but also in coal from different parts of the same mine. Some rock and earthy materials find their way into the mined pro-duct. Before marketing, some commercial coals are cleaned or washed to remove a portion of what would be reported as ash in laboratory determinations. In any case, the ash determinations of significance to the user are those made at the point of use, and the values noted below are on that basis.

The bulk of bituminous coal used for power generation in the U.S. has an ash content within the range of 6 to 20%. Low values of 3% or 4% are encountered infrequently, and such coals find other commercial uses, particularly in the metallurgical field. On the other hand, some coals may have an ash content as high as 30%. Many high-ash fuels are successfully burned in the Cyclone Furnace as well as in pulverized-coal-fired units. Their use is increasing in localities where the fuel costs indicate a favorable overall economy.

Nature of coal ash

The presence of ash is accounted for by minerals associated with initial vegetal growth or those which entered the coal seam from external sources during or after the period of coal formation. Appreciable quantities of inorganic material may be contributed to the commercial fuel by partial inclusion of adjacent rock strata in the process of mining.

Since quantitative evaluation of mineral forms is extremely difficult, the composition of the coal ash is customarily determined by chemical analysis of the residue produced by burning a sample of coal at a slow rate and at moderate temperature (1 350 °F) under oxidizing conditions in a laboratory furnace. It is thus found to be composed chiefly of compounds of silicon, aluminum, iron, and calcium, with smaller amounts of magnesium, titanium, sodium and potassium.

The element sulfur is present in practically all coal, and its effect on equipment performance has been given much attention. Sulfur itself burns as a fuel with a relatively low heating value (3 980 Btu/lb when burned to SO_2), but its reputation, which is nearly all bad, results from the effect of its chemical combination with other elements. Under certain conditions some of these compounds corrode boiler components; others contribute to the fouling and slagging of gas passages and heating surfaces.

Some of the sulfur in coal is in combination with iron as FeS_2. Sulfur may also be present in the form of complex organic compounds and, in minor amounts, in combination with the alkaline earths (calcium and magnesium). When the fuel is burned, the sulfur compounds are normally converted to more or less stable mineral oxides and sulfur dioxide gas, SO_2. A very small part of the SO_2 thus formed is further oxidized to SO_3. These sulfur gases are carried along with the other combustion gases, and their presence, under certain conditions, can contribute to corrosion of boiler heating surfaces and to air pollution problems.

Coals may be classified into two groups based on the nature of their ash constituents. One is the bituminoustype ash and the other is the lignite-type ash. The term "lignite-type" ash is defined as an ash having more CaO plus MgO than Fe_2O_3. By contrast, the "bituminoustype" ash will have more Fe_2O_3 than CaO plus MgO.

Ash fusibility

The preferred procedure for the determination of ash fusion temperatures is outlined in ASTM Standard D-1857. Earlier procedure used only a reducing atmosphere for ash-fusibility determination whereas the standard adopted in 1968 offers the use of both reducing and oxidizing atmospheres. The previous method had loosely defined softening and fluid critical points; the new procedure uses improved definitions, as follows:

Initial deformation temperature, at which the first rounding of the apex of the cone occurs.

Softening temperature, at which the cone has fused down to a spherical lump in which the height is equal to the width at the base.

Hemispherical temperature, at which the cone has fused down to a hemispherical lump at which point the height is one half the width of the base.

Fluid temperature, at which the fused mass has spread out in a nearly flat layer with a maximum height of one sixteenth in.

The determination of ash fusion temperatures is strictly a laboratory procedure, developed in standardized form, which experience shows can be duplicated with some degree of accuracy. For example, the permissible differences of reproducibility between two furnace runs may range from 100 to 150 °F. However, some bituminoustype ash, containing relatively large amounts of silica, may exhibit low ash-softening temperatures, yet exhibits high viscosity characteristics in its plastic range. Some lignite-type ash, containing large amounts of calcium and magnesium, may react with the refractory base (kaolin and alumina), or it may evolve gaseous products and swell, thereby causing changes in density of the ash cone. Methods for determining fusibility of coal ash used by countries outside the U. S. may also vary considerably. Thus, ash fusibility data should be used with care and its limitations recognized.

Ash melts when heated to a sufficiently high temperature. Following combustion, individual ash particles are generally in the form of tiny spheres (cenospheres) that appear hollow when viewed under a microscope. The form of the ash particles indicates that, during combustion of the coal, the particles were actually liquid and the spheres were formed as tiny bubbles by evolved gases trying to escape. What happens to these particles depends on their physical and chemical characteristics and on furnace conditions. If cooled promptly and sufficiently, the result is a dusty ash that may travel through the equipment, lodge on heating surfaces, drop out in soot hoppers and along flues, or collect at the base of the stack. Those particles that remain in suspension are carried out with the flue gases to the particulate-removal equipment and stack. The individual ash particles do not, however, always cool quickly to a solid state. If insufficiently cooled, they remain molten or sticky and tend to coalesce into large masses in the boiler furnace or other heat-absorption surfaces. This problem is dealt with by adequate design of burners and furnace arrangement for the fuels to be burned and by proper attention to boiler operation.

Words and Expressions

fuel-ash   n. 燃料灰
bulk   [bʌlk]   n. 大部分,堆
bituminous   [bi'tjuːminəs]   a. 烟煤的
cyclone   ['saikləun]   a. 旋风的
vegetal   ['vedʒitl]   a. 植物的,蔬菜的
slag   [slæg]   n. 熔渣,渣滓
sulfur   ['sʌlfə]   n. 硫磺,含硫磺的
fusibility   [ˌfjuːzə'biliti]   n. (可)熔性,熔度
deformation   [ˌdiːfɔː'meiʃən]   n. 变形
lump   [lʌmp]   n. 堆
hemispherical   [ˌhemi'sferrikəl]   a. 半球状的,半球体的

3.4 The Mechanisms of Gaseous Fuels Combustion

As has been found by experiment, the rates of combustion reactions substantially exceed the rates calculated using the law of mass action and Arrhenius'law by considering the number of active molecules of the initial substances entering a reaction. Actually, reactions do not occur immediately between the original molecules, but pass through a number of intermediate stages in which active molecular fragments (radicals and atoms of H, OH, O, etc.) participate along with molecules. As a result, each of these intermediate reactions has a low level of the activation energy E, since radicals and individual atoms possess a free valency, and can therefore form free-valency particles. Such reactions can proceed at a high rate. The start of a reaction between substances is preceded by a period during which active reaction centres in the form of charged particles accumulate in the medium, owing to the partial destruction of original molecules by other molecules which possess an energy higher than the energy of the atomic bonds in the original molecules. This is what is called the *induction period*.

The combustion of gaseous fuels. Combustion of gaseous fuels occurs by the laws of branched chain reactions which were discovered by Soviet Academician N. N. Semenov and C. N. Hinshelwood. The conversion of the original substances to the final products passes through a sequence of reaction links which are connected in succession with one another and develop in the volume of a combustible mixture like the branches of a tree develop from its trunk. This results in the formation of the final reaction products and of an even greater number of active centres which further ensure the development of the reaction in the confining volume.

Let us consider the mechanism of branched chain reactions, taking as an example the combustion of hydrogen in air. By the stoichiometric equation

$$2H_2 + O_2 = 2H_2O$$

the rate of the reaction between molecules of the combustible substance

$$w_{H_2O} = k_0 e^{-E/RT} C_{H_2}^2 C_{O_2} \qquad (3.3)$$

cannot be very large. Actually, however, combustion of hydrogen at temperatures above 500 ℃ is an explosive chain reaction proceeding at a very high rate. Indeed, according to N. N. Semenov, the beginning of the active reaction is preceded by the formation of active centres:

$$H_2 + M^a \longrightarrow 2H + M$$
$$H_2 + O_2^a \longrightarrow 2OH$$

where M^a and O_2^a are active molecules which possess high energy levels in the volume.

Fuels and Combustion 61

Atoms and radicals formed by this mechanism actively enter the reactions with the surrounding molecules, i. e. chains of successive reactions develop which result in the formation of the final reaction products and ever greater number of active centres.

Fig. 3. 2 schematically shows the first cycle of this reaction. As may be seen, each of the active hydrogen atoms H that has given rise to a chain reaction has produced three new active centres, owing to which the reaction progressively develops in the volume confining the gas mixture. As the reaction products accumulate and the concentrations of the starting substances become lower, chains are disrupted more often in the volume and at the walls of the reactor:

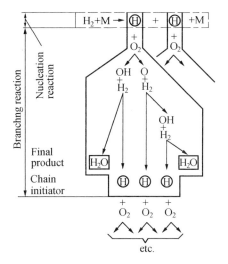

Fig. 3. 2 Chain reaction cycle of hydrogen burning
○—chain reaction exciter;
□—final product

$$H+H \longrightarrow H_2$$

$$OH+H \longrightarrow H_2O$$

The actual reaction rate is described by the equation:

$$w_H = 10^{11}\sqrt{T}C_H C_{O_2} e^{-E'/RT} \quad (3.4)$$

The decisive factors for the reaction rate are the concentrations of hydrogen atoms (reaction centres) and oxygen molecules, with the activation energy E' of the reaction between them being substantially lower than E in equation(3.3). Similar laws of chain reactions govern the combustion of carbon monoxide CO, methane CH_4 and other combustible gases.

It follows from the foregoing that a short time, the induction period, precedes the beginning of an active reaction, during which a sufficiently large quantity of active centres (atoms and radicals) accumulates in the reaction volume. During this period, the reaction is almost unnoticeable and its thermal effect is negligible. After this period, the reaction rate increases due to the development of a large number of parallel reaction chains over the whole volume, until an equilibrium between the appearance and disappearance of active centres is established. The reaction then attains its maximum rate and will proceed at this rate, provided that fresh portions of starting substances are regularly supplied to the combustion zone.

Combustion of a gaseous fuel in a mixture with air occurs at a very high rate (a ready methane-air mixture burns in a volume of 10 m^3 in 0.1 s). For this reason, the intensity of combustion of natural gas in steam boiler furnaces is limited by the speed at which it mixes with air in the burner, i.e. by physical factors. The difficulties which arise when high flows of gas and air should be mixed thoroughly in a very short time in a burner are linked with the fact that the volume flow rates of the gas and air differ substantially, as approximately 10 m^3 of air are needed for the combustion of 1 m^3 of gas. For thorough intermixing, gas must be introduced into the air flow in the form of numerous fine jets and at a high rate. For the same purpose, the air flow is thoroughly turbulized by special swirling arrangements.

Words and Expressions

mechanism ['mekənizəm] n. 机理,机构
intermediate [ˌintə'miːdjət] a. 中间的 n. 中间物
valency ['veilənsi] n. (化合)价,(原子)价
medium ['miːdiəm] n. 媒体
induction [in'dʌkʃən] n. 感应,诱导
sequence ['siːkwəns] n. 连续,次序
trunk [trʌŋk] n. 树干,主要部分
confine [kən'fain] v. 限制
concentration [ˌkɔnsen'treiʃən] n. 浓度,浓缩
thermal ['θəːməl] a. 热的
parallel ['pærəlel] a. 相似的,相同的 n. 相似处
approximately [ə'prɔksimətli] adv. 大概,近乎
swirl [swəːl] n. 旋涡,涡动

3.5 The Combustion of Liquid Fuels and Solid Fuels

The combustion of liquid fuels

In the combustion of liquid fuels (petroleum, fuel oil), both the ignition and combustion temperatures (especially the latter) turn out to be higher than the boiling temperature of the individual fuel fractions. For this reason, liquid fuel first evaporates from the surface under the effect of the supplied heat, then its vapours are mixed with air, preheated to the ignition temperature and start burning. A stable flame forms at a certain distance from the surface of liquid fuel (0.5 ~ 1 mm or more).

Fig. 3.3 schematically shows the combustion of a liquid fuel droplet in stagnant air. A vapour cloud forms around the droplet and diffuses into the environment, with the diffusion of oxygen of the air occurring in the opposite direction. As a result, the stoichiometric relationship between the combustible gases and oxygen is established at a certain distance r_{st} from the droplet, i.e. the burning fuel vapours form a spherical combustion front around it. The magnitude of r_{st} is equal to 4 ~ 10 droplet radii, i.e. $r_{st} = 4 \sim 10 r_d$, and depends heavily on the droplet size and the temperature in the combustion zone. In the zone where $r < r_{st}$, fuel vapours prevail, but their concentration decreases inversely with the distance from the liquid surface. The zone with $r > r_{st}$ contains primarily combustion products mixed with the oxygen that has diffused into the combustion zone. The highest temperature is established in the reaction zone. Although at both sides of this zone the temperature decreases gradually, its decrease is more intensive in the inside direction, i.e. on approaching the droplet, since some heat is spent there for heating fuel vapours.

Thus, the burning rate of a liquid fuel droplet is determined by the rate of evaporation from its surface, the rate of chemical reaction in the combustion zone, and the rate of oxygen diffusion to this zone. As stated earlier, the reaction rate in a gaseous medium is very high and cannot limit the total rate of combustion. The quantity of oxygen diffused through the spherical surface is proportional to the square of sphere diameter, and therefore, a slight removal of the combustion zone from the surface of the droplet (under oxygen deficiency) noticeably increases the mass flow rate of supplied oxygen. Thus, the rate of combustion of the droplet is mainly determined by evaporation from its surface. The combustion rate of liquid fuels is increased by atomizing the fuel just before burning, which substantially increases the total

Fuels and Combustion 65

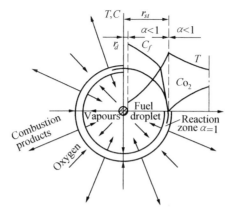

Fig. 3.3 Mechanism and combustion characteristics of a liquid fuel droplet

surface of evaporation. Besides all this, as the size of the droplets decreases, the intensity of evaporation per unit area of their surface increases. Fine liquid fuel droplets suspended in an air flow move at low Reynolds numbers, $Re \ll 4$. In such cases, the heat flow through a spherical surface is determined solely by the conductivity λ through the boundary layer, which is much thicker than the droplet diameter. Under such conditions, the heat-transfer coefficient α is given by Sokolsky's formula:

$$Nu = \alpha d/\lambda = 2 \qquad (3.5)$$

whence

$$\alpha = 2\lambda/d = \lambda/r \qquad (3.6)$$

where Nu is the Nusselt number.

As follows from formula (3.6), the heat exchange between a droplet and the surrounding medium increases as the size of the droplet decreases, i.e. with a decrease in its mass. It turns out that the evaporation time of a droplet is proportional to the square of its initial diameter.

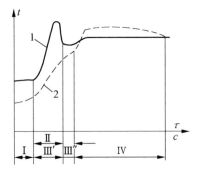

Fig. 3.4 Temperature conditions of burning of an individual solid fuel particle
1—temperature of gaseous medium around the particle;
2—particle temperature;
I—thermal preparation zone;
II—zone of burning of volatiles;
III′—heating of coke particle due to burning of its volatiles;
III″—heating of coke particle from an external source;
IV—burning of coke particle

The combustion of solid fuel

When combined with air in a furnace, pulverized coal first passes through the stage of thermal preparation (Fig. 3.4, I) , which consists in the evaporation of residual moisture and separation of volatiles. Fuel particles are heated up to a temperature at which volatiles are evolved intensively (400 ~ 600 ℃) in a few tenths of a second. The volatiles are then ignited, so that the temperature around a coke particle increases rapidly and its heating is accelerated (III′). The intensive burning of the volatiles (II) takes up 0.2 ~ 0.5 s. A high yield of volatiles (brown coal, younger coals, oil shales, peat) , produces enough heat through combustion to ignite coke particles. When the yield of volatiles is low, the coke particles must be heated additionally form an external source (III″). The final stage is the combustion of coke particles at a temperature above 800 ~ 1 000 ℃ (IV). This is a heterogeneous process whose rate is determined by the oxygen supply to the reacting surface. The burning of a coke particle proper takes up the greater portion(1/2 to 2/3) of the total time of combustion which may constitute 1 to 2.5 s, depending on the kind of fuel and the initial size of particles.

The reacting mechanism between carbon and oxygen seems to be as follows. Oxygen is adsorbed from the gas volume on the surface of particles and reacts chemically with carbon to form complex carbon-oxygen compounds of the type C_xO_y which then dissociate with the formation of CO_2 and CO. The resulting reaction at temperatures near 1 200 ℃ can be written as follows:

$$4C+3O_2 = 2CO+2CO_2 \qquad (3.7)$$

As has been established by experiment(L. Meyer, L. X. Khitrin), the ratio of the primary products. CO/CO_2, increases sharply with the increasing temperature of burning particles. For instance, the resulting equation at temperatures near 1 700 ℃ can be written in the form:

$$3C+2O_2 = 2CO+CO_2 \qquad (3.8)$$

where the CO/CO_2 ratio is equal to two.

The primary reaction products are continuously removed from the surface of particles to the environment. In this process, carbon monoxide encounters the diffusing oxygen, which moves in the opposite direction, and reacts with it within the boundary gas film to be oxidized to CO_2, with the result that the concentration of supplied oxygen decreases sharply on approaching the surface of particles, while the concentration of CO_2 increases(Fig. 3.5(a)). At a high combustion temperature, carbon monoxide can consume all the oxygen supplied, which, consequently, will not reach the solid surface of particles(Fig.

3.5(b)). Under such conditions, the endothermic reduction reaction will occur on the surface of particles, i.e. CO_2 will be partially reduced to CO.

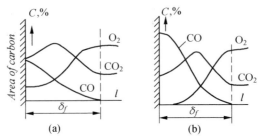

Fig. 3.5 Variations of concentration of gaseous substances at the surface of burning carbon
(a) burning at moderate temperatures;
(b) burning at high temperatures;
δ_f—thickness of boundary film

Thus, heterogeneous combustion of a carbon particle from its surface can be represented as a process embracing four subsequent reactions (according to A. S. Predvoditelev), two of which are the main ones:

$$C+O_2 = CO_2+q_1$$
$$2C+O_2 = 2CO+2q_2$$

the other two being secondary

$$2CO+O_2 = 2CO_2-2q_3$$
$$C+CO_2 = 2CO-q_4$$

where q is the thermal effect of a reaction, MJ/mol.

The thermal effect of the first reaction $q_1 = q_2+q_3$. while $q_4 = 0.57 q_3$. The latter equation implies that even when the endothermic reaction takes place, the temperature of combustion is maintained at a rather high level due to a higher heat evolution in the volume.

As follows from an analysis of these reactions, the combustion of carbon from the surface takes place with partial gasification (formation of CO and its afterburning in the volume). This process accelerates the burning-off of coke particles.

Words and Expressions

evaporate [i'væpəreit] v. 使蒸发,使挥发
droplet ['drɔplit] n. 小滴
diffuse [di'fju:z] v. 扩散,散开
spherical ['sferikəl] a. 球的,球形的
deficiency [di'fiʃənsi] n. 缺乏,不够
solely ['səulli] adv. 单独地,完全
pulverize ['pʌlvəraiz] v. 将……粉碎
residual [ri'zidjuəl] a. 残留,剩余的
peat [pi:t] n. 泥煤块
boundary ['bəundəri] n. 界线,边界
embrace [im'breis] v. 包含

3.6 Nuclear Fuels

The principal source of heat energy, other than the sun, has traditionally been the combustion of fossil fuels such as wood, coal, oil and gas. A new source of energy, popularly called "atomic" energy was dramatically demonstrated during World War II when the Manhattan Project in the U.S. developed the atomic bomb. The subsequent naval propulsion and civilian power programs have successfully harnessed the fission of the atomic nucleus as a practical source of heat. This source, properly called "nuclear" energy, converts by fission some of the matter in the nucleus of the atom into energy, in accordance with Einstein's mass-energy equation:

$$E = mc^2 \qquad (3.9)$$

where E is energy, m is mass and c is the velocity of light.

All practical applications of nuclear energy for the production of steam utilize the process of fission. The nucleus of a heavy atom splits into two principal fragments, each of which is the nucleus of a lighter atom. This is accompanied by the release of a very considerable amount of energy. In addition neutrons are released which can be used to fission additional atoms producing a "chain reaction," which is controlled to maintain a continuous production of heat.

Uranium

Uranium is the basic raw material of the nuclear power industry. It is a heavy, slightly radioactive chemical element of atomic number 92—the heaviest element that occurs in nature in more than trace quantities.

Chemically, uranium is a highly reactive metal with three principal valences, +3, +4 and +6. It has three crystalline phases and melts at 2 070 °F. In the alpha phase, it is reasonably ductile and can be fabricated by standard metalworking techniques. Since small particles or chips of uranium are highly pyrophoric, machining operations and the storage of scrap require special precautions, such as use of coolant or an inert atmosphere.

Natural uranium is a mixture of three isotopes, uranium-234 (0.01%), uranium-235 (0.71%), and uranium-238 (99.28%). Uranium-234 is present in small amounts and is not significant. Uranium-235 is a fissionable isotope, and uranium-238 is generally known as a fertile isotope.

These three natural isotopes of uranium are radioactive and emit alpha particles. However, they have sufficiently long half lives so that only a minimum of precaution is required in handling natural uranium. Uranium is chemically toxic and must not be ingested. In areas where uranium is handled, the amount of uranium in the air must be kept below prescribed tolerances.

Uranium-235 is fissionable as a result of the absorption of a neutron by its nucleus. When one gram of uranium-235 is fissioned, the heat released is equivalent to approximately one megawatt-day (24 000 kwhr or 82 000 000 Btu). When one short ton of uranium-235 is fissioned, the heat released is equivalent to 22 billion kwhr or 75 thousand billion Btu, which is the quantity of heat contained in approximately three million tons of coal.

Uranium-235 can be fissioned by neutrons at various energy levels and a chain reaction can be maintained. It is a fissile material, which means that it can be fissioned by "slow" (low energy or thermal) neutrons.

Uranium-238 is not capable of sustaining a nuclear chain reaction but it is fissioned to some extent by high energy neutrons. When exposed to neutrons, as in a nuclear reactor, the uranium-238 nucleus, upon capture of a neutron, is ultimately transformed into plutonium-239, a fissile isotope of a new element. Plutonium-239 is capable of sustaining a chain reaction and, when fissioned, produces about the same amount of heat per gram as uranium-235. Because of this ability to be transmuted to a fissionable material, uranium-238 is known as a fertile material.

Uranium has become the basic raw material of the nuclear power industry because of its two principal isotopes, uranium-235 and uranium-238. The first is the only fissile material found in quantity in nature; the second is a fertile material from which fissile plutonium is produced. Since uranium-238 is 140 times as abundant as uranium-

235, its ultimate potential as a source of power is very large.

Another fertile element, thorium, can be used for the production of power, but uranium is required for the conversion of thorium to a fissionable material.

Utilization of uranium

Unlike fossil fuels for steam generation which require a continuous feed of fuel for good combustion, nuclear fuel is utilized by a batch process. It is introduced into the nuclear furnace, or reactor, in the form of fabricated packages called "fuel assemblies."

These are assemblies of fuel rods, consisting of uranium oxide pellets contained in alloy cladding tubes. The term "cladding" does not imply deposition of one metal on another, but simply refers to the outer jacket of the nuclear fuel, which is used to prevent corrosion and the release of fission products to the coolant. For a large power reactor using fuel assemblies of this type, each assembly may be 14 ft or more in length and 8 in. square, or larger, in cross section. In pressurized water reactors, fuel rods must be designed to accommodate differential pressures of as much as 2 500 psi that occur early in life as a result of system pressure external to the cladding tubes. These tubes must also contain the internal pressure from gaseous fission products that accumulate during the life of the fuel.

The following requirements are basic to the utilization of fuel for the production of steam, whether the fuel is nuclear or fossil:

1. Control of heat release rate in the reactor or furnace.

2. Transfer of heat developed by the fuel into water for the production of steam.

3. Protection of the operators and control of the byproducts of the reaction.

4. A design which results in good fuel economics.

Words and Expressions

atomic　　[ə'tɔmik]　　*a.* 原子的,核子的,核能的
dramatically　　[drə'mætikəli]　　*adv.* 明显地,显著地
split　　[split]　　*v.* 劈开,分裂
uranium　　[ju'reiniəm]　　*n.* 铀
radioactive　　[ˌreidiəu'æktiv]　　*a.* 放射性的,放射引起的
isotope　　['aisəutəup]　　*n.* 同位素,核素
toxic　　['tɔksik]　　*a.* 有毒的,有害的
tolerance　　['tɔlərəns]　　*n.* 容忍,抗拒药物的能力
plutonium　　[plu:təuniəm]　　*n.* 钚
thorium　　['θɔ:riəm]　　*n.* [化]钍
pellet　　['pelit]　　*n.* 小球,弹丸,锭片
coolant　　['ku:lənt]　　*n.* 冷却剂,载热剂,冷却油

3.7　Liquid By-product Fuels

Pitch and tar

　　The liquid and semiliquid residues from the distillation of petroleum and coal are known as pitch and tar. Most of these residues are suitable for use as boiler fuels. Some handle as easily and burn as readily as does kerosine, whereas others give considerable trouble. To determine whether a particular pitch or tar might be a suitable fuel for a given installation, the following items are important:

　　Moisture. If the fuel contains moisture, it must be well emulsified to avoid reaching the burner in slugs. If there is a brief break in the continuous flow of fuel to the burners, the fires will be extinguished. Upon reestablishing the fuel flow, a furnace explosion might occur if there is any delay in reigniting the burners. Consequently, a slug of water in the fuel supply can be disastrous if it extinguishes the flame briefly. Tars and pitches containing as much as 35% moisture may be burned in properly designed units.

Flash and fire points. Flash point is defined as the lowest temperature at which, under specified conditions, a liquid fuel will vaporize sufficiently to flash into momentary flame when ignited. Fire point is the lowest temperature at which, under given conditions, a liquid fuel will vaporize to an extent to burn continuously when ignited. Many liquid fuels are blends of two or more different liquids. One of these might have low flash and fire points, whereas the other might have high flash and fire points. Such a fuel usually burns with a bright flame at the burner, where the low-flash-point constituents are burning off; but beyond, where the components whith the higher flash and fire points are burning, the flame is a dark yellow. Actually, if there is too little turbulence at the burner or if the burning products are quenched by passing too quickly from the active combustion zone, combustion is incomplete, and high unburned combustible olss results. Consequently, while the flash temperature is useful for determining the possible hazard involved in storing the fuel, the fire point determines its suitability for firing in a boiler. Fuels with fire points as high as 600 °F can be burned in properly designed equipment.

Viscosity. Practically all tars and pitches are burned in the same manner as fuel oil. They are reduced to a foglike dispersion in an atomizer located in a burner and then vaporized and burned. To produce the fine particles, the viscosity of the fuel must be correct—not over 180 Saybolt Universal Seconds(SUS) for most atomizers, although if favored by the burnerfurnace arrangement, viscosities as high as 1 000 SUS may be used.

Suspended matter. Many of these fuels contain suspended matter.

If they are delivered to the burners in this condition, there will be:
1. Abnormal fouling of the atomizers, requiring frequent cleaning.
2. Excessive rate of wear of burner parts.
3. Deposition of unburned carbon throughout the unit or objectionable stack emission.

Such fuels should therefore be passed through strainers before they are fed to the burners.

Compatibility. When some of these fuels come into contact with ordinary fuel oil, they combine to form liver-like substances. If this happens in tanks or piping, trouble results. The mixture cannot be pumped from the tanks, and plugging of the piping often requires complete dismantling for cleaning. Burner operation, too, is erratic and spasmodic. Therefore, before mixing large quantities of tar or pitch with fuel oil, laboratory tests should be made at both storage and pumping temperatures to determine the compatibility of the fuels.

Words and Expressions

petroleum [pi'trəuliəm] *n.* 石油
moisture ['mɔistʃə] *n.* 水分,湿气
emulsify [i'mʌlsifai] *vt.* 使乳化
extinguish [iks'tiŋgwiʃ] *vt.* 使熄灭,扑灭,使……不复存在
reestablish ['riːis'tæbliʃ] *vt.* 重建,恢复,另行安装,使复原
viscosity [vis'kɔsəti] *n.* 黏稠,黏性
compatibility [kəmˌpæti'biliti] *n.* 兼容性

4

Air-conditioning and Refrigeration

4.1 Air-conditioning

Air-conditioning

Air-conditioning is a process that simultaneously conditions air, distributes it combined with the outdoor air to the conditioned space; and at the same time controls and maintains the required space's temperature, humidity, air movement, air cleanliness, sound level, and pressure differential within predetermined limits for the health and comfort of the occupants, for product processing, or both.

The acronym HVAC & R stands for heating, ventilating, air-conditioning, and refrigerating. The combination of these processes is equivalent to the functions performed by air-conditioning.

Air-conditioning systems

An air-conditioning or HVAC & R system consists of components and equipment arranged in sequential order to heat and cool, humidify or dehumidify, clean and purify, attenuate objectionable equipment noise, transport the conditioned outdoor air and recirculate air to the conditioned space, and control and maintain an indoor or enclosed environment at optimum energy use.

The types of buildings which the air-conditioning system serves can be classified as:

- Institutional buildings, such as hospitals and nursing homes
- Commercial buildings, such as offices, stores, and shopping centers
- Residential buildings, including single-family and multifamily low-rise buildings of three or fewer stories above grade
- Manufacturing buildings, which manufacture and store products

Types of air-conditioning systems

In institutional, commercial, and residential buildings, air-conditioning systems are mainly for the occupants' health and comfort. They are often called comfort air-conditioning systems. In manufacturing buildings, air-conditioning systems are provided for product processing, or for the health and comfort of workers as well as processing, and are called processing air-conditioning systems.

Based on their size, construction, and operating characteristics, air-conditioning systems can be classified as the following.

Individual Room or Individual Systems. An individual air-conditioning system normally employs either a single, self-contained, packaged room air conditioner (installed in a window or through a wall) or separate indoor and outdoor units to serve an individual room. "Self-contained, packaged" means factory assembled in one package and ready for use.

Space-conditioning Systems or Space Systems. These systems

have their air-conditioning—cooling, heating, and filtration performed predominantly in or above the conditioned space. Outdoor air is supplied by a separate outdoor ventilation system.

Unitary Packaged Systems or Packaged Systems. These systems are installed with either a single self contained, factory-assembled packaged unit or two split units: an indoor air handler, normally with duct work, and an outdoor condensing unit with refrigeration compressor(s) and condenser. In a packaged system, air is cooled mainly by direct expansion of refrigerant in coils called DX coils and heated by gas furnace, electric heating, or a heat pump effect, which is the reverse of a refrigeration cycle.

Central Hydronic or Central Systems. A central system uses chilled water or hot water from a central plant to cool and heat the air at the coils in an air handling unit (AHU). For energy transport, the heat capacity of water is about 3 400 timesgreater than that of air. Central systems are built-up systems assembled and installed on the site.

Packaged systems are comprised of only air system, refrigeration, heating, and control systems. Both central and space-conditioning systems consist of the following.

Air Systems. An air system is also called an air handling system or the air side of an air-conditioning or HVAC & R system. Its function is to condition the air, distribute it, and control the indoor environment according to requirements. The primary equipment in an air system is an AHU or air handler; both of these include fan, coils, filters, dampers, humidifiers (optional), supply and return duct work, supply outlets and return inlets, and controls.

Water Systems. These systems include chilled water, hot water, and condenser water systems. A water system consists of pumps, piping work, and accessories. The water system is sometimes called the water side of a central or space-conditioning system.

Central Plant Refrigeration and Heating Systems. The refrigeration system in the central plant of a central system is usually in the form of a chiller package with an outdoor condensing unit. The refrigeration system is also called the refrigeration side of a central system. A boiler and accessories make up the heating system in a central plant for a central system, and a direct-fired gas furnace is often the heating system in the air handler of a rooftop packaged system.

Control Systems. Control systems usually consist of sensors, a microprocessor-based direct digital controller(DDC), a control device, control elements, personal computer (PC), and communication network.

Words and Expressions

simultaneously [ˌsɪməl'teɪnɪlslɪ] adv. 同时地
humidity [hjuː'mɪdəti] n. 湿度
occupant ['ɒkjəpənt] n. 居住者；占有人
acronym ['ækrənɪm] n. 首字母缩略词
ventilating ['ventɪleɪtɪŋ] v. 通风；使通风
refrigerating [rɪ'frɪdʒəˌreɪtɪŋ] v. 冷冻；冷藏
component [kəm'pəʊnənt] n. 成分；组分；零件
sequential [sɪ'kwenʃl] adj. 序贯；时序；按次序的，相继的
recirculate [rɪ'sɜːkjʊleɪt] v. 再通行，再流通
institutional building   机构建筑
residential building   住宅建筑
manufacturing building   制造业建筑
individual [ˌɪndɪ'vɪdʒuəl] adj. 个人的
packaged ['pækɪdʒd] adj. 包装过的
filtration [fɪl'treɪʃn] n. 过滤；筛选；滤清；滤除

predominantly [prɪˈdɑmɪnəntli] adv. 占主导地位地；显著地
installed [ɪnsˈtɔːld] v. 安置；安装
expansion [ɪkˈspænʃn] n. 扩大；膨胀
hydronic [haɪˈdrɑnɪk] adj. 液体循环加热(或冷却)的
chilled water 冷冻水
comprised [kəmpˈraɪzd] v. 组成；包括；构成
filter [ˈfɪltə(r)] n. 过滤器
damper [ˈdæmpə(r)] n. 减震器
humidifier [hjuːˈmɪdɪfaɪə(r)] n. 加湿器
ductwork [ˈdʌktˌwɜːk] n. 管道系统
direct digital controller 直接数字控制器

4.2 Air-conditioning Cycle

An air-conditioning cycle comprises several air-conditioning processes that are connected in a sequential order. An air-conditioning cycle determines the operating performance of the air system in an air-conditioning system. The working substance to condition air may be chilled or hot water, refrigerant, desiccant, etc.

Each type of air system has its own air-conditioning cycle. Psychrometric analysis of an air-conditioning cycle is an important tool in determining its operating characteristics and the state of moist air at various system components, including the volume flow rate of supply air, the coil's load, and the humidifying and dehumidifying capacity.

According to the cycle performance, air-conditioning cycles can be grouped into two categories:

• Open cycle, in which the moist air at its end state does not resume its original state. An air conditioning cycle with all outdoor air is an open cycle.

• Closed cycle, in which moist air resumes its original state at its end state. An air-conditioning cycle that conditions the mixture of recirculating and outdoor air, supplies it, recirculates part of the return air, and mixes it again with outdoor air is a closed cycle.

Based on the outdoor weather and indoor operating conditions, the operating modes of air-conditioning cycles can be classified as:

· Summer mode: when outdoor and indoor operating parameters are in summer conditions.

· Winter mode: when outdoor and indoor operating parameters are in winter conditions.

· Air economizer mode: when all outdoor air or an amount of outdoor air that exceeds the minimum amount of outdoor air required for the occupants is taken into the AHU or PU for cooling. The air economizer mode saves energy use for refrigeration.

Continuous modes operate 24 hr a day and 7 days a week. Examples are systems that serve hospital wards and refrigerated warehouses. An intermittently operated mode usually shuts down once or several times within a 24-hr operating cycle. Such systems serve offices, class rooms, retail stores, etc. The 24-hr day-and-night cycle of an intermittently operated system can again be divided into:

1. Cool-down or warm-up period. When the space is not occupied and the space air temperature is higher or lower than the predetermined value, the space air should be cooled down or warmed up before the space is occupied.

2. Conditioning period. The air-conditioning system is operated during the occupied period to maintain the required indoor environment.

3. Nighttime shut-down period. The air system or terminal is shut down or only partly operating to maintain a set-back temperature.

Summer, winter, air economizer, and continuously operating

modes consist of full-load (design load) and part-load operations. Part load occurs when the system load is less than the design load. The capacity of the equipment is selected to meet summer and winter system design loads as well as system loads in all operating modes.

Words and Expressions

working substance　工作介质
desiccant　['desɪkənt]　*n.* 干燥剂
psychrometric　[ˌpsaikrəu'metrik]　*n.* 空气线图
humidifying and dehumidifying capacity　加湿和除湿能力
moist air　湿空气
resume　[rɪ'zjuːm]　*v.* 继续;重新开始
operating parameter　运行参数
exceed　[ɪk'siːd]　*vt.* 超过;超越;胜过
warehouse　['weəhaus]　*n.* 仓库
intermittently　[ˌɪntə'mɪtəntlɪ]　*adv.* 间歇地;断断续续
nighttime　['naɪttaɪm]　*n.* 夜间

4.3 Refrigeration

Refrigeration and refrigeration systems

Refrigeration is the cooling effect of the process of extracting heat from a lower temperature heat source, a substance or cooling medium, and transferring it to a higher temperature heat sink, probably atmospheric air and surface water, to maintain the temperature of the heat source below that of the surroundings.

A refrigeration system is a combination of components, equipment, and piping, connected in a sequential order to produce the refrigeration effect. Refrigeration systems that provide coolingfor air-conditioning are classified mainly into the following categories:

1. Vapor compression systems. In these systems, a compressor(s) compresses the refrigerant to a higher pressure and temperature from an evaporated vapor at low pressure and temperature. The compressed refrigerant is condensed into liquid form by releasing the latent heat of condensation to the condenser water. Liquid refrigerant is then throttled to a low-pressure, low-temperature vapor, producing the refrigeration effect during evaporation. Vapor compression is often called mechanical refrigeration, that is, refrigeration by mechanical compression.

2. Absorption systems. In an absorption system, the refrigeration effect is produced by means of thermal energy input. After liquid refrigerant produces refrigeration during evaporation at very low pressure, the vapor is absorbed by an aqueous absorbent. The solution is heated by a direct-fired gas furnace or waste heat, and the refrigerant is again vaporized and then condensed into liquid form. The liquid refrigerant is throttled to a very low pressure and is ready to produce the refrigeration effect again.

3. Gas expansion systems. In an air or other gas expansion system, air or gas is compressed to a high pressure by compressors. It is then cooled by surface water or atmospheric air and expanded to a low pressure. Because the temperature of air or gas decreases during expansion, a refrigeration effect is produced.

Refrigerants, cooling mediums, and absorbents

A refrigerant is a primary working fluid used to produce refrigeration in a refrigeration system. All refrigerants extract heat at low temperature and low pressure during evaporation and reject heat at high temperature and pressure during condensation.

A cooling medium is a working fluid cooled by the refrigerant during evaporation to transport refrigeration from a central plant to remote cooling equipment and terminals. In a large, centralized air-conditioning system, it is more economical to pump the cooling medium to the remote locations where cooling is required. Chilled water and brine are cooling media. They are often called secondary refrigerants to distinguish them from the primary refrigerants.

A liquid absorbent is a working fluid used to absorb the vaporized refrigerant (water) after evaporation in an absorption refrigeration system. The solution that contains the absorbed vapor is then heated. The refrigerant vaporizes, and the solution is restored to its original concentration to absorb water vapor again.

A numbering system for refrigerants was developed for hydrocarbons and halocarbons. According to ANSI/ASHRAE Standard 34-1992, the first digit is the number of unsaturated carbon-carbon bonds in the compound. This digit is omitted if the number is zero. The second digit is the number of carbon atoms minus one. This is also omitted if the number is zero. The third digit denotes the number of hydrogen atoms plus one. The last digit indicates the number of fluorine atoms. For example, the chemical formula for refrigerant R-123 is $CHCl_2CF_3$. In this compound:

No unsaturated carbon-carbon bonds, first digit is   0

There are two carbon atoms, second digit is $2-1=1$

There is one hydrogen atom, third digit is $1+1=2$

There are three fluorine atoms, last digit is   3

To compare the relative ozone depletion of various refrigerants, an index called the ozone depletion potential (ODP) has been introduced. ODP is defined as the ratio of the rate of ozone depletion of 1 lb of any halocarbon to that of 1 lb of refrigerant R-11. For R-11, $ODP=1$.

Words and Expressions

refrigeration [rɪˌfrɪdʒəˈreɪʃən] n. 制冷
extracting heat 提取热量
cooling medium 冷却介质
sink [sɪŋk] vi. 淹没；下落
atmospheric air 大气
combination [kɑmbɪˈneɪʃn] n. 结合；联合体
category [ˈkætɪɡərɪ] n. 种类，类别
vapor compression system 蒸汽压缩系统
absorption system 吸收系统
gas expansion system 气体膨胀系统
brine [breɪn] n. 盐水
vaporized refrigerant 汽化的制冷剂
hydrocarbon [ˌhaɪdrəˈkɑːbən] n. 碳氢化合物，烃
halocarbon [ˈhæləˌkɑːbən] n. 卤烃
unsaturated [ˈʌnˈsætʃəreɪtɪd] adj. 不饱和的
be omitted [əʊˈmɪtɪd] v. 被遗漏；被省略
fluorine atom 氟原子
ozone depletion potential 臭氧消耗潜能

4.4 Ideal Single-stage Vapor Compression Cycle

Refrigeration Cycles

When a refrigerant undergoes a series of processes like evaporation, compression, condensation, throttling, and expansion, absorbing heat from a low-temperature source and rejecting it to a higher temperature sink, it is said to have undergone a refrigeration cycle. If its final state is equal to its initial state, it is a closed cycle; if the final state does not equal the initial state, it is an open cycle.

Vapor compression refrigeration cycles can be classified as single stage, multistage, compound, and cascade cycles.

A pressure-enthalpy diagram or p-h diagram is often used to calculate the energy transfer and to analyze the performance of a refrigeration cycle, as shown in Fig. 4.1. In a p-h diagram, pressure p, in psia or psig logarithmic scale, is the ordinate, and enthalpy h, in Btu/lb, is the abscissa. The saturated liquid and saturated vapor line encloses a two-phase region in which vapor and liquid coexist. The two-phase region separates the subcooling liquid and superheated vapor regions. The constant-temperature line is nearly vertical in the subcooling region, horizontal in the two-phase region, and curved down sharply in the superheated region.

In the two-phase region, a given saturated pressure determines the saturated temperature and vice versa. The constant-entropy line is curved upward to the right-hand side in the superheated region. Each kind of refrigerant has its own p-h diagram.

Refrigeration Processes in an Ideal Single-stage cycle

An ideal cycle has isentropic compression, and pressure losses in the pipeline, valves, and other components are neglected. All refrigeration cycles covered in this section are ideal. Single stage means a single stage of compression.

There are two refrigeration processes in an ideal single-stage vapor compression cycle, as shown in Fig. 4.2(a) and Fig. 4.2(b):

1. Isothermal evaporation process 4 − 1—The refrigerant evaporates completely in the evaporator and produces refrigeration effect q_{rf}, in Btu/lb:

$$q_{rf} = (h_1 - h_4) \qquad (4.1)$$

where h_1, h_4 = enthalpy of refrigerant at state points 1 and 4,

Refrigeration and Airconditioning 87

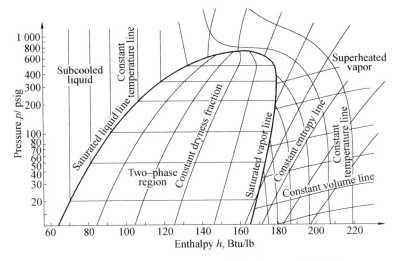

Fig. 4.1 Skeleton of pressure-enthalpy diagram for R-22

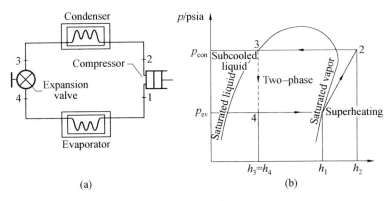

Fig. 4.2 A single-stage ideal vapor compression refrigeration cycle

respectively, Btu/lb.

2. Isentropic compression process 1 – 2—Vapor refrigerant is extracted by the compressor and compressed isentropically from point 1 to 2. The work input to the compressor W_{in}, in Btu/lb, is

$$W_{in} = (h_2 - h_1) \qquad (4.2)$$

where h_2 = enthalpy of refrigerant at state point 2, Btu/lb.

The greater the difference in temperature/pressure between the condensing pressure p_{con} and evaporating pressure p_{ev}, the higher will be the work input to the compressor.

3. Isothermal condensation process 2-3—Hot gaseous refrigerant discharged from the compressor is condensed in the condenser into liquid, and the latent heat of condensation is rejected to the condenser water or ambient air. The heat rejection during condensation, q_{2-3}, in Btu/lb, is

$$-q_{2-3} = (h_2 - h_3) \qquad (4.3)$$

where h_3 = enthalpy of refrigerant at state point 3, Btu/lb.

4. Throttling process 3 - 4—Liquid refrigerant flows through a throttling device (e.g., an expansion valve, a capillary tube, or orifices) and its pressure is reduced to the evaporating pressure. A portion of the liquid flashes into vapor and enters the evaporator. This is the only irreversible process in the ideal cycle, usually represented by a dotted line. For a throttling process, assuming that the heat gain from the surroundings is negligible:

$$h_3 = h_4 \qquad (4.4)$$

The mass flow rate of refrigerant $\overset{o}{m}_r$, n lb/min, is

$$\overset{o}{m}_r = q_{rc}/60 q_{rf} \qquad (4.5)$$

where q_{rc} = refrigeration capacity of the system, Btu/hr.

The ideal single-stage vapor compression refrigeration cycleon a $p-h$ diagram is divided into two pressure regions: high pressure (p_{con}) and low pressure (p_{ev}).

Coefficient of Performance of Refrigeration Cycle

The coefficient of performance (COP) is a dimensionless index used to indicate the performance of a thermodynamic cycle or thermal system. The magnitude of COP can be greater than 1.

- If a refrigerator is used to produce a refrigeration effect, COP_{ref} is

$$COP_{ref} = q_{rf}/W_{in} \qquad (4.6)$$

- If a heat pump is used to produce a useful heating effect, its performance denoted by COP_{hp} is

$$COP_{hp} = q_{2-3}/W_{in} \qquad (4.7)$$

- For a heat recovery system when both refrigeration and heating effects are produced, the COP_{hr} is denoted by the ratio of the sum of the absolute values of q_{rf} and q_{2-3} to the work input, or

$$COP_{hr} = (|q_{rf}| + |q_{2-3}|)/W_{in} \qquad (4.8)$$

Words and Expressions

undergo [ˌʌndə'gəʊ] *vt.* 经历,经验
evaporation [ɪˌvæpə'reɪʃn] *n.* 蒸发
compression [kəm'preʃn] *n.* 压缩
condensation [ˌkɒnden'seɪʃn] *n.* 冷凝
throttling [θ'rɒtlɪŋ] *n.* 节流
vapor compression refrigeration cycle 蒸汽压缩制冷循环
multistage ['mʌltɪsteɪdʒ] *adj.* 多级的
compound ['kɒmpaʊnd] *n.* 复合物
cascade [kæ'skeɪd] *n.* 串联
enthalpy [en'θælpɪ] *n.* 焓
logarithmic [ˌlɑgə'rɪðmɪk] *adj.* 对数的
ordinate ['ɔːdɪnət] *n.* 纵坐标
abscissa [æb'sɪsə] *n.* 横坐标
subcooling [sʌb'kuːlɪŋ] *adj.* 过冷的
superheated [ˌsuːpə'hiːtɪd] *adj.* 过热的
horizontal [ˌhɒrɪ'zɒntl] *adj.* 水平的

isentropic [aɪsen'trɒpɪk] *adj.* 等熵的
isothermal ['aɪsəʊ'θɜːməl] *adj.* 等温的
respectively [rɪ'spektɪvli] *adv.* 各自地；分别地
ambient ['æmbiənt] *adj.* 环境；周围的，包围着的
throttling [θ'rɒtlɪŋː] *v.* 压制
capillary tube 毛细管
portion ['pɔːʃn] *n.* 一部分
dimensionless [də'menʃənləs] *adj.* 无量纲的
index ['ɪndeks] *n.* 指数；标志
magnitude ['mægnɪtjuːd] *n.* 量级

4.5 Refrigeration Compressors

A refrigeration compressor is the heart of a vapor compression system. It raises the pressure of refrigerant so that it can be condensed into liquid, throttled, and evaporated into vapor to produce the refrigeration effect. It also provides the motive force to circulate the refrigerant through condenser, expansion valve, and evaporator.

According to the compression process, refrigeration compressors can be divided into positive displacement and nonpositive displacement compressors. A positive displacement compressor increases the pressure of the refrigerant by reducing the internal volume of the compression chamber. Reciprocating, scroll, rotary, and screw compressors are all positive displacement compressors. The centrifugal compressor is the only type of nonpositive displacement refrigeration compressor widely used in refrigeration systems today.

Based on the sealing of the refrigerant, refrigeration compressors can be classified as

· Hermetic compressors, in which the motor and the compressor are sealed or welded in the same housing to minimize leakage of refrigerant and to cool the motor windings by using suction vapor

· Semihermetic compressors, in which motor and compressor are enclosed in the same housing but are accessible from the cylinder head for repair and maintenance

· Open compressors, in which compressor and motor are enclosed in two separate housings

Refrigeration compressors are often driven by motor directly or by gear train.

Reciprocating Compressors

In a reciprocating compressor, as shown in Fig. 4.3 (a), a crankshaft connected to the motor shaft drives 2, 3, 4, or 6 single-acting pistons moving reciprocally in the cylinders via a connecting rod.

The refrigeration capacity of a reciprocating compressor is a fraction of a ton to about 200 tons. Refrigerants R-22 and R-134a are widely used in comfort and processing systems and sometimes R-717 in industrial applications. The maximum compression ratio R_{com} for a single-stage reciprocating compressor is about 7. Volumetric efficiency h_v drops from 0.92 to 0.65 when R_{com} is raised from 1 to 6. Capacity control of reciprocating compressor including: on-off and cylinder unloader in which discharge gas is in short cut and return to the suction chamber.

Although reciprocating compressors are still widely used today in small and medium-sized refrigeration systems, they have little room for significant improvement and will be gradually replaced by scroll and screw compressors.

Scroll Compressors

A scroll compressor consists of two identical spiral scrolls assembled opposite to each other, as shown in Fig. 4.3(b). One of the scrolls is fixed, and the other moves in an orbit around the motor shaft whose amplitude equals the radius of the orbit. The two scrolls are in contact at several points and therefore form a series of pockets.

Vapor refrigerant enters the space between two scrolls through lateral openings. The lateral openings are then sealed and the formation of the two trapped vapor pockets indicates the end of the suction process. The vapor is compressed and the discharge process begins when the trapped gaseous pockets open to the discharge port. Compressed hot gas is then discharged through this opening to the discharge line. In a scroll compressor, the scrolls touch each other with sufficient force to form a seal but not enough to cause wear.

The upper limit of the refrigeration capacity of currently manufactured scroll compressors is 60 tons. A scroll compressor has $h_v > 95\%$ at $R_{com} = 4$ and $h_{isen} = 80\%$. A scroll compressor also has only about half as many parts as a reciprocating compressor at the same refrigeration capacity. Few components result in higher reliability and efficiency. Power input to the scroll compressor is about 5% to 10% less than to the reciprocating compressor. A scroll compressor also operates more smoothly and is quieter.

Rotary Compressors

Small rotary compressors for room air conditioners and refrigerators have a capacity up to 4 tons. There are two types of rotary compressors: rolling piston and rotating vane. A typical rolling piston rotary compressor is shown in Fig. 4.3(c). A rolling piston mounted on an eccentric shaft is kept in contact with a fixed vane that slides in a slot. Vapor refrigerant enters the compression chamber and is compressed by the eccentric motion of the roller. When the rolling piston contacts the top housing, hot gas is squeezed out from the discharge valve.

Screw Compressors

These are also called helical rotary compressors. Screw compressors can be classified into single-screw compressors, in which there is a single helical rotor and two star wheels, and twin-screw compressors. Twin-screw compressors are widely used.

A typical twin-screw compressor, as shown in Fig. 4.3 (d) consists of a four-lobe male rotor and a six-lobe female rotor, a housing with suction and discharge ports, and a sliding valve to adjust the capacity during part load. Normally, the male rotor is the driver. Twin-screw compressors are often direct driven and of hermetic type.

Vapor refrigerant is extracted into the interlobe space when the lobes are separated at the suction port. During the successive rotations of the rotor, the volume of the trapped vapor is compressed. When the interlobe space is in contact with the discharge port, the compressed hot gas discharges through the outlet. Oil injection effectively cools the rotors and results in a lower discharge temperature. Oil also provides a sealing effect and lubrication. A small clearance of 0.000 5 in. as well as the oil sealing minimizes leakage of the refrigerant.

The refrigeration capacity of twin-screw compressors is 50 to 1 500 tons. The compression ratio of a twin-screw compressor can be up to 20:1. R-22 and R-134a are the most widely used refrigerants in comfort systems. In a typical twin-screw compressor, h_v decreases from 0.92 to 0.87 and h_{isen} drops from 0.82 to 0.67 when R_{com} increases from 2 to 10. Continuous and stepless capacity control is provided by moving a sliding valve toward the discharge port, which opens a shortcut recirculating passage to the suction port.

Twin-screw compressors are more efficient than reciprocating compressors. The low noise and vibration of the twin-screw compressor together with its positive displacement compression results in more applications today.

Centrifugal Compressors

A centrifugal compressor is a turbomachine and is similar to a centrifugal fan. A hermetic centrifugal compressor has an outer casing with one, two, or even three impellers internally connected in series and is driven by a motor directly or by a gear train. At the entrance to the first-stage impeller are inlet guide vanes positioned at a specific opening to adjust refrigerant flow and therefore the capacity of the centrifugal compressor.

Fig. 4.3 (e) shows a two-stage hermetic centrifugal compressor. The total pressure rise in a centrifugal compressor, often called head lift, in psi, is due to the conversion of the velocity pressure into static pressure. Although the compression ratio R_{com} of a single-stage centrifugal compressor using R-123 and R-22 seldom exceeds 4, two or three impellers connected in series satisfy most of the requirements in comfort systems.

Because of the high head lift to raise the evaporating pressure to condensing pressure, the discharge velocity at the exit of the second-stage impeller approaches the acoustic velocity of saturated vapor v_{ac} of R-123, 420 ft/sec at atmospheric pressure and a temperature of 80 °F. Centrifugal compressors need high peripheral velocity and rotating speeds (up to 50 000 rpm) to produce such a discharge

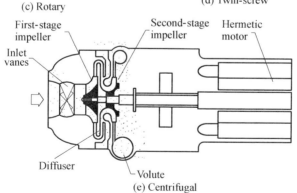

Fig. 4.3 Various types of refrigeration compressors

velocity. It is not economical to manufacture small centrifugal compressors. The available refrigeration capacity for centrifugal compressors ranges from 100 to 10 000 tons. Centrifugal compressors have higher volume flow per unit refrigeration capacity output than positive displacement compressors. Centrifugal compressors are efficient and reliable. Their volumetric efficiency almost equals 1. At design conditions, their h_{isen} may reach 0.83, and it drops to 0.6 during part-load operation. They are the most widely used refrigeration compressors in large air-conditioning systems.

Words and Expressions

nonpositive ['nɒn'pɒzɪtɪv] adj. 非正的,(整数)负的
chamber ['tʃeɪmbə(r)] n. 室
hermetic compressor 密封式压缩机
semihermetic compressor 半封闭压缩机
open compressor 开式压缩机
reciprocating compressor 往复式压缩机
crankshaft ['kræŋkʃɑːft] n. 曲轴
piston ['pɪstən] n. 活塞
cylinder ['sɪlɪndə(r)] n. 气缸
fraction ['frækʃn] n. 分数
unloader ['ʌn'ləʊdə] n. 减荷器,减压器
scroll compressor 涡旋式压缩机
amplitude ['æmplɪtjuːd] n. 振幅
orbit ['ɔːbɪt] n. 轨道
rotary compressor 旋转式压缩机
rotating vane 旋转叶片
eccentric [ɪk'sentrɪk] adj. 离心的
screw compressor 螺杆式压缩机
helical rotor 螺旋转子
interlobe space (容积式压气机)叶间容积

centrifugal compressor 离心式压缩机
turbomachine 涡轮机
hermetic [hɜːˈmetɪk] adj. 密封的
impeller [ɪmˈpelə] n. 叶轮

4.6 Refrigeration Systems

Classifications of Refrigeration Systems

Most of the refrigeration systems used for air-conditioning are vapor compression systems. Because of the increase in the energy cost of natural gas in the 1980s, the application of absorption refrigeration systems has dropped sharply. According to Commercial Buildings Characteristics 1992, absorption refrigeration system have a weight of less than 3% of the total amount of refrigeration used in commercial buildings in the United States. Air expansion refrigeration systems are used mainly in aircraft and cryogenics.

Refrigeration systems used for air-conditioning can be classified mainly in the following categories:
- Direct expansion(DX) systems and heat pumps
- Centrifugal chillers
- Screw chillers
- Absorption systems

Each can be either a single-stage or a multistagesystem.

Direct Expansion Refrigeration Systems

A direct expansion refrigeration (DX) system, or simply DX system, is part of the packaged air-conditioning system. The DX coil in the packaged unit is used to cool and dehumidify the air directly as shown in Fig. 4.4. According to EIA Commercial Buildings

Characteristics 1992, about 74% of the floor space of commercial buildings in the United States was cooled by DX refrigeration systems.

Refrigerants R-22 and R-134a are widely used. Azeotropics and near azeotropics are the refrigerants often used for low-evaporating-temperature systems like those in supermarkets. Because of the limitation of the size of the air system, the refrigeration capacity of DX systems is usually 3 to 100 tons.

Components and Accessories. In addition to the DX coil, a DX refrigeration system has the following components and accessories:

· Compressor(s)—Both reciprocating and scroll compressors are widely used in DX systems. Scroll compressors are gradually replacing reciprocating compressors because they have fewer parts and comparatively higher efficiency. For large DX systems, multiple compressors are adopted.

· Condensers—Most DX systems in rooftop packaged units are air cooled. Water-cooled condensers are adopted mainly for DX systems in indoor packaged units due to their compact volume. Evaporative-cooled condensers are also available.

· Refrigerationfeed—Thermostatic expansion valves are widely used as the throttling and refrigerant flow control devices in medium and large DX systems, whereas capillary tubes are used in small and medium-sized systems.

· Oil lubrication—R-22 is partly miscible with mineral oil. Since R-134a is not miscible with mineral oil, synthetic polyolester oil should be used. For medium and large reciprocating compressors, an oil pump of vane, gear, or centrifugal type is used to force the lubricating oil to the bearings and moving surfaces via grooves. For small reciprocating compressors, splash lubrication using the rotation of the crankshaft and the connecting rod to splash oil onto the bearing surface and the cylinder walls is used.

A scroll compressor is often equipped with a centrifugal oil pump to force the oil to lubricate the orbiting scroll journal bearing and motor bearing. For the scroll contact surfaces, lubrication is provided by the small amount of oil entrained in the suction vapor.

• Refrigerant piping—Refrigerant piping transports refrigerant through the compressor, condenser, expansion valve, and DX coil to provide the required refrigeration effect. As shown in Fig. 4.4, from the exit of the DX coil to the inlet of the compressor(s) is the suction line. From the outlet of the compressor to the inlet of the air-cooled condenser is the discharge line. From the exit of the condenser to the inlet of the expansion valve is the liquid line.

Heat Pumps

A heat pump in the form of a packaged unit is also a heat pump system. A heat pump can either extract heat from a heat source and reject heat to air and water at a higher temperature for heating, or provide refrigeration at a lower temperature and reject condensing heat at a higher temperature for cooling. During summer, the heat extraction, or refrigeration effect, is the useful effect for cooling in a heat pump. In winter, the rejected heat and the heat from a supplementary heater provide heating in a heat pump.

There are three types of heat pumps: air-source, water-source, and ground-coupled heat pumps. Ground-coupled heat pumps have limited applications. Water-source heat pump systems are covered in detail in a later section.

Air-Source Heat Pump. An air-source heat pump, or air-to-air heat pump, is a DX system with an additional four-way reversing valve to change the refrigerant flow from cooling mode in summer to heating

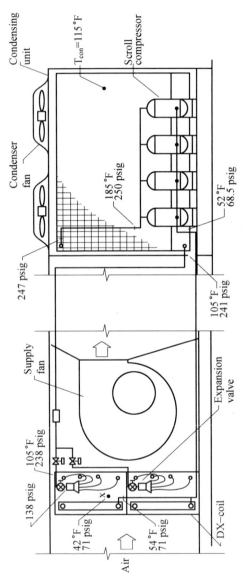

Fig.4.4 The schematic diagram of a DX refrigeration system

mode in winter and vice versa. The variation in connections between four means of refrigerant flow—compressor suction, compressor discharge, DX coil exit, and condenser inlet—causes the function of the indoor and outdoor coils to reverse. In an air-source heat pump, the coil used to cool or to heat the recirculating/outdoor air is called the indoor coil. The coil used to reject heat to or absorb heat from the outside atmosphere is called the outdoor coil. A short capillary or restrict tube is often used instead of a thermostatic expansion valve. Both reciprocating and scroll compressors are used in air-source heat pumps. R-22 is the refrigerant widely used. Currently available air-source heat pumps usually have a cooling capacity of 1.5 to 40 tons.

Cooling and Heating Mode Operation. In cooling mode operation, as shown in Fig. 4.5(a), the solenoid valve is deenergized and drops downward. The high-pressure hot gas pushes the sliding connector to the left end. The compressor discharge connects to the outdoor coil, and the indoor coil connects to the compressor inlet.

In heating mode operation, as shown in Fig. 4.5(b), the solenoid plunger moves upward and pushes the slide connector to the right-hand side. The compressor discharge connects to the indoor coil, and the outdoor coil exit connects to the compressor suction.

System Performance. The performance of an air-source heat pump depends on the outdoor air temperature To in °F as well as the required space heating load q_{rh}. During cooling mode operation, both the refrigeration capacity q_{rc}, in Btu/hr, and EER for the heat pump EER_{hp}, in Btu/hr.W, increase as To drops. During heating mode operation, the heating capacity q_{hp}, in Btu/hr, and COP_{hp} decrease, and q_{rh} increases as the To drops. When $q_{rh} > q_{hp}$, supplementary heating is required. If COP_{hp} drops below 1, electric heating may be more economical than a heat pump.

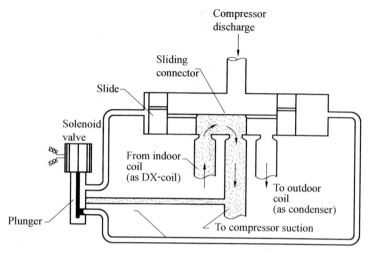

(a) four-way reversing valve, cooling mode

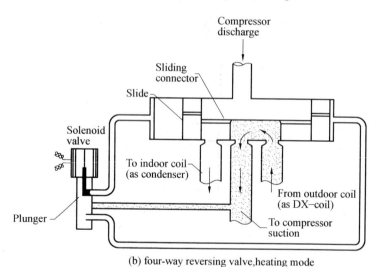

(b) four-way reversing valve, heating mode

Fig. 4.5 A DX refrigeration system

If on-off is used for compressor capacity control for an air-source heat pump in a split packaged unit, refrigerant tends to migrate from the warmer outdoor coil to the cooler indoor coil in summer and from the warmer indoor coil to the cooler outdoor coil in winter during the off period. When the compressor starts again, 2 to 5 min of reduced capacity is experienced before the heat pump can be operated at full capacity. Such a loss is called a cycling loss.

In winter, most air-source heat pumps switch from the heating mode to cooling mode operation and force the hot gas to the outdoor coil to melt frost. After the frost is melted, the heat pump is switched back to heating mode operation. During defrosting, supplementary electric heating is often necessary to prevent a cold air supply from the air-source heat pump.

Centrifugal Chillers

A chiller is a refrigeration machine using a liquid cooler as an evaporator to produce chilled water as the cooling medium in a central air-conditioning system. A centrifugal chiller is a refrigeration machine using a centrifugal compressor to produce chilled water. It is often a factory-assembled unit with an integrated DDC control system and sometimes may separate into pieces for transportation. A centrifugal chiller is also a centrifugal vapor compression refrigeration system.

System Components. A centrifugal chiller consists of a centrifugal compressor, an evaporator or liquid cooler, a condenser, a flash cooler, throttling devices, piping connections, and controls. A purge unit is optional.

· Centrifugal compressor—According to the number of internally connected impellers, the centrifugal compressor could have a single, two, or more than two stages. A two-stage impeller with a flash cooler is most widely used because of its higher system performance and comparatively simple construction. Centrifugal compressors having a refrigeration capacity less than 1 200 tons are often hermetic. Very large centrifugal compressors are of open type. A gear train is often required to raise the speed of the impeller except for very large impellers using direct drive.

· Evaporator—Usually a liquid cooler of flooded shell-and-tube type evaporator is adopted because of its compact size and high rate of heat transfer.

· Condenser—Water-cooled, horizontal shell-and-tube condensers are widely used.

· Flash cooler—For a two-stage centrifugal compressor, a single-stage flash cooler is used. For a three-stage compressor, a two-stage flash cooler is used.

· Orifice plates and float valves—Both multiple-orifice plates and float valves are used as throttling devices in centrifugal chillers.

· Purge unit—R-123 has an evaporating pressure $p_{ev} = 5.8$ psia at 40 °F, which is lower than atmospheric pressure. Air and other noncondensable gases may leak into the evaporator through cracks and gaps and usually accumulate in the upper part of the condenser. These noncondensable gases raise the condensing pressure, reduce the refrigerant flow, and lower the rate of heat transfer. A purge unit uses a cooling coil to separate the refrigerant and water from the noncondensable gases and purge the gases by using a vacuum pump.

Screw Chillers

A screw chiller or a helical rotary chiller is a refrigeration machine using a screw compressor to produce chilled water. A factory-fabricated and assembled screw chiller itself is also a screw vapor compression refrigeration system.

Twin-screw chillers are more widely used than single-screw

chillers. A twin-screw chiller consists of mainly a twin-screw compressor, aflooded shell-and-tube liquid cooler as evaporator, a water-cooled condenser, throttling devices, an oil separator, an oil cooler, piping, and controls. The construction of twin-screw compressors has already been covered. For evaporator, condenser, and throttling devices, they are similar to those in centrifugal chillers. Most twin-screw chillers have a refrigeration capacity of 100 to 1 000 tons.

Following are the systems characteristics of screw chillers.

Economizer. The hermetic motor shell is connected to an intermediate point of the compression process and maintains an intermediate pressure p_i between p_{con} and p_{ev}. Liquid refrigerant at condensing pressure p_{con} is throttled to p_i, and a portion of the liquid is flashed into vapor. This causes a drop in the temperature of the remaining liquid refrigerant down to the saturated temperature corresponding to p_i. Although the compression in a twin-screw compressor is in continuous progression, the mixing of flashed gas with the compressed gas at the intermediate point actually divides the compression process into two stages. The resulting economizing effect is similar to that of a two-stage compound refrigeration system with a flash cooler: an increase of the refrigeration effect and a saving of the compression power from $(p_{con}-p_{ev})$ to $(p_{con}-p_i)$.

Oil Separation, Oil Cooling, and Oil Injection. Oil entrained in the discharged hot gas enters an oil separator. In the separator, oil impinges on an internal perforated surface and is collected because of its inertia. Oil drops to an oil sump through perforation. It is then cooled by condenser water in a heat exchanger. A heater is often used to vaporize the liquid refrigerant in the oil sump to prevent dilution of the oil. Since the oil sump is on the high-pressure side of the refrigeration system, oil is forced to the rotor bearings and injected to the rotors for lubrication.

Oil slugging is not a problem for twin-screw compressors. When suction vapor contains a small amount of liquid refrigerant that carries over from the oil separator, often called wet suction, it often has the benefit of scavenging the oil from the evaporator.

Twin-screw compressors are positive displacement compressors. They are critical in oil lubrication, sealing, and cooling. They are also more energy efficient than reciprocating compressors. Twin-screw chillers are gaining more applications, especially for ice-storage systems with cold air distribution.

Words and Expressions

direct expansion system　直接膨胀式系统
centrifugal chiller　离心式冷水机组
screw chiller　螺杆式冷水机组
azeotropic　[ˌəˌziːəˈtrɒpɪk]　*adj.* 共沸的,恒沸点的
accessary　[əkˈsesəri]　*n.* 附件
lubrication　[luːbrɪˈkeɪʃən]　*n.* 润滑
synthetic polyolester oil　合成多元醇酯油
splash lubrication　[splæʃˌluːbrɪˈkeɪʃən]　*n.* 飞溅润滑
crankshaft　[ˈkræŋkʃɑːft]　*n.* 曲轴
refrigerant piping　冷媒管道
ground-coupled heat pumps　地面耦合热泵
deenergized　[ˈdiːnədʒaɪzd]　*v.* 被断电的
solenoid plunger　电磁柱塞
orifice plates　孔板
float valves　浮阀
multiple　[ˈmʌltɪpl]　*adj.* 多重的;多个的
shell-and-tube liquid　管壳式液体

4.7 Absorption System

Absorption systems use heat energy to produce refrigeration as well as heating if it is required. Water is the refrigerant and aqueous lithium bromide (LiBr) is widely used as the carrier to absorb the refrigerant and provide a higher coefficient of performance.

The mixture of water and anhydrous LiBr is called solution. The composition of a solution is usually expressed by its mass fraction, or percentage of LiBr, often called concentration. When the water vapor has boiled off from the solution, it is called concentration solution. If the solution has absorbed the water vapor, it is called diluted solution.

Absorption systems can be divided into the following categories:

· Absorption chillers use heat energy to produce refrigeration.

· Absorption chiller/heaters use direct-fired heat input to provide cooling or heating separately.

· Absorption heat pumps extract heat energy from the evaporator, add to the heat input, and release them both to the hot water for heating.

· Absorption heat transformers raise the temperature of the waste heat source to a required level.

Most recently installed absorption chillers use direct-fired natural gas as the heat source in many locations in the United States where there are high electric demand and electric rate at on-peak hours. Absorption chillers also are free from CFC and HCFC. An energy cost analysis should be done to determine whether an electric chiller or a gas-fired absorption chiller is the suitable choice.

Absorption heat pumps have only limited applications in district heating. Most absorption heat transformers need industrial waste heat. Both of them will not be covered here.

Double-effect Direct-fired Absorption Chillers

Fig. 4.6 shows a double-effect direct-fired absorption chiller. Double effect means that there are two generators. Direct fired means that gas is directly fired at the generator instead of using steam or hot water. A single-effect absorption chiller using steam as the heat input to its single generator has a COP only from 0.7 to 0.8, whereas a double-effect direct-fired absorption chiller has a COP approximately equal to 1 and therefore is the mot widely used absorption chiller in the United States for new and retrofit projects today. The refrigeration capacity of double-effect direct-fired absorption chillers varies from 100 to 1 500 tons.

A double-effect direct-fired absorption chiller mainly consists of the following components and controls:

• Evaporator—An evaporator is comprised of a tube bundle, spray nozzles, a water trough, a refrigerant pump, and an outer shell. Chilled water flows inside the tubes. A refrigerant pump sprays the liquid refrigerant over the outer surface of the tube bundle for a higher rate of evaporation. A water trough is located at the bottom to maintain a water level for recirculation.

• Absorber—In an absorber, there are tubebundles in which cooling water flows inside the tubes. Solution is sprayed over the outer surface of the tube bundle to absorb the water vapor. A solution pump is used to pump the diluted solution to the heat exchanger and low-temperature generator.

• Heat exchangers—There are two heat exchangers: low-temperature heat exchanger in which the temperature of hot concentrated solution is lower, and high-temperature heat exchanger in which the temperature of hot concentrated solution is higher. In both heat exchangers, heat is transferred from the hot concentrated solution to the cold diluted solution. Shell-and-tube or plate-and-frame heat exchangers are most widely used for their higher effectiveness.

· Generators—Generators are also called desorbers. In the direct-fired generator, there are the fire tube, flue tube, vapor/liquid separator, and flue-gas economizer. Heat is supplied from the gas burner or other waste heat source. The low-temperature generator is often of the shell-and-tube type. The water vapor vaporized in the direct-fired generator is condensed inside the tubes. The latent heat of condensation thus released is used to vaporize the dilute solution in the lowtemperature generator.

· Condenser—A condenser is usually also of the shell-and-tube type. Cooling water from the absorber flows inside the tubes.

· Throttling devices—Orifices and valves are often used as throttling devices to reduce the pressure of refrigerant and solution to the required values.

· Air purge unit—Since the pressure inside the absorption chiller is below atmospheric pressure, air and other noncondensable gases will leak into it from the ambient air. An air purge unit is used to remove these noncondensable gases from the chiller. A typical air purge unit is comprised of a pickup tube, a purge chamber, a solution spray, cooling water tubes, a vacuum pump, a solenoid valve, and a manual shut-off valve.

When noncondensable gases leak into the system, they tend to migrate to the absorber where pressure is lowest. Noncondensable gases and water vapor are picked from the absorber through the pickup tube. Water vapor is absorbed by the solution spray and returned to the absorber through a liquid trap at the bottom of the purge chamber. Heat of absorption is removed by the cooling water inside the tubes.

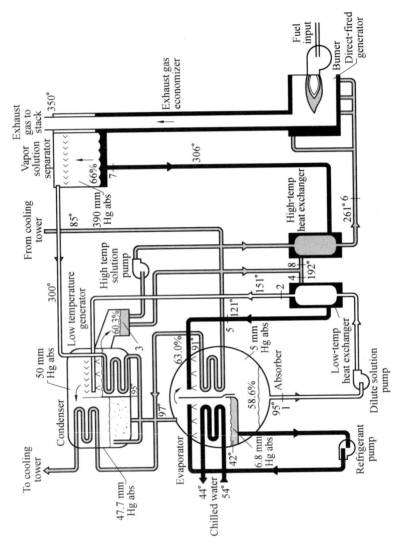

Fig. 4.6 A double-effect direct-fired reverse-parallel-flow absorption chiller; schematic diagram (reprinted by permission from the Trane catalog)

Noncondensable gases are then evacuated from the chamber periodically by a vacuum pump to the outdoor atmosphere.

Palladium cells are used to continuously remove a small amount of hydrogen that is produced due to corrosion. Corrosion inhibitors like lithium chromate are needed to protect the machine parts from the corrosive effect of the absorbent when air is present.

Absorption Cycles, Parallel-, Series-, and Reverse-parallel Flow

An absorption cycle shows the properties of the solution and its variation in concentrations, temperature, and pressure during absorbing, heat exchanging, and concentration processes on an equilibrium chart as shown in Fig. 4.7. The ordinate of the equilibrium chart is the saturated temperature and pressure of water vapor in °F and mm Hg abs. The abscissa is the temperature of the solution in °F. Concentration lines are incline lines. At the bottom of the concentration lines, there is a crystallization line or saturation line. If the mass of fraction of LiBr in a solution which remains at constant temperature is higher than the saturated condition, that part of LiBr exceeding the saturation condition tends to form solid crystals.

Because there are two generators, the flow of solution from the absorber to generators can bein series flow, parallel flow, or reverse-parallel flow. In a series-flow system, the diluted solution from the absorber is first pumped to the direct-fired generator and then to the low-temperature generator. In a parallel-flow system, diluted solution is pumped to both direct-fired and low-temperature generators in parallel. In a reverse-parallel-flow system as shown in Fig. 4.6, diluted solution is first pumped to the lowtemperature generator. After that, the partly concentrated solution is then sent to the direct-fired generator as

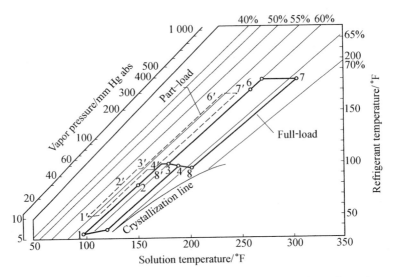

Fig. 4.7 A double-effect direct-fired reverse-parallel-flow absorption chiller: absorption cycle

well as to the intermediate point 4 between high- and low-temperature heat exchangers in parallel. At point 4, partly concentrated solution mixes with concentrated solution from a direct-fired generator. A reverse-parallel-flow system is more energy efficient.

Solution and Refrigerant Flow

In a typical double-effect direct-fired reverse-parallel-flow absorption chiller operated at design full load, water is usually evaporated at a temperature of 42 °F and a saturated pressure of 6.8 mm Hg abs in the evaporator. Chilled water returns from the AHUs or fan coils at a temperature typically 54 °F, cools, and leaves the evaporator at 44 °F. A refrigeration effect is produced due to the vaporization of water vapor and the removal of latent heat of vaporization from the chilled water.

Water vapor in the evaporator is then extracted to the absorber due to its lower vapor pressure. It is absorbed by the concentrated LiBr solution at a pressure of about 5 mm Hg abs. After absorption, the solutionis diluted to a concentration of 58.6% and its temperature increases to 95 °F (point 1). Most of the heat of absorption and the sensible heat of the solution is removed by the cooling water inside the tube bundle. Diluted solution is then pumped by a solution pump to the low-temperature generator through a low-temperature heat exchanger.

In the low-temperature generator, the dilute solution is partly concentrated to 60.3% at a solution temperature of 180 °F (point 3). It then divides into two streams: one ofthem is pumped to the directfired generator through a high-temperature heat exchanger, and the other stream having a slightly greater mass flow rate is sent to the intermediate point 4. In the direct-fired generator, the concentrated solution leaves at a concentration of 66% and a solution temperature of 306 °F (point 7).

The mixture of concentrated and partly concentrated solution at point 4 has a concentration of 63% and a temperature of 192 °F. It enters the low-temperature heat exchanger. Its temperature drops to 121 °F before entering the absorber (point 5).

In the direct-fired generator, water is boiled off at a pressure of about 390 mm Hg abs. The boiled off water vapor flows through the submerged tube in the low-temperature generator. The release of latent heat of condensation causes the evaporation of water from the dilution solution at a vapor pressure of about 50 mm Hg abs. The boiled-off water vapor in the low-temperature generator flows to the condenser through the top passage and is condensed into liquid water at a temperature of about 99 °F and a vapor pressure of 47.7 mm Hg abs.

This condensed liquid water is combined with the condensed water from the submerged tube at the trough. Both of them return to the evaporator after its pressure is throttled by an orifice plate.

Part-load Operation and Capacity Control

During part-load operation, a double-effect direct-fired reverse-parallel-flow absorption chiller adjusts its capacity by reducing the heat input to the direct-fired generator through the burner. Lower heat input results at less water vapor boiled off from the solution in the generators. This causes the drop in solution concentration, the amount of water vapor extracted, the rate of evaporation, and the refrigeration capacity. Due to less water vapor being extracted, both evaporating pressure and temperature will rise. Since the amount of water vapor to be condensed is greater than that boiled off from the generators, both the condensing pressure and condensing temperature decrease.

Coefficient of Performance (COP)

The COP of an absorption chiller can be calculated as
$$COP = 12\ 000/q_{lg} \qquad (4.9)$$
where q_{lg} = heat input to the direct-fired generator per ton of refrigeration output (Btu/hr. ton).

Safety Controls

Safety controls in an absorption chiller include the following:
· Crystallization controls are devices available to prevent crystallization and dissolve crystals. Absorption chillers are now designed to operate in a region away from the crystallization line. It is no longer a serious problem in newly developed absorption systems. One such device uses a bypass valve to permit refrigerant to flow to the

concentration solution line when crystallization is detected. Condenser water temperature is controlled by using a three-way bypass valve to mix the recirculating water with the evaporated cooled water from the tower to avoid the sudden drop of the temperature of concentrated solution in the absorber.

· Low-temperature cut-out control shuts down the absorption chiller if the temperature of the refrigerant in the evaporator falls below a preset limit to protect the evaporator from freezing.

· Chilled and cooling water flow switches stop the absorption chiller when the mass flow rate of chilled water or the supply of cooling water falls below a preset value.

· A high-pressure relief valve is often installed on the shell of the direct-fired generator to prevent its pressure from exceeding a predetermined value.

· Monitoring of low and high pressure of gas supply and flame ignition are required for direct-fired burner(s).

· Interlocked controls between absorption chiller and chilled water pumps, cooling water pumps, and cooling tower fans are used to guarantee that they are in normal operation before the absorption chiller starts.

Words and Expressions

aqueous lithium bromide　溴化锂溶液
double-effect direct-fired absorption chiller　双效直燃型吸收式制冷机
the latent heat　潜热
throttling device　节流装置
air purge unit　空气净化装置
vacuum pump　真空泵
solenoid valve　电磁阀
manual shut-off valve　手动截止阀

equilibrium chart 平衡图
crystallization [ˌkrɪstəlaɪ'zeɪʃn] n. 结晶
saturation line 饱和线
reverse-parallel flow 反向平行流
diluted solution 稀溶液
submerged tube 埋管
part-load operation 部分负荷运行
monitoring ['mɒnɪtərɪŋ] n. 监测
interlocked control 联锁控制

4.8 Air-Conditioning Systems

Basics in classification

The purpose of classifing air-conditioning or HVAC & R systems is to distinguish one type from another so that an optimum air-conditioning system can be selected according to the requirements. Proper classification of air-conditioning systems also will provide a background for using knowledge-based expert systems to help the designer to select an air-conditioning system and its subsystems.

Since air system characteristics directly affect the space indoor environmental parameters and the indoor air quality, the characteristics of an air system should be clearly designated in the classification.

The system and equipment should be compatible with each other. Each system has its own characteristics which are significantly different from others.

Individual Systems

As described in Section 4.1, air conditoning or HVAC & R systems can be classified as individual, space, packaged, and central systems.

Individual systems usually have no duct and are installed only in rooms that have external walls and external windows. Individual systems can again be subdivided into the following.

Room Air-conditioner Systems

A room air conditioner is the sole factory-fabricated self-contained equipment used in the room airconditioning system. It is often mounted on or under the window sill or on a window frame. A room air-conditioner consists mainly of an indoor coil, a small forward-curved centrifugal fan for indoor coil, a capillary tube, a low-efficiency dry and reusable filter, grilles, a thermostat or other controls located in the indoor compartment, and a rotary, scroll, or reciprocating compressor, an outdoor coil, and a propeller fan for the outdoor coil located in the outdoor compartment. There is an outdoor ventilation air intake opening and a manually operated damper on the casing that divides the indoor and outdoor compartments. Room air-conditioners have a cooling capacity between 1/2 to 2 tons.

Packaged Terminal Air-conditioner (PTAC) Systems

A packaged terminal air-conditioner is the primary equipment in a PTAC system. A PTAC system is similar to a room air-conditioner system. Their main differences are

· A PTAC uses a wall sleeve and is intended to be mounted through the wall.

· Heating is available from hot water, steam, heat pump, electric heater, and sometimes even directfired gas heaters.

PTACs are available in cooling capacity between 1/2 to $1\frac{1}{2}$ tons and a heating capacity of 2 500 to 35 000 Btu/hr.

Space (space-conditioning) Systems

Most space conditioning air-conditioning systems cool, heat, and filtrate their recirculating space air above or in the conditioned space. Space conditioning systems often incorporate heat recovery by transferring the heat rejected from the interior zone to the perimeter zone through the condenser(s). Space systems often have a separate outdoor ventilation air system to supply the required outdoor ventilation air.

Space systems can be subdivided into four-pipe fan-coil systems and water-source heat pump systems.

Four-pipe Fan-coil Systems

In a four-pipe fan-coil unit system, space recirculating air is cooled and heated at a fancoil by using four pipes: one chilled water supply, one hot water supply, one chilled water return, and one hot water return. Outdoor ventilation air is conditioned at a make-up AHU or primary AHU. It is then supplied to the fan coil where it mixes with the recirculating air, or is supplied to the conditioned space directly.

Water-source Heat Pump Systems

Water-source heat pumps(WSHPs) are the primary equipment in a water-source heat pump system. A water-source heat pump usually consists of an air coil to cool and heat the air; a water coil to reject and extract heat from the condenser water; a forward-curved centrifugal fan; reciprocating, rotary, or scroll compressor(s); a short capillary tube; a reversing valve; controls; and an outer casing. WSHPs could be either a horizontal or vertical unit. WSHPs usually have cooling capacities between 1/2 to 26 tons. Small-capacity WSHPs of 3 tons or less without ducts are used in perimeter zones, whereas large-capacity WSHPs with ductwork are used only in interior zones.

Packaged Systems

In packaged systems, air is cooled directly by a DX coil and heated by direct-fired gas furnace or electric heater in a packaged unit (PU) instead of chilled and hot water from a central plant in a central system. Packaged systems are different from space conditioning systems since variable-air-volume supply and air economizer could be features in a packaged system. Packaged systems are often used to serve two or more rooms with supply and return ducts instead of serving individual rooms only in an individual system.

Packaged units are divided according to their locations into rooftop, split, or indoor units. Based on their operating characteristics, packaged systems can be subdivided into the following systems:

Single-zone constant-volume (CV) packaged systems

Although a single-zone CV packaged system may have duct supplies to and returns from two or more rooms, there is only a single zone sensor located in the representative room or space. A CV system has a constant supply volume flow rate during operation except the undesirable reduction of volume flow due to the increase of pressure drop across the filter.

A single-zone CV packaged system consists mainly of a centrifugal fan, a DX coil, a direct-fired gas furnace or an electric heater, a low or medium efficiency filter, mixing box, dampers, DDC controls, and an outer casing. A relief or a return fan is equipped for larger systems.

Constant-volume zone-reheat packaged systems

System construction and system characteristics of a CV zone-reheat system are similar to the singlezone CV packaged systems except:

1. It serves multizones and has a sensor and a DDC controller for each zone.

2. There is a reheating coil or electric heater in the branch duct for each zone.

A CV zone-reheat packaged system cools and heats simultaneously and therefore wastes energy. It is usually used for the manufacturing process and space needs control of temperature and humidity simultaneously.

Variable-air-volume packaged systems

A variable-air-volume(VAV) system varies its volume flow rate to match the reduction of space load at part load. A VAV packaged system, also called a VAV cooling packaged system, is a multizone system and uses a VAV box in each zone to control the zone temperature at part load during summer cooling mode operation.

A VAV box is a terminal in which the supply volume flow rate of the conditioned supply air is modulated by varying the opening of the air passage by means of a single blade damper, or a moving disc against a cone-shaped casing.

VAV reheat packaged systems

A VAV reheat packaged system has its system construction and characteristics similar to that in a VAV packaged system except in each VAV box there is an additional reheating coil. Such a VAV box is called a reheating VAV box. VAV reheat packaged systems are used to serve perimeter zones where winter heating is required.

Fan-powered VAV packaged systems

A fan-powered VAV packaged system is similar to that of a VAV packaged system except fan-powered VAV boxes are used instead of VAV boxes.

There are two types of fan-powered VAV boxes: parallel-flow and series-flow boxes. In a parallel flow fan-powered box, the plenum air flow induced by the fan is parallel with the cold primary air flow through the VAV box. These two air streams are then combined and mixed together. In a series-flow box, cold primarily from the VAV box is mixed with the induced plenum air and then flows through the small fan. The parallel-flow fan-powered VAV box is more widely used.

Central systems

Central systems use chilled and hot water that comes from the central plant to cool and heat the air in the air-handling units (AHUs). Central systems are built-up systems. The most clean, most quiet thermalstorage systems, and the systems which offer the most sophisticated features, are always central systems. Central systems can be subdivided into the following.

Single-zone constant-volume central systems

A single-zone CV central system uses a single controller to control the flow of chilled water, hot water, or the opening of dampers to maintain a predetermined indoor temperature, relative humidity, or air contaminants. They are often used in manufacturing factories. The system characteristics of a single-zone CV central system are

Single-zone CV air washer central system uses air washer to control both space relative humidity and temperature. This system is widely used in textile mills. The reason to use constant volume is to dilute the fiber dusts produced during manufacturing. A rotary filter is often used for high dust-collecting capacity.

Single-zone CV clean room systems

This is the central system which controls the air cleanliness, temperature, and relative humidity in Class1, 10, 100, 1000, and 10,000 clean rooms for electronic, pharmaceutical, and precision manufacturing and other industries. The recirculating air unit (RAU) uses prefilter, HEPA filters, and a water cooling coil to control the space air cleanliness and required space temperature, whereas a make-up air unit (MAU) supplies conditioned outdoor air, always within narrow dew point limits to the RAU at any outside climate. A unidirectional air flow of 90 fpm is maintained at the working area. For details, refer to ASHRAE Handbook 1991 HVAC Applications and Wang's Handbook of Air Conditioning and Refrigeration.

CV zone-reheat central systems

These systems have their system construction and characteristics similar to that for a single-zone CV central system, except they serve multizone spaces and there is a reheating coil, hot water, or electric heating in each zone. CV zone-reheat central systems are often used for health care facilities and in industrial applications.

VAV central systems

A VAV central system is used to serve multizone space and is also called VAV cooling central system. It is similar to that of a VAV packaged system except air will be cooled or heated by water cooling or heating coils in the AHUs.

Single-zone VAV central system differs from a VAV central system only because it serves a single zone, and therefore there is no VAV box in the branch ducts. Supply volume flow is modulated by inlet vanes and AC inverter.

VAV reheat central systems

A VAV reheat system is similar in system construction and characteristics to that in a VAV central system except that reheating boxes are used instead of VAV boxes in a VAV central system.

Fan-powered VAV central systems

A fan-powered VAV central system is similar in system

construction and characteristics to that in a VAV central system except that fan-powered VAV boxes are used instead of VAV boxes.

Dual-duct VAV central systems

A dual-duct VAV system uses a warm air duct and a cold air duct to supply both warm and cold air to each zone in a multizone space. Warm and cold air are first mixed in a mixing VAV box, and are then supplied to the conditioned space. Warm air duct is only used for perimeter zones.

A mixing VAV box consists of two equal air passages, one for warm air and one for cold air, arranged in parallel. Each of them has a single blade damper and its volume flow rate is modulated. Warm and cold air are then combined, mixed, and supplied to the space.

A dual-duct VAV system is usually either a single supply fan and a relief/return fan combination, or a warm air supply fan, a cold air supply fan, and a relief/return fan. A separate warm air fan and cold air supply fan are beneficial in discharge air temperature reset and fan energy use.

Dual-duct CV central system

This is another version of a dual-duct VAV central system and is similar in construction to a dual-duct VAV system, except that a mixing box is used instead of a mixing VAV box. The supply volume flow rate from a mixing box is nearly constant. Dual-duct CV central systems have only limited applications, like health care facilities, etc.

An ice- or chilled-water storage system is always a central system plus a thermal storage system. The thermal storage system does not influence the system characteristics of the air distribution, and air cooling and heating—except for a greater head lift for a refrigeration compressor—is needed for ice-storage systems. Therefore, the following central systems should be added:

- VAV ice-storage or chilled-water systems
- VAV reheat ice-storage or chilled-water storage systems
- Fan-powered VAV ice-storage systems

Words and Expressions

distinguish [dɪˈstɪŋgwɪʃ] vi. 区分
individual system 独立系统
room air-conditioner system 房间空气调节系统
scroll [skrəʊ] n. 滚动
packaged terminal air-conditioner system 组装式终端空调器系统
sleeve [sliːv] n. 套筒
space(space-conditioning) system 空间(空间空调)系统
four-pipe fan-coil system 四管式风机盘管系统
water-source heat pump system 水源热泵系统
single-zone constant-volume packaged system 单区定容量成套系统
constant-volume zone-reheat packaged system 恒容区再热成套系统
variable-air-volume packaged system 变风量成套系统
VAV reheat packaged system 变风量再热成套系统
fan-powered VAV packaged system 风机驱动的变风量成套系统
parallel flow 平行流,层流
single-zone constant-volume central system 单区恒容中央系统
single-zone CV clean room system 单区恒容洁净室系统
pharmaceutical [ˌfɑːməˈsuːtɪkl] adj. 制药的;配药的
CV zone-reheat central system 恒容区再热中央系统
VAV central system 变风量中央系统
dual-duct VAV central system 双风道变风量中央系统
dual-duct CV central system 双风道定容量中央系统

5

Boiler

5.1 Fossil-fuel Boilers for Electric Utilities

Selection of steam generating equipment

Most of the electric power used in the U. S. is produced in steam plants using fossil fuels and high-speed turbines.

Each steam generating unit must satisfy the user's specific needs in the most economical manner. Achieving this requires close cooperation between the designer and the user's engineering staff or consultants.

Before the specifications for a steam generator can be written, the user or plant designer must conduct a cost evaluation of the entire electric generating plant. In areas where fossil-fuel costs are high, it may be necessary to evaluate both nuclear and fossil units to determine which best satisfies the user's needs.

The cost of electricity from a steam plant has three principal elements: (1) capital equipment, (2) fuel, and (3) other operating and maintenance costs.

The capital cost survey must include the steam generator, steam turbine and electric generator, condenser, feedwater heaters and pumps, fuel handling facilities, buildings and real estate costs. The fuel cost survey must include the costs of the various fuels which may be used, and the probable changes in cost of these fuels during plant lifetime. There is a direct relation between plant efficiency and fuel used, and an important interrelation between plant efficiency and equipment cost.

Other important items are the location of the electric generating plant with respect to fuel supply and the areas where electricity is used. In some cases it is more economical to transport electricity than fuel, and some large steam generating stations are being built at the coal-mine mouth to generate electricity which is used several hundred miles away. If the user is a member of a grid system, the probable requirements of other grid members may be an important factor. Anticipated costs of operation and maintenance must also be included in the evaluation.

Considerable time and effort are required to establish sufficiently accurate basic data with comprehensive consideration of engineering factors, judgment in planning for future expansion or changes, and evaluation of the tangibles and intangibles, so that the experience and craftsmanship of the boiler manufacturer and other suppliers can be applied to the full benefit of the plant designer and the owner. The user should, at the outset, decide who is to prepare this data. If he lacks personnel with the necessary qualifications, the services of consulting engineers should be utilized. A thorough discussion with the boiler manufacturer will provide many details which will aid the user in making correct decisions.

Before the equipment can be selected, the basis of operation and arrangement of the entire steam plant must be planned. Ultimately the available data must be translated into the form of equipment specifications so that the manufacturers of various components can provide apparatus in accordance with the user's requirements. After equipment selection, construction drawings must be prepared for the foundations, building, piping and walkways. The construction work must be coordinated utilizing modern schedule and control techniques for effective management and completion of erection.

Boiler designer's requirements

Most important to the boiler designer are the amount of steam required, the fuel to be used, and the steam conditions which are specified as a result of the user's cost evaluation. These steam conditions include temperature and pressure of the primary and reheat steam.

The boiler designer needs all data pertinent to steam generation to enable him to produce the most economical steam-generating equipment to satisfy the needs of the user. This requires close cooperation between the boiler designer and the user's engineering staff or consultants.

The requirements and conditions that form the basis for the designer's selection of equipment can be outlined as follows:

1. Fuel (s)—sources presently available, analyses, costs, and future trends.

2. Steam requirements

(a) Pressure and temperature—at points of use, at outlet of steam generating units, allowable temperature variations.

(b) Rate of heat delivery (or steam flow)—to points of end use, to boiler house auxiliaries and feed water heating, to blowdown, from outlet of steam generating unit, variations (minimum, average and maximum), and predictable future requirements.

3. Boiler feedwater—source and analysis, and temperature entering steam generating unit.

4. Space and geographical considerations—space limitations, relation of new equipment to existing boiler house equipment, environmental requirements and restrictions of local laws, earthquake and wind requirements, elevation above sea level, foundation conditions, climate, and accessibility for service and construction.

5. Kind and cost of energy for driving auxiliaries.

6. Operating personnel—experience level of workmen for operation and maintenance, and cost of labor.

7. Guarantess.

8. Evaluation basis—for unit efficiency, auxiliary power required, building volume, and various fixed charges.

With this information, the boiler designer is able to analyze the user's specific needs and coordinate the many components that make up a steam generator into the most economical design, by balancing first cost charges with long-term savings.

Design practice

The boiler designer usually works with standardized (pre-engineered) components. Detailed engineering of these components has been completed, hence shop fabrication is expedited and operating experience is proved. Examples of these are fuel burners, pulverizers, furnace sections, steam drums, and pressure parts. These components can be transformed readily into units of various capacities and dimensions. This results in lower costs, more rapid delivery schedules and improved availability of equipment in service.

There has been little standardization of complete unit designs for utility application primarily because of the distinctive nature of each user's conditions. The variables are not so much steam capacity, pressure and temperature as the types of fuels that are fired and the user's plans for utilizing the steam generating unit within his system. Variations of this type require changes in detail and overal arrangement of components. This, together with ever-changing costs of money, fuel, materials and labor, has made full unit standardization impracticable.

Words and Expressions

utility   [juˈtiliti]   n. 实用,公用事业
staff   [staːf]   n. 全体职员
tangible   [ˈtændʒəbl]   a. 确实的,实质的
qualification   [ˌkwɔlifiˈkeiʃən]   n. 限定,条件
schedule   [ˈskedʒul]   n. 时刻表,进度
erection   [iˈrekʃən]   n. 建筑,安装
pertinent   [ˈpəːtinənt]   a. 相关的,有关系的
guarantee   [ˌɡærənˈtiː]   n. 保证,保证书
hence   [hens]   adv. 从此,今后,因此
expedite   [ˈekspidait]   v. 使加速,迅速完成
dimension   [diˈmenʃən]   n. 尺寸

5.2 Selection of Coal-burning Equipment

The selection of the most suitable equipment for a particular job consists of balancing the investment, operating characteristics, efficiency, and type of coal to give the most economical installation.

Almost any coal can be burned successfully in pulverized form or on some type of stoker. Cyclone-Furnace firing has special advantages for certain coals for which it is suited.

The capacity limitations imposed by stokers have been overcome by the development of pulverized-coal and Cyclone-Furnace firing. These improved methods of burning coal also provide:

1. Ability to use any size of coal available.
2. Improved response to load changes.
3. Increase in thermal efficiency because of lower excess air for combustion and lower carbon loss than with stoker firing.
4. A reduction in manpower required for operation.
5. Improved ability to burn coal in combination with oil and gas.

Experience shows that stoker firing is more economical for steam generating units of capacity less than 100 000 lb of steam per hr, where the lower efficiency of a stoker can be tolerated. In larger plants, where fuel cost is a larger fraction of the operating cost, pulverized-coal or Cyclone-Furnace firing is more economical except in special cases.

Operating characteristics may be of controlling significance in the choice of firing methods. For example, where unit size is suitable for pulverized-coal, Cyclone-Furnace, or stoker firing, an extremely wide load range may make stoker firing preferable. Where rotary kilns and industrial furnaces are fired by coal, pulverized-coal firing is generally used.

The type of coal influences the choice of the method of firing for boiler furnaces with the primary considerations as follows:

Pulverized-coal firing: grindability, rank, moisture, volatile matter, and ash.

Stoker firing: rank of coal, volatile matter, ash, and ashsoftening temperature.

Cyclone-Furnace firing: volatile matter, ash, and ash viscosity.

Convenient approximations for the selection of bituminous coals for the firing of boilers are given in Table 5.1.

Table 5.1 Coal characteristics and the method of firing

	Stoker	Pulverized Coal	Cyclone Furnace
Max. total moisture * (as fired), %	15 ~ 20	15	20
Min. Volatile matter (dry basis), %	15	15	15
Max. total ash (dry basis), %	20	20	25
Max. sulfur (as fired), %	5	—	—

Pulverized-coal systems

The function of a pulverized-coal system is to pulverize the coal, deliver it to the fuel-burning equipment, and accomplish complete combustion in the furnace with a minimum of excess air. The system must operate as a continuous process and, within specified design limitations, the coal supply or feed must be varied as rapidly and as widely as required by the combustion process.

A small portion of the air required for combustion (15 to 20% in current installations) is used to transport the coal to the burner. This is known as primary air. In the direct-firing system, primary air is also used to dry the coal in the pulverizer. The remainder of the combustion air (80 to 85%) is introduced at the burner and is known as secondary

---

* These limits may be exceeded for lower rank, higher inherent-moisture-content coals, i. e., subbituminous and lignite.

air.

The two basic equipment components of a pulverized coal system are:

1. The pulverizer which pulverizes the coal to the fineness required.

2. The burner which accomplishes the mixing of the pulverized-coal-primary-air mixture with secondary air in the right proportions and delivers the mixture to the furnace for combustion.

Other necessary requirements are:

3. Hot air for drying the coal for effective pulverization.

4. Fan(s) to supply air to the pulverizer and deliver the coal-air mixture to the burner(s).

5. Coal feeder to control the rate of coal feed to each pulverizer.

6. Coal and air conveying lines.

Two principal systems-the bin system and the direct-firing system-have been used for processing, distributing and burning pulverized coal. The direct-firing system is the one being installed almost exclusively today.

Bin system

The bin system is primarily of historical interest, although a large number of units of this type remain in operation. Its use was required before pulverizing equipment had reached the stage of development where it could be relied upon for uninterrupted operation, flexibility and consistent performance.

In this system the coal is processed at a location apart from the furnace, and the end product is pneumatically conveyed to cyclone collectors which recover the fines and clean the moisture-laden air before returning it to the atmosphere. The pulverized coal is discharged into storage bins and later conveyed by pneumatic transport through pipelines to utilization bins which may be as far as 5 000 ft from the point of preparation.

For the coal-air transport system, a differential-pitch screw pump, is provided to feed pulverized coal continuously into a pipeline, where coal is aerated or fluidized at the entrance so that it flows through the pipe somewhat like a viscous fluid. Through a system of two-way valves the coal can be distributed to any number of bins. The system may be arranged for manual, remote or automatic control. These air-transport systems are built in sizes from 1 to 100 tons of coal per hour. For successful operation, the surface moisture in the pulverized coal must not exceed 3%, and the fineness should not be less than 90% through a 50-mesh sieve.

Although bin systems installed in older plants are still operating quite satisfactorily, this system is no longer competitive with the direct-firing system. Furthermore, the drying, transportation and storage of pulverized coal, other than anthracite, involves a fire hazard from spontaneous combustion.

Direct-firing system

The bin system has been superseded by the direct-firing system because of improvements in safety conditions, plant cleanliness, greater simplicity, lower initial investment, lower operating cost, and less space requirement.

The pulverizing equipment developed for the direct-firing system permits continuous utilization of raw coal directly from the bunkers where coal is stored in the condition in which it is received at the plant. This is accomplished by feeding the raw coal directly into the pulverizer, where it is dried as well as pulverized, and then delivering it to the burners in a single continuous operation.

Components of the direct-firing system are as follows:

1. Raw-coal feeder.

2. Source (steam or gas air heater) to supply hot primary air to the pulverizer for drying the coal.

3. Pulverizer fan, also known as the primary-air fan, arranged as a blower (or exhauster).

4. Pulverizer arranged to operate under pressure (or suction).

5. Coal-and-air conveying lines.

6. Burners.

There are two direct-firing methods in use-the pressure type, which is more commonly used, and the suction type. The principal differences between the two methods are summarized in Table 5.2.

Table 5.2 Comparative features of direct-firing pressure and suction systems

System	Pressure	Suction
Type of fan	Blower	Exhauster
Location of fan	Pulverizer inlet	Pulverizer outlet
Fan construction	Standard	Explosion-proof
Fan handles	Air only	Pulverized coal and air
Relative fan efficiency	High	Low
Fan wear	Low to none	High
Pulverized coal distribution to burners	Good	Distributor required

In the pressure method, the primary-air fan, located on the inlet side of the pulverizer, forces the hot primary air through the pulverizer where it picks up the pulverized coal, and delivers the proper coal-air mixture to the burners. Where a separate air heater is provided, the fan operates on cold air, forcing the air first through the air heater and then the pulverizer. In either event, the coal is delivered to the burners by a fan operating entirely on air, so that no entrained dust passes through the fan. One pulverizer generally furnishes the coal for several burners. With the pressure method, it is usual to supply each burner with a single conveying line direct from the pulverizer, thus eliminating the expense of a distributor.

In the suction method, the air and entrained coal are drawn through the pulverizer under negative pressure by an exhauster located on the outlet side of the pulverizer. With this arrangement the fan handles a mixture of coal and air, and distribution of the mixture to more than one burner must be obtained by a distributor beyond the fan discharge.

The feeding of coal and air to the pulverizer is controlled by either of two methods: (1) The coal feed is proportioned to the load demand, and the primary-air supply is adjusted to the rate of coal feed; or (2) the primary air through the pulverizer is proportioned to the load demand, and the coal feed is adjusted to the rate of air flow. In either case, a predetermined air-coal ratio is maintained for any given load.

The direct-firing system, in addition to eliminating separately fired dryers and storage facilities for pulverized coal, permits the use of inlet air temperatures to the pulverizer up to 650 °F and higher for drying high-moisture coals (total moisture 20%, surface moisture 15%) or high-moisture lignites (20 to 40% total moisture) in the pulverizer.

The direct-firing system has one minor disadvantage. The operating range of a pulverizer is usually not more than 3 to 1 (without change in the number of burners in service) because the air velocities in lines and other parts of the system must be maintained above the minimum values to keep the coal in suspension. In practice most boiler units are provided with more than one pulverizer, each feeding multiple burners. Load variations beyond 3 to 1 are generally accommodated by shutting down (or starting up) a pulverizer and the burners it supplies.

Words and Expressions

investment ['in'vestmənt] n. 投资,投资额
rotary ['rəutəri] a. 旋转的,转动的
grindability [ˌgraində'biliti] n. 可磨性,磨削性
rank [ræŋk] n. 等级
volatile ['vɔlətail] a. 挥发性的,易变的
pulverize ['pʌlvəraiz] v. 将……弄碎,磨碎
convey [kən'vei] v. 传送,输运
uninterrupted [ˌʌnˌintə'rʌptid] a. 不间断的
bin [bin] n. 仓,箱
anthracite ['ænθrəsait] n. 无烟煤,白煤,硬煤
hazard ['hæzəd] n. 危险,机会,偶然
raw-coal 原煤,未加工的煤

5.3 Superheaters and Reheaters

Early in the eighteenth century, it was demonstrated that substantial savings in fuel could be experienced when steam engines were run with some superheat in the steam. In the late 1800's, lubrication problems were encountered with reciprocating engines, but once these were overcome, development of superheaters continued.

Commercial development of the steam turbine hastened the general use of superheat. By 1920 steam temperatures of 650 °F, representing superheats of 250 °F, were generally accepted. In the early 1920's the regenerative cycle, using steam bled from turbines for feedwater heating, was developed to improve station economy without going to higher steam temperatures. At the same time, superheater development permitted raising the steam temperature to 725 °F. A further gain in economy by still higher temperature was at that time limited by allowable superheater tube-metal temperature. This led to the commercial use of reheat, where the steam leaving the high-pressure stage of the turbine was reheated in a separate reheat superheater and returned at higher temperature and enthalpy to the low-pressure stage.

The first reheat unit for a central station was proposed in 1922 and went into service in September,1924. It was designed for 650 psi and operated at 550 psi and 725 °F. Exhaust steam from the high-pressure turbine was reheated to 725 °F at 135 psi.

Amuch higher-pressure reheat unit, designed in 1924 for 1 200 psi and 700 °F primary steam temperature with reheat at 360 psi and 700 °F, went into service in December,1925.

Advantages of superheat and reheat

When saturated steam is utilized in a steam turbine, the work done results in a loss of energy by the steam and consequent condensation of a portion of the steam, even though there is a drop in pressure. The amount of work that can be done by the turbine is limited by the amount of moisture which can be handled by the turbine without excessive wear on the turbine blades. This is normally somewhere between 10% and 15%. It is possible to increase the amount of work done by moisture separation between turbine stages, but this is economical only in special cases. Even with moisture separation, the total energy that can be transformed to work in the turbine is small compared to the amount of heat required to raise the water from feedwater temperature to saturation and then evaporate it.

Thus moisture constitutes the basic limitation in turbine design.

Because a turbine generally transforms the heat of superheat into work without forming moisture, the heat of superheat is essentially all recoverable in the turbine. This is illustrated in the temperature-entropy diagram of the ideal Rankine cycle. Where the heat added to the right of the saturated vapor line is shown as 100% recoverable. While this is not always entirely correct, the Rankine cycle diagrams indicate that this is essentially true.

The foregoing discussion is not specifically applicable at steam pressures in the vicinity of the critical point. The term "superheat" is not really appropriate in defining the temperature of the working fluid at or above the critical point. However, even at pressures exceeding 3 208 psia, heat added at temperatures above 705 °F is essentially all recoverable in a turbine.

The benefits of superheat are illustrated graphically in Fig. 5. 1, which shows the reduction in cycle heat rate by increasing the steam temperature from 900 to 1 100 °F at pressures from 1 800 to 3 500 psi.

Superheater types

The original and somewhat basic type of superheater and reheater was the convection unit, for gas temperatures where heat transfer by radiation was very small. With a unit of this type the steam temperature leaving the superheater increases with boiler output because of the decreasing percentage of heat input that is absorbed in the furnace, leaving more heat available for superheater absorption. Since convection heat transfer rates are almost a direct function of output, the total absorption in the superheater per lb of steam increases with increase in boiler output(see Fig. 5. 2). This effect is increasingly pronounced the further the superheater is removed from the furnace,

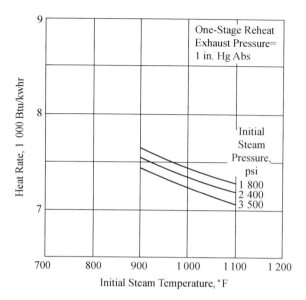

Fig. 5.1 Effect of changes in steam temperature and pressure on performance of ideal Rankine cycle with one-stage reheat

i. e. , the lower the gas temperature entering the superheater.

On the other hand, the radiant superheater receives its heat through radiation and practically none from convection. Because the heat absorption of furnace surfaces does not increase in direct proportion to boiler output but at a considerably lesser rate, the curve of radiant superheat as a function of load slopes downward with increase in boiler output.

In certain cases the two opposite-sloping curves have been coordinated by the combination of radiant and convection superheaters to give flat superheat curves over wide ranges in load, as typically indicated in Fig. 5.2. A separately fired superheater has the characteristic that it can be fired to produce a flat superheat curve.

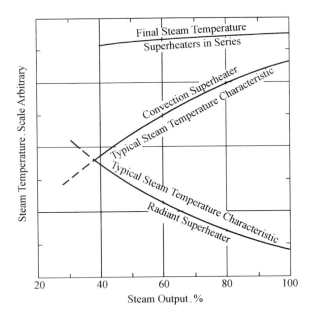

Fig. 5. 2 A substantially uniform final steam temperature over a range of output can be attained by a series arrangement of radiant and convection superheater components

Development of superheaters

The early convection superheaters were placed above or behind a deep bank of boiler tubes in order to shield them from the fire or from the higher temperature gases. The greater heat absorption required in the superheater for higher steam temperatures made it necessary to move the superheater closer to the fire. This new location brought with it problems which were not apparent with the superheaters located in the original lower-gas-temperature zone. Steam- and gas-distribution difficulties and instances of general overheating of tube metal were ultimately resolved by improved superheater design, including higher mass velocity of the steam. This increased the heat conductance through the steam film, resulting in lower tube-metal temperatures, and also improved steam distribution by increasing pressure drop through the tubes.

Steam mass velocity in modern super-heaters ranges from as low as 100 000 to 1 000 000 lb/sq ft, hr or higher depending on pressure, steam and gas temperatures, and the tolerable pressure drop in the superheater.

The fundamental considerations governing super-heater design apply also to reheater design. However, the pressure drop in reheaters is critical because the gain in heat rate with the reheat cycle can be completely nullified by too much pressure drop through the reheater system. Hence, steam mass flows are generally somewhat lower in the reheater.

Tube sizes. Plain cylindrical tubes of 2-in. or $2\frac{1}{2}$-in. outside diameter predominate in superheaters and reheaters in stationary practice. Smaller diameters (1-in. or $1\frac{1}{4}$-in.) are used to conserve weight and space in marine units. Steam pressure drop is higher and alignment more difficult with the smaller diameters. Larger diameters bring about higher pressure stresses.

Recent designs have called for greater spans between supports for horizontal superheater tubes, and for wider tube spacing or fewer tubes per row to avoid slag accumulation. The $2\frac{1}{2}$-in. tube has met these new conditions with a minimum sacrifice of the smaller-tube advantages, and 3-in. tubes are used to advantage in some cases. When steam temperatures increase, the allowable stresses may force a return to the smallerdiameter thinner-wall tube.

Plain tubes are used almost exclusively in modern superheater practice. Extended surface on superheater tubes in the form of fins, rings, or studs not only makes gas-side cleaning difficult, but the added thickness increases metal temperature and thermal stress beyond tolerable limits.

Relationships in superheater design

Effective superheater design calls for the resolution of several factors. The outstanding considerations are:

1. The steam temperature desired.

2. The superheater surface required to give this steam temperature.

3. The gas temperature zone in which the surface is to be located.

4. The type of steel, alloy, or other material best suited to make up the surface and the supports.

5. The rate of steam flow through the tubes (mass velocity), which is limited by the permissible steam pressure drop but which, in turn, exerts a dominant control over tube-metal temperatures.

6. The arrangement of surface to meet the characteristics of the fuels anticipated, with particular reference to the spacing of the tubes to prevent accumulations of ash and slag or to provide for the removal of such formations in their early stages.

7. The physical design and type of superheater as a structure.

A change in any one of the first six items will call for a counterbalancing change in all other items.

The steam temperature desired in advanced power station design is the maximum for which the superheater designer and manufacturer can produce an economical structure. Economics in this case requires the resolution of two interrelated factors-first, or investment cost and the later cost of upkeep for minimum operating troubles, outages, and replacements. A higher first cost is warranted if the upkeep cost is thereby reduced sufficiently to cover, in a reasonable time, the extra initial cost. The steam temperature desired is, therefore, based on the complete coordinated knowledge available for the optimum evaluation of the combination of the other five items and the necessities of the particular project. Operating experience in recent years has resulted in the use of approximately 1 000 °F steam temperature both for primary superheat and reheat in nearly all large units purchased for installation in the U. S.

After the steam temperature desired is actually set or specified, the next consideration is the amount of surface necessary to give this superheat. The amount of superheater surface required is dependent on the four remaining items and, since there is no single correlation, the amount of surface must be determined by trial, locating it in a zone of gas temperature that is likely to be satisfactory. In the so-called standard boilers, the zone is fairly well established by the physical arrangements and by the space preempted for superheater surface.

Steam mass velocity, steam pressure drop, and super-heater tube-metal temperatures are calculated after the amount of surface is established for the trial location and the trial tube spacing. The proper type of material is then selected for the component tubes, headers, and other parts. It may be necessary to compare several arrangements to obtain an optimum combination that will:

1. Require an alloy of lesser cost.

2. Give a more reasonable steam pressure drop without jeopardizing the tube temperatures.

3. Give a higher steam mass velocity in order to lower the tube temperatures.

4. Give a different spacing of tubes that will provide more protection against the ash accumulations with uncertain types of fuel.

5. Permit closer spacing of the tubes, thereby making a more economical arrangement for a fuel supply that is known to be favorable.

6. Give an arrangement of tubes which will reduce the draft loss for an installation where draft loss evaluation is crucial.

7. Permit the superheater surface to be located in a zone of a higher gas temperature, with a consequent saving in surface, that will compensate for deviation from a standard arrangement.

It is possible to achieve a practical design with optimum economic and operational characteristics and with all criteria reasonably satisfied, but a large measure of experience and the application of sound physical principles are required for satisfactory results.

Relationships in reheater design

The same general similarity exists between superheater and reheater considerations, but the reheater is limited in ruggedness of design by the permissible steam pressure drop. Steam mass velocities in reheater tubes should be sufficient to keep the steam-film temperature drop below 150 °F. Ordinarily this may be done with less than 5% pressure drop through the reheater tubes. This allows another 5% pressure drop for the reheater piping and valves without exceeding the usual 10% total allowable.

Metals for tubes

Oxidation resistance, maximum allowable stress, and economics determine the choice of materials for superheater and reheater tubes. The use of carbon steel should be extended as far as these considerations permit. Beyond this point, carefully selected alloy steels should be used.

Words and Expressions

superheater　['sju:pəhi:tə]　*n.* 过热器
reheater　['ri:'hi:tə]　*n.* 再热器
exhaust　[ig'zɔ:st]　*vt.* 取出,弄空
temperature-entropy diagram　温熵图
saturated vapor　饱和蒸汽
upkeep　['ʌpki:p]　*n.* 保养,维修,维持
installation　[,instə'leiʃən]　*n.* 安装,设置,装置
accumulation　[əkju:mju'leiʃ(ə)n]　*n.* 积聚,堆积物

5.4　Boiler and Its Role Playing in National Economy

A boiler is a closed vessel in which water, under pressure, is transformed into steam by the application of heat. In china, usually those devices generating steam and/or hot water at atmospheric pressure are also considered to be boilers.

A boiler has emerged as an important tool of industry with a high degree of versatility. In addition to the generation of electricity, as a source of hot water and/or steam it has found applications in a variety of industries likealuminium, automobiles, concrete block and bricks, ceramic glass, inorganic and organic chemicals, copper primary and secondary, lumber pulp and paper, selected plastics, rubber, textiles and sugar etc.

In its essentials a boiler consists of a furnace in which any fuel-oil, coal, wood, husk, or gas are burnt to produce combustion products and thereby generate heat and an arrangement of heating surfaces to contain and heat water or produce steam.

The people dealing with boiler are also called as water-heaters in folk Chinese language. Indeed, the boiler is mainly associated with water, although the working fluid of a boiler can be a liquid other than water in special circumstances.

As well known to all, water can exist in three states in nature, which are solid (ice) , liquid (water) and gas (vapor) respectively. Being heated, the temperature of water will be elevated with the absorption of heat, and the water boils a certain temperature. The temperature at which the water boils is known as boiling point or saturation temperature. The boiling water is called as saturated water. The heat the water of 1 kg absorbs from 0 ℃ to saturation temperature is named as named as liquid heat.

If heat is exerted further after the saturation temperature is reached, the water starts evaporating, but the temperature does not continue to rise. The heat added makes water turn into steam . Actually, the boiling is a process in which a great number of vapor bubbles are formed and rise to surface. During this process, the temperature of the steam maintains unchanged at the saturation temperature, the vapor is known as saturated steam. The heat needed to change the saturated water of 1 kg into saturated steam completely is named as latent heat.

The temperature of saturated vapor will rise up if it continues to be heated at a constant pressure. The steam whose temperature is higher than saturation temperature has the name of superheated steam. The number of degrees beyond the saturated temperature is referred to as superheat. The heat for superheating the steam is named as superheating heat.

At different pressures, the saturation temperature, liquid heat and latent heat of water are quite different. Their values corresponding to several pressures are listed in Table 5.3. The state at which the latent heat is zero is known as critical state, and the corresponding parameters are called critical parameters.

Table 5.3 Thermophysical characteristics of water at different pressures

Absolute pressure/MPa	0.1	1	10	22.12
Saturation temperature/℃	99.6	179.9	310.9	374.15
Liquid heat/($kJ \cdot kg^{-1}$)	417.5	762.6	1 409	2 095
Latent heat/($kJ \cdot kg^{-1}$)	2 258	2 014	1 316	0

If 1 kg of water at 0 ℃ is heated at constant pressure to certain state, the heat absorbed by the water is defined as the enthalpy of the water or the steam. If the water has been heated to superheated state, the enthalpy will be the sum of liquid heat, latent heat and superheat. The heat absorbed by 1 kg of water when heated by boiler is the difference between the enthalpy of the steam at outlet and the enthalpy of water entering the boiler.

In order to realize heating and evaporating the water and superheating the steam, a boiler shall have the equipment that can acquire heat energy from fuels, i. e. , the furnace, the pressure vessel containing the water and the heating surface absorbing sufficient heat. Whether or not the heating surface is sufficient depends on the amount of the steam required, and the temperature and pressure.

If a strict definition is given for boiler, it may be described as, boiler is a device in which fuels are burned, the chemical energy is released as heat energy, and the heat is transferred to the water (or other working fluid), finally the water is transformed into the steam or hot water with certain pressure and temperature.

As mentioned above, current structure of global energy resources is that coal, crude oil and natural gas are given priority to. In addition, hydropower and unclear energy are playing more and more important role. Up to now, solar, windpower, geothermal, and tidal energy have also been rather highly developed. Whether or no, the main form of energy utilized by the modern people is electricity, and various energy resource are being converted into the electricity.

The gross installation capacity of China has been 6×10^2 kW. The changes of the installed capacity and the generation capacity are listed in Table 5.4 (The figures are exclusive of Hong Kong, Macao and Taiwan). Since 1996, both the installed capacity and the generation capacity of China have exceeded those of Japan, and ranked No. 2 in the word.

Table 5.4 The installation capacity and the generation capacity of China

Year	Installed capacity($\times 10^4$ kW)				Generation capacity($\times 10^4$ kW · h)			
	Total	Hydropower	Thermal	Nuclear	Total	Hydropower	Thermal	Nuclear
1980	6 586.9	2 032.0	4 555.0		3 006	582	2 424	
1985	8 705.3	2 641.0	6 064.01		4 107	924	3 183	
1900	13 789.0	3 604.5	10 184.5		6 213	1 264	4 950	
1995	21 722.4	5 218.4	16 294.0	210	10 069	1 868	8 073	128
1996	23 654.2	5 557.8	17 886.4	210	10 974	1 869	8 781	143
1997	25 423.8	5 973.0	19 240.8	210	11 342	1 946	9 249	144
1998	27 728.9	6 505.5	21 012.4	210	11 577	2 043	9 388	141
1999	29 876.8	7 297.1	22 343.4	210	12 331	2 129	10 017	148
2000	31 932.1	7 935.2	23 754.0	210	13 685	2 431	11 079	167
2005	51 718.48	11 738.79	39 137.56	684.60	24 975.26	3 963.96	20 437.30	530.88
2006	62 200	12 857	48 405	685	28 311	4 167	23 573	543

The energy resource structure determines the guidelines of

electric power development. In China, the guidelines are as follows; thermal power generation shall be optimized, hydropower shall be developed actively, nuclear power shall be developed moderately, and new energy sources shall be developed by adjusting measures to local conditions. The development of new electrical grids and the upgrading of existent electrical grids shall be resource, even more attention shall be paid to environmental protection and the efficiency of energy utilization shall be improved by all means.

Up to now, in China more than 80% of the gross electric power generation is from thermal power generation. The installed thermal gross capacity is about 75%. The proportions of the generation and the installation capacity of hydropower are 20% and 25%, respectively. The corresponding figures for nuclear power are 1.2% and 0.66%, respectively. Others are negligible. In the thermal power generations, coals are taken as the major fuels, whereas oil and natural gas are seldom used to generate electric power. Roughly speaking, 1/3 of the coal produced is for power generation, 1/3 for industrial and residential purposes, and 1/3 for metallurgical and chemical industries etc.

The proportion of thermal power generation in the total generation has been maintained to a level of more than 80% over the past decade, and the proportion from coal is over 90% in thermal power generation. During the period of 9th Five Year Plan, the proportion from coal is over 95%, and the proportion from oil is less than 5%, and that from gas is negligible, as shown in Table 5.5. It can be predicted that in China the pattern in which coal is the dominating energy resource for power generation will continue.

Boiler is indispensable in fossil fuel fired power plants and industrial productions. The steam generated by boiler can be directly utilized for production, or for space heating. There are also the residential boilers for supplying hot water and space heating. Wherever you go, you can find a boiler.

Table 5.5 Pattern of energy resources for power generation (1990 ~ 2000)

Year	Coal	Oil	Gas	Hydropower	Nuclear
1990	72.09	7.57	—	20.34	—
1996	77.65	3.70	—	17.32	1.27
1997	77.92	3.66	—	17.15	1.27
1998	77.17	3.92	—	17.66	1.22
1999	77.68	3.80	—	17.27	1.20
2000	77.18	3.78	—	17.77	1.22

Boilers are consuming more and more fuels. Many problems have been incurred with the widespread use of boilers. These problems include

(1) Huge amount of primary unrenewable energy resources are consumed, and their exhaust is approaching.

(2) The emitted greenhouse gases such as CO_2 can lead to global warming, melting of glaciers, and increase of sea level, the living space of human being is imperiled, although they may be helpful to the growth of vegetations.

(3) The evolution and growth of animals and plants are being threatened due to the emissions of soot and dust, SO_2, NO_2, heavy metals, dioxin and other harmful substances.

On one hand, our capability of conquering and transforming the nature is expanding. On the other hand, human beings have been punished be the nature. The exemplifications include serious soil erosion, land desertification, grassland retrogradation, frequent occurrence of sandstorms in the west area of China, especially the northwest area. These natural disasters have become an obstacle of sustainable development, and lessening the space for living and evolution.

Currently, every country is taking up with the research and development of high efficiency and low pollution boilers in order to minimize the detrimental impact to the environment due to the burning of fuels.

Words and Expressions

vessel　['ves(ə)l]　*n.* 船,舰;血管;容器
aluminium　[æl(j)ʊ'mɪnɪəm]　*n.* 铝
heat　[hiːt]　*n.* 高温;压力;热度　*v.* 使激动;把…加热
vapor　['veipə(r)]　*n.* 蒸汽;烟雾　*v.* 蒸发
saturated　['sætʃəreɪtɪd]　*adj.* 饱和的;渗透的
steam　[stiːm]　*v.* 蒸,散发　*n.* 蒸汽
superheated　[ˌsjuːpə'hiːtɪd]　*adj.* 过热的
bubble　['bʌb(ə)l]　*n.* 气泡,泡沫　*v.* 沸腾,冒泡
latent　['leɪt(ə)nt]　*adj.* 潜在的;潜伏的
enthalpy　[en'θælpi]　*n.* 焓;热含量

5.5　Technical Economic Indices of Boiler

Technical indices of boiler are generally indicated by economics, reliability and flexibility.

(1) Economics.

Economics of boiler includes thermal efficiency, initial cost, fuel consumption rate and auxiliary power consumption.

Thermal efficiency is the ratio of available heat to total heat entering the boiler, that is, the ratio of the available heat Q_1 to the heat Q_r released by the fuel consumed in unit time.

$$\eta = \frac{Q_1}{Q_r}$$

Available heat is the total heat absorbed by the working fluid in unit time, including the heat absorbed by water and steam and the heat contained in blowoff water and steam consumed by boiler itself. The input heat of boiler is the total heat entering the boiler along with fuel per kg or per m^3, which includes the as-received basis net calorific value, the sensible heat of fuel and the heat entrained by heating the fuel or combustion air with external heat sources. Thermal efficiency η is also referred to as gross efficiency of a boiler.

In practices, it is insufficient that only thermal efficiency is used to characterize the economics of boiler operation, because thermal efficiency can only reflect the completeness of combustion and heat transfer processes. But, from the point of view of the end use of a boiler, only the exported steam or heat from the boiler is the end effective product, the heat contained in blowoff water the steam consumed by boiler itself are not for end use. Furthermore, additional power consumption for running all the auxiliary equipments is necessary to maintain normal operation of a boiler.

Net efficiency of a boiler is obtained by deducting the plant energy consumption (heat rate and auxiliary power consumption) for its operation from the gross. Net efficiency of a boiler η_j can be expressed as:

$$\eta_j = \frac{Q_1}{Q_r + \Sigma Q_{zy} + \frac{b}{B} 29\ 300 \Sigma P} \times 100\%$$

where B—fuel consumption rate, kg/h;

Q_{zy}—Q boiler heat rate, kJ/kg;

ΣP—power consumed by auxiliary equipments, kW;

b—equivalent coalconsumption of power generation, kg/(kW·h);

29 300—calorific value of equivalent coal, kJ/kg.

Majority of modern utility boilers have a thermal efficiency of higher than 90%.

In China, it is compulsory that the thermal efficiencies of the industrial boiler that take water as the working fluid should be not less than the values listed in Table 5.6. For residential boilers, they should be not less than the values listed in Table 5.7.

Table 5.6 Thermal efficiencies of industrial boilers (GB/T17954-2000)

Rated heat output/MW	Operation class	Used fuel								
		Low rank bituminous	Bituminous			Lean coal	Anthracite			Lignite	Oli & gas
			I	II	III		I	II	III		
0.7	1	61	68	70	72	68	60	58	64	67	83
	2	56	63	65	67	64	56	54	58	63	79
	3	52	59	61	63	60	51	50	53	60	75
1.4	1	63	70	72	74	70	63	62	67	70	85
	2	59	65	68	70	67	60	58	63	67	82
	3	55	63	65	67	65	56	54	59	65	78
2.8~5.6	1	67	72	75	77	73	66	64	72	74	87
	2	64	70	72	74	71	64	62	69	72	83
	3	62	68	70	72	70	63	60	66	70	80
7~14	1	69	74	76	78	77	72	69	75	77	88
	2	66	72	75	77	75	69	66	72	75	85
	3	64	71	71	76	74	67	64	70	74	82

Table 5.6

Rated heat output/MW	Operation class	Used fuel									
		Low rank bituminous	Bituminous			Lean coal	Anthracite			Lignite	Oli & gas
			I	II	III		I	II	III		
>11	1	71	76	78	81	79	74	71	77	79	89
	2	68	74	76	79	77	71	68	75	77	86
	3	66	72	75	77	75	69	66	73	75	83

Table 5.7　Thermal efficiencies of residential boilers(GB/T18292–2001)

Rated heat output/MW	Operation class	Used fuel								
		Gas	Bituminous			Anthracite			Lignite	Oli
			I	II	III	I	II	III		
≥0.05 ~ <0.1	1	85	58	60	62	60	52	51	55	60	80
	2	80	56	58	60	58	50	49	53	58	75
	3	76	54	56	58	56	48	47	50	56	71
≥0.1 ~ <0.35	1	87	61	63	65	64	56	54	58	62	82
	2	82	58	60	62	60	52	51	54	60	77
	3	77	56	58	60	58	49	48	50	58	72
≥0.35 ~ 0.7	1	88	68	70	72	68	60	58	64	67	83
	2	84	63	65	67	64	56	54	58	63	79
	3	79	59	64	63	60	51	50	63	60	75
>0.7 ~ 1.4	1	89	70	72	74	70	63	62	67	70	85
	2	86	65	68	70	67	60	58	63	67	82
	3	81	63	65	67	63	56	54	59	65	78
>1.4 ~ 2.8	1	91	72	75	77	73	66	64	72	74	87
	2	87	70	72	74	71	64	62	69	72	83
	3	83	68	70	72	70	63	60	66	70	80

Boiler cost is generally represented by steel consumption rate, which is the most important economical index. Steel consumption rate is defined as the steel weight consumed by unit capacity of boiler, expressed as t · h/t. Many factors can affect steel consumption rate, including boiler conditions, small capacity, coal being fired, tubular air heater and steel framework have a high steel consumption rate. The boilers with low conditions, large capacity, once-through type oil or gas being fired, regeneration type air heater and steel reinforced concrete column framework have a low steel consumption rate.

Because of the variability of the prices of steel, refractory materials, for the sake of convenient comparisons, steel consumption rate is frequently used to represent boiler cost. In general, to raise single-unit capacity and steam conditions is an effective approach to reduce metal consumption and investment cost. For instance, the investment per kW can be reduced by 10% ~ 15% when the single-unit capacity is raised to 600 MW from 300 MW. If the pressure is increased from subcritical to supercritical the investment per kW is boosted by 1% ~ 5%. Obviously, by the appropriate combination of supercritical pressure and larger capacity, the comprehensive economic benefit of the unit can be appreciably increased. Related sources show that the cost of 600 MW boiler can be reduced by 10% compared to that of 300 MW boilers, the cost for personnel and maintenance can be reduced by 50%, metal consumption can be reduced by 20%, capital construction labor consumption can be reduced by 30%.

The metal consumption for steel framework of a large capacity boiler takes a very large part of its total metal consumption. 300 MW boilers manufactured in 70's of last century in China used steel reinforced concrete structures to save total metal consumption and shorten construction period.

The steel consumption rate of industrial boilers is 5 ~ 6 (t · h/ h), that of electric utility boilers is around 2.5 ~ 5 (t · h/t). The consumption rate of steel, in particular heat-resisting alloy steel, should be rationally reduced at the prerequisites of safe, reliable, economic operations.

Coal consumption and auxiliary power consumption are frequently taken as assessment indices of economics. Power generating (supplying) coal consumption rate is defined as the coal consumed to generate (supply) 1 (kW · h) of electricity. Auxiliary power consumption ratio is defined as the ratio of the electric power consumed by auxiliary equipment to total power generation.

Auxiliary power consumption ratio is intimately associated with the arrangement and selection of auxiliary equipments, especially, fuel preparation system. Besides, fuel type and firing method also have an influence.

Coal consumption rate is related to the conditions of the boiler, the higher the conditions, the lower is the coal consumption rate. However, fuel type, load pattern, layout of powerhouse, single-unit capacity and so on can have an effect as well. As such, the relationship between coal consumption rate and conditions can be compared only under the same conditions. For instance, the power generating coal consumption rate of a coal fired variable load supercritical pressure boiler can be higher than that of a coal fired variable load supercritical pressure boiler. But, the power generating coal consumption rate of a supercritical unit is lower than that of a subcritical unit.

In china, high conditions and large capacity units have been installed and many old units have been retrofitted. The coal conditions rate averaged nationwide was reduced to 392 g/(kW · h) in 2 000 from 412 g/(kW · h) in 1995. If the annual power generation was estimated to be 1×10^{12} (kW · h), 2×10^7 tce had been saved in 2000, compared to 1995.

(2) Reliability.

The reliability of a boiler can often be evaluated by following 3 indexes;

①Continuous operation hours = time interval between upkeeps;

②Outage rate = $\dfrac{\text{hours due to forced outage}}{\text{overall operational hours+hours due to forced outage}} \times 100\%$;

③Availability = $\dfrac{\text{overall operational hours+standby hours}}{\text{total time (hours)}} \times 100\%$.

In china, the continuous operation hours for electrical power generation units are required to be greater than 4 000 hours, the availability as high as 90%.

(3) Flexibility.

Modern lifestyle and electrical load as demands have more and more new requirements for the operation of a boiler. These include maneuverability and adjustability. For utility boilers, they should be operated at as low load as possible, in addition to base, peak-shaving and cyclic load. There are two modes of operating boiler, constant pressure and variable pressure. For example, a domestically manufactured subcritical pressure and variable pressure operation, and can be used to under take base load and peak-shaving load as well. The load changed rate is 5% MCR/min for constant pressure operation, 3% MCR/min for variable pressure operation. The steam temperature regulation employs single stage or two-stage spray with tilting burners. The reheat steam temperature is mainly regulated by tilting burners. Steam temperatures can be ensured in the load range of (70% ~ 100%) MCR for constant pressure operation and (50% ~ 100%) MCR for variable pressure operation. Stable combustion without oil supporting can be maintained at as low as (30% ~ 40%) MCR for bituminous coal and (55% ~ 65%) MCR for lean coal.

Therefore, the flexibility refers to that steam load should be changed fast, should be capable of frequent shut down and sequent quick startup, long time operation at allowable low load. These requirements have become most important indexes of boiler performances. The flexibility of coal fired boiler will be impaired when low rank coal is fired or coal is changed.

Words and Expressions

thermal ['θɜːm(ə)l] *adj.* 热的;热量的
auxiliary [ɔːg'zɪljəri] *n.* 辅助物;附属机构 *adj.* 辅助的
calorific [kælə'rɪfɪk] *adj.* 发热的,生热的
regeneration [rɪdʒenə'reɪʃn] *n.* 再生,重生
framework ['freɪmwɜːk] *n.* 框架;结构
variability [ˌveərɪə'bɪlətɪ] *n.* 可变性,变化性
metal ['met(ə)l;] *n.* 金属;合金 *adj.* 金属制的
subcritical [sʌb'krɪtɪk(ə)l] *adj.* 次临界的
flexibility [ˌfleksɪ'bɪlɪtɪ] *n.* 灵活性;弹性;适应性

5.6 Brief History of Boiler

It has been believed that in 200 B.C. a Greek named Hero invented a simple machine shown in Fig. 5.3, which was mainly used for enjoying in imperial palace. The water in the cauldron was transformed into steam be the heat from the fire beneath the cauldron, the hollow ball turned around its axis because of the bounce-back of steam. This machine is considered to be the earliest one generating power by water and steam. Hence, it is considered to be the earliest boiler.

This machine had not been improved at all until the industrial revolution. The industrial revolution starting in England stimulated the development of steam use. In particular, as coal mines became deeper, they were often flooded with underground water. How to pump the water more economically from the mines led to greater needs for power. Based on the invention by Newcomen. Watt further improved the steam engine, as known in Fig. 5.4 and Fig. 5.5 respectively. The boiler producing steam for engine at that time was cylindrical shell type, and heated from outside of the shell, as shown in Fig. 5.6.

Fig. 5.3　Invention of Hero

With industrial progress, boilers had been evolved in two directions;

Way 1: To increase the heat transfer surface inside the shell. Initially, one furnace tube that is surrounded by water was added inside the shell, and the fuel was fired inside the furnace tube, then two were added, later multiple tubes added. Finally, modern fire tube boiler evolved.

There are mainly two types of furnace tube boiler, single furnace tube boiler and twin furnace tube boiler. In 1860 or so, the fire tube

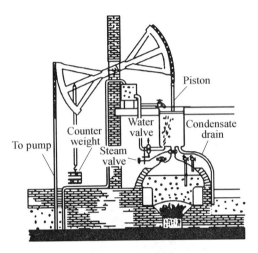

Fig. 5.4 Invention of Newcomen

boiler appeared. In this boiler, small tubes were used instead of the large diameter furnace tube, resulting in the increase of heat transfer surface. The combustion chamber (furnace), formed be firebricks, was still outside the shell, and the combustion products passed through the tubes. Later, fire tube and furnace tube combined boiler was evolved.

Way 2: To increase the heat transfer surface outside the shell, i. e. , to increase the number of cylinders. The fuel was fired still outside the shell. Similar to fire tube boiler, the increase of cylinder number led to the utilization of small diameter tubes. Because the water flows inside the tube, the boiler is known as water tube boiler.

Practices show that the use of small diameter tubes is conducive to the improvement of heat transfer, the reduction of metal consumption, the increase of output and pressure, since the fist water tube boiler emerged in 1840, various types of water tube boilers have been developed. The water tube boiler has become the sole choice for large capacity, high conditions electricity generating boilers.

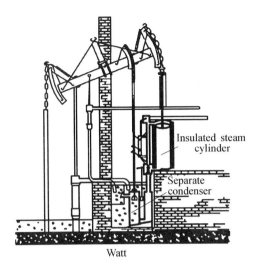

Fig. 5.5 Invention of Watt

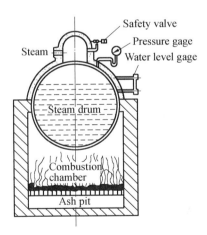

Fig. 5.6 Simple cylindrical

There are two types of water tubes boilers, horizontal tube and vertical tube. Early horizontal water tube boilers were integral header type, in which all the tubes were connected to two large diameter headers. The header is low in pressure bearing capability because of its large diameter. Thus, horizontal sub-header type boilers were developed, in which many small diameter subheaders were used to replace the large diameter headers, pressure-bearing capability was significantly increased. Because the tubes were arranged close to the horizontal, the flow of water inside the tubes was not satisfactory. In addition, the increase of heating surface was still limited by drum diameter. Hence, this type of boiler was gradually out of use.

Vertical water tube boilers, which occurred firstly in 1900, take most shares in modern boilers. The early vertical tube boilers used straight tubes, which had been gradually replaced by bent tubes. The number of drums had to be increased to accommodate more absorbing surfaces. Afterwards, the achievements in heat transfer confirmed that the heat absorption of the water cooled wall tubes from the flame infurnace by radiation can be much more effective than by the heat absorption of common tube bank by convection. Hence, water cooled wall surface was increased, convective bank surface was reduced. Accordingly, the number of drums was reduced. Nowadays, the large capacity boilers with single drum and without drum have been very common.

In one word, the evolution of boiler is a history of raising output, boosting parameters, reducing coal consumption, saving metal consumption and improving technological process.

With the fast development of national economy, the manufacturing industry of China has been continuously progressing in technological level and production scope. Boiler manufactories are categorized as Class A, B, C, D, Table 5. 8 lists the status of manufacturing industry of China as of the end of 2005.

Table 5.8 Status of boiler manufacturing industry in China

Class	Qualified range	Number of manufacturers
A	$P>2.45$ MPa	534
B	$P\leqslant 2.45$ MPa	739
C	$P\leqslant 0.8$ MPa, $D\leqslant 1$ t/h	2 060
D	$P\leqslant 0.1$ MPa(Drum type steam boiler); $t<120$ ℃, $Q\leqslant 2.8$ MW Hot water boiler	1 675
YJ		62
Others	Individual Parts	114

Currently, China faces many problems for industrial boilers, which are mainly:

(1) Low thermal efficiency. The industrial boilers in China take raw coals, which are hardly water washed, as fuels of boiler.

(2) Small single-unit capacity. The averaged capacity of residential and industrial boilers is only 2.28 t/h.

(3) Severe pollution to the environment. Majority of small capacity boilers, in particular smaller than 2 t/h, have imperfect smoke and dust eliminating devices, sometimes even no such devices. Besides, desulfurization devices are hardly used in these small capacity boilers.

(4) Low level of mechanization andautomatization. Small capacity boilers are still fired with coal being added and with ash and slag being removed be manpower. Professional levels of boiler operators differ greatly.

(5) Low boiler manufacturing capability and level. In China there

are quite a number of small sized boiler manufactories. They did contribute to the development of boiler manufacturing industry. However, some of them are short in professional personnel, incomplete in drawings and data, simple and backward in examining devices.

Oil-and gas-fired boilers, because of high thermal efficiency, low pollutant emission, have been widely used, abroad in particular. Statistic data show that in developed countries oil-and gas-fired boilers take a quite large share among the space heating boilers, for instance, in Russia they take 60%, in the USA 98%, in Japan 99%.

Over the past years, the demand for environment protection is continuing to rise. Hence, oil-and gas-fired boilers have found wider and wider applications in China.

In China, the first power generation plant was put into run in Shanghai in 1882. In 1919 the total installed capacity was only 185 MW, with an electric energy production of 43×10^8 (kW · h), there was hardly boiler manufacturing industry. In 1953, Shanghai Boiler Works was founded. In 1954, Harbin Boiler Works was established. Afterwads, Wuhan Boiler Corresponding disciplines and specialties were also established in universities and colleges. An intergrated system of education, research, design, manufacture, installation had been formulated. At present, China is capable of designing, manufacturing a variety of boilers, and domestic demands can be basically met. Large capacity boilers made in China have been exported to many countries, and power generating equipments have become important export products.

Modern utility boilers are developing toward high efficiency (partial reduction of pollution), large capacity, high conditions, minimum pollution, automation, high reliability, low initial cost (steel consumption). For industrial boilers, high efficiency, minimum pollution, automation, low initial cost (metal consumption) are emphasized. For residential boilers, minimum pollution, automation, safety and reliability are sought.

Words and Expressions

furnace ['fɜːnɪs] n. 火炉,熔炉
tube [tjuːb] n. 管
cylinder ['sɪlɪndə] n. 圆筒;汽缸
chamber ['tʃeɪmbə] n. 室,膛
firebrick ['faɪəbrɪk] n. 耐火砖
vertical ['vɜːtɪk(ə)l] adj. 垂直的,直立的

5.7 Basic Components and General Working Processes of a Boiler

A boiler consists of many parts, and these parts can be classified into two categories, boiler proper (also called as major components) and auxiliaries.

Talking a modern large-capacity natural circulation high pressure boiler as an example, the major components and their functions are described as follows.

The boiler proper

(1) Furnace. It is the place where fuel is combusted, and the combustion products (also known as flue gases) are cooled to such a low exit temperature that the successive convective heating surfaces can work reliably enough.

(2) Firing equipment. It conveys the fuel and the combustion air into the furnace, and ensures stable ignition, complete combustion of fuel.

(3) Boiler drum. It is a closing component of heating surfaces for

a natural circulation boiler, which brings the water cooled walls (risers) and downcomers together to form a circulating circuitry. The steam and water mixture is stored inside the to follow the variation of steam load, and the quality of the steam leaving the drum is ensured by arranging drum internals. Drum is unnecessary for a once-through boiler.

(4) Water cooled wall. It is the major radiant heating surface, which absorbs the radiant heat from the flame inside the furnace and protects the boiler setting. The tubes that are widely spaced from rear water cooled wall are referred to as slag screening tubes, which can prevent the successives uperheater tubes from slagging.

(5) Superheater. It heats the saturated steam further to the desired temperature. There is no superheater for the boilers that generate saturated steam or hot water.

(6) Reheater . It heats the steam that has expanded and done work in the high pressure cylinder of a turbine to a higher temperature, then is led into the medium pressure cylinder in order to continue to do work. The cyclic thermal efficiency of a power plant can be improved by using reheater.

(7) Economizer. It is used to heat feedwater by recovering the heat in the flue gases of a boiler. Therefore, thermal efficiency of the boiler can be increased and fuel consumption can be reduced.

(8) Air heater. It is used to heat the combustion air in order to enhance ignition and combustion. Since the waste heat of the flue gases can be recovered by doing so, the flue gases temperature leaving the boiler can be lowered, thus the thermal efficiency of the boiler can be improved. The hot air is also the drying medium of pulverizing system.

(9) Boiler setting. It is the protective casing of a boiler, which is

gas tight and components of the boiler.

(10) Framework. It supports and fixes all the components of a boiler, and retains the relative location of them.

The auxiliaries

(1) Fuel feeding equipment. It stores and transports fuels.

(2) Pulverizing and milling equipment. It is used to pulverize the coal and transports the pulverized coal to burners for combustion.

(3) Forced draft fan. It is used to transports air to air heater, the preheated air then goes to furnace for combustion orpulverizer for coal drying.

(4) Induced draft fan. It is used to discharge flue gases through stack to the atmosphere.

(5) Feedwater pump. It is used to provide the water treated in water treatment devices to boiler.

(6) Ash and slag disposal devices. By them the ash and slag from boiler are removed and carried away.

(7) Dust precipitators. They are used to catch the flyash entrained in flue gases to meet the requirements due to environmental protection.

(8) Automatic control devices. They are used for automatic inspection, programming control, protection and regulation.

The working processes

(1) Combustion of fuels, during which the chemical energy of fuels is released, transformed into the heat energy stored in the products of combustion. This process is also known as fire side process, as shown in Fig. 5.7.

(2) Heat transfer, in which the heat in flue gases is transferred to the

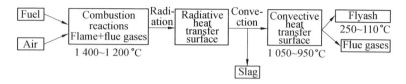

Fig. 5.7 Combustion process

working fluid through various heating surfaces, as shown in Fig. 5.8.

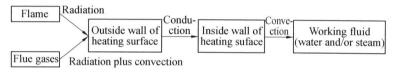

Fig. 5.8 Heat transfer process

(3) Fluid heating-up, vaporization and superheating, during this process, the working fluid is promoted to the desired temperature due to heat absorption, as shown in Fig. 5.9.

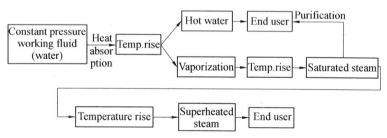

Fig. 5.9 Temperature rise, vaporization and superheating of working fluid

The working processes of a boiler can be elucidated by a pulverized coal fired, natural circulation boiler shown in Fig. 5.10.

The raw coal is fed into coal bunker through traveling belt, then by coal feeder into mill for pulverizing. The pulverized coal is separated and led to storage bin after passing through vent collector. The pulverized coal is distributed to individual transporting pipes by the feeders, and entrained by the air coming from the air heater or the

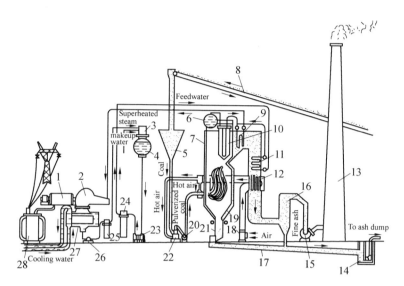

Fig. 5. 10 Working processes of boiler

exhaust air out of the vent collector into the furnace through the burner for combustion. The remaining part of the combustion air is directed into the furnace be the secondary air nozzles connected to the air heater. A great amount of heat is released due to the combustion of pulverized coal in the furnace. The hot combustion products go upwards and in the same time exchange heat with water cooled wall. The flue gases are reduced to a temperature of 140 ~ 170 ℃ after passing through superheaters, economizer and air heater, and drawn off by an induced fan and discharged to the atmosphere through chimney.

The water chemically treated (demineralized and deaerated) is pumped into the heating surfaces. In an electrical power plant, the water will be heated by low pressure heaters and high pressure heaters in the turbine room before entering boiler to 150 ~ 175 ℃ (medium pressure boilers) or 215 ~ 240 ℃ (high pressure boilers) , then fed through feedwater piping into the economizer. After having been heated to a certain temperature, the feedwater is led into drum, then the water flows downwards in downcomers into the inlet header of the water-cooled walls, where the water is distributed into the individual wall tubes. The water inside the wall tubes is partially transformed into steam due to radiative heat absorption from the flame in the furnace. The formed steam and water mixture rises and returns into the drum, in which the mixture is separated, and the steam enters superheaters through the main steam piping. The saturated steam continues to absorb heat in the low temperature superheater and high temperature superature and family becomes superheated steam. The superheated steam is led to turbine-generator unit for generating electricity.

Cool air is sent to air heater for preheating by a forced draft fan. The air absorbing heat from flue gases is divided into primary and secondary air and leads topulverizers and burners, respectively.

The ash discharged from the boiler bottom falls into sluice trough and transported to ash dump by water power.

Words and Expressions

downcomer ['daʊn,kʌmə] n. 下水管
circuitry ['sɜːkɪtrɪ] n. 电路;电路系统
drum [drʌm] v. 击鼓,大力争取
superheater [ˌsjuːpə'hiːtə] n. 过热器
slag [slæg] n. 炉渣
reheater [riː'hiːtə] n. 再热器
economizer [iː'kɑnəˌmaɪzə] n. 节约装置;省煤器
pulverize ['pʌlvəraɪz] v. 粉碎;研磨
preheated [ˌpriː'hiːt] adj. 预先加热的
feedwater ['fiːdwɔːtə] n. 给水,锅炉给水
flyash [f'laɪ'æʃ] n. 飞灰
bunker ['bʌŋkə] n. 沙坑;煤仓;燃料库

5.8 Classifications and Types of Boilers

Boilers can be classified by many different methods or criteria.

By end use, boilers can be classified into utility, industrial, and heating or residential. Utility boilers are used to generate electricity. These boilers are usually suspension-fired with high capacity, high pressure and high temperature, high thermal efficiency, and provide superheated steam. Industrial boilers are usually grate-fired with relatively low capacity, low pressure and low temperature, and low thermal efficiency. The boiler that provides steam is referred to as industrial steam boiler. The heating or residential boilers are used for space heating or for supplying residential hot water.

By structure, boilers can be classified into fire-and water-tube. As their names imply, combustion products flow inside the tubes of a fire-tube boiler. Usually, fire tube boilers are low in capacity, pressure, temperature and thermal efficient, but can operate well with the water of poor quality. Both operation and maintenance are convenient. Water and/or steam flow inside the tubes of a water tube boiler. Water tube boilers can be low capacity, low pressure and low temperature, and large capacity, high pressure and high temperature as well. Utility boilers are generally water tube with high efficiency, but require high quality water.

By water circulation mode, boilers can be classified into natural circulation, controlled circulation and once-through. Natural circulation boiler requires drum, and the fluid flow is driven be the density difference between water and steam. It can be applied only at subcritical pressures because the density difference when pressure is at or above the critical point. Drum is unnecessary for a once-through boiler, in which the feedwater is driven by pump to pass through all the heating surfaces once. Once-through boilers can be used under various pressures. A pump is equipped between downcomer and riser section in the controlled circulation boiler to assist the recirculation of working fluid, sometimes, controlled circulation boiler is known as assisted circulation boiler. The controlled circulation boiler includes three different types: ① Drum type controlled circulation boiler evolving from natural circulation boiler (circulation ratio is 2. 4 ~ 3. 5); ② Low circulation ratio (1. 2 ~ 2) boiler evolving from once-through boiler with water-steam separators. These two types of boilers are based on the same principles of the water circulation, that is, the circulation is established due to the density differences of the working fluids inside downcomers and risers and or the driving force provided by circulating pump. ③ Combined circulation boiler that operates as once-through boiler at high loads and operates as low circulation ratio boiler with circulation pump in operation at low loads.

By pressure of working fluid, boilers can be divided into atmospheric pressure, micro-pressurized, low pressure, medium pressure, high pressure, ultra high pressure, subcritical pressure, supercritical pressure, and ultra supercritical. For an atmospheric pressure boiler, the gauge pressure is zero. The gauge pressure of a micro-pressurized boiler is only several millimeters of H_2O column. Low pressure boilers are those with a pressure lower than 1. 275 MPa. A medium pressure boiler has a pressure around 3. 825 MPa. High pressure boiler has a pressure of 9. 8 MPa or so. The pressure of the ultra high pressure boiler is generally 13. 73 MPa. The boilers with a pressure around 16. 67 MPa are referred to as subcritical pressure boilers. The pressure of a supercritical pressure boiler is in the rage of 23 ~ 25 MPa. The pressure of an ultra supercritical pressure boiler is generally higher than 27 MPa. The above designations with respect to pressure are mainly in fashion in China.

By firing method, boilers can be divided into grate or stoker fired, space fired, fluidized bed combustion, and cyclone furnace. Grate fired boilers, including stationary grate, hand-wobbed grate, forward-moving spreader stoker, vibrating grate stoker, underfeed stoker and reciprocating shoving feed stoker, are used mostly as industrial boilers. Occasionally, they can find allocations in small utility and cogeneration boilers. In these boilers, fuel is fired on the grates. Space fired boilers are mostly used for utility boilers. All the boilers using liquid-gas and pulverized coal as fuel must be space-fired. In these boilers, fuels are burned in suspension in furnace. In a fluidized bed combustion boiler, the coal particles float over the distributor (grates) due to the lift of the air fed from under the distributor, and behave like fluid, the finer particles burn as they rise with the air. The boiler working under such conditions is often used for industrial purpose. If the velocity of the air from under the distributor is so increased that the particles are entrained out of the furnace, and go into a separator, the precipitated parcticles re-enter the furnace for further combustion. The boiler under such conditions is referred to as circulating fluidized bed combustion boiler, which mostly finds applications for generating electricity. In a cyclone furnace boiler, the fuel particles and the combustion air rotate with high speed within a cylinder, the finer particles are burned in suspension, and the coarser particles are tossed onto the liquefied slag layer where combustion is taking place.

By fuel fired, boilers can be classified into solid fuel fired, liquid fuel fired, gaseous fuel fired, waste heat, refuse fired and nuclear fuel. In a solid fuel fired boiler, coal etc is fired. In a liquid fuel fired boiler, heavy oil or light oil etc is fired. In a gaseous fuel fired boiler, natural gas etc is fired. In a waste heat boiler, the high temperature flue gases from metallurgical, petroleum and chemical processes etc are taken as the heat source. A nuclear fuel boiler is a steam generator utilizing the heat energy released in a reactor. In a refuse fired boiler, various residential and commercial solid wastes are used as the fuel of the boiler.

By ash tapping mode, boilers can be divided into dry bottom and slag tapping. In a dry bottom boiler, the ash due to combustion of solid fuels is discharged in solid state. This kind of boiler is dominating when coal is fired. In a slag tapping boiler, the ash due to combustion of solid fuels flows out of slag drip opening in liquid state, which is cracked by the water in granulating pool into small particulates, then swept into ash sluice.

By flue gas pressure in furnace, boilers can be classified as balanced draft, micro-pressurized and pressurized. In a balanced draft furnace boiler, some vacuum is established within the furnace by both forced draft fan and induced draft fan. This type of boiler finds widest applications in coal fired boilers. A micro-pressurized boiler has a flue gas gauge pressure of 2 ~ 5 kPa in the furnace, this boiler does not require induced fan, and suitable for low oxygen combustion. In a pressurized furnace boiler, a gauge pressure greater than 0.3 MPa usually is maintained in the furnace, mostly applied to steam-gas combined cycle.

By number of drums, boilers can be classified into single drum type and multiple drum type. The drums may be in longitudinal arrangement or transverse arrangement. All the modern drum type utility boilers are single drum type. For industrial boilers, both single drum and double drum type can be employed.

By configuration, boilers can be divided into inverted U type, tower type, box type, T type, U type, N type, L type, D type and A type. A and D types are usually applied to industrial boiler, other types are used for utility boiler.

By type of boiler house, boilers can be divided as open air, semi open air, in-room, underground, and in-cave. In-room arrangements are usually considered for industrial boilers, but, utility boilers generally take open-air or semi open-air arrangements.

Boilers can also be divided into packaged, semi-packaged and field-erected. Small capacity boilers can be packed, but utility boilers are commonly semi-packaged and field-erected.

Words and Expressions

criteria [kraɪ'tɪərɪə] n. 标准;条件
suspension [sə'spenʃ(ə)n] n. 悬浮,暂停
pump [pʌmp] n. 泵;抽水机 v. 抽水
supercritical [ˌsjuːpə'krɪtɪkəl] adj. 超临界的
ultra ['ʌltrə] adj. 极端的;过分的
grate [greɪt] v. 装格栅于;摩擦 n. 壁炉;格栅
float [fləʊt] v. 使漂浮
cyclone ['saɪkləʊn] n. 旋风;气旋
toss [tɔs] n. 投掷;摇荡
gaseous ['gæsɪəs] adj. 气态的,气体的

5.9 Basic Operating Principles

The operation of a boiler means that all of the factors that went into the design and construction of the facility are put into the test. A principal objective of proper operation is sustained service between outages while, at the same time, obtaining the highest possible efficiency from all the plant components. Effective operation of a boiler is critical to maintaining system efficiency, reliability and availability. The procedures used to operate a boiler vary widely, depending upon the type of system, fuel and application. Systems can range from simple and fully automated requiring a minimum of attention, such as small gas-fired package boilers, to the very complex requiring constant operator attention and interaction, such as a large capacity utility boiler. There are, however, a set of relatively common fundamental operating guidelines which safeguard personnel and optimize equipment performance and reliability. When combined with equipment specific procedures, these guidelines promote the best possible operations.

Because of the intimate relationship between equipment design and operation, in fact, some operating guidelines have been discussed in the previous chapters.

The most overwhelming consideration for all operations is the safety of people and equipment. Whenever there is any doubt about an unsafe condition, the operator must take immediate action to return the unit to a known safe condition even if it means tripping the unit. Safe operation is a result of comprehensive training programs for operators, well-designed furnace safeguard systems, and an effective preventative-maintenance program.

Although boiler design and power production have become sophisticated, basic operating principles still apply. Combustion safety and proper steam/water cooling are always essential.

The operation of a boiler is balance of inputs to outputs. The better the balance, the smoother the operation is. Producing steam from a boiler requires that the mass of water entering the boiler should be equal to the steam leaving, and firing the furnace requires a balance of fuel and air. To equalize these inputs and outputs, operator must understand the system. This understanding is the principal ingredient of successful operation.

Before firing a furnace, there must be no lingering combustible material inside the unit. Purging, or removal of this material, assures that the furnace is ready for firing. A standard operating rule is to purge the unit for five minutes at no less than 25% of the maximum continuous rating (MCR) air flow.

Once combustion is established, the correct air/fuel ratio must be maintained. Insufficient air flow may permit the formation of combustible gas pockets and, thereby, provide an explosion potential. Sufficient air flow to match the combustion requirements of the fuel should be maintained and a small amount of excess air should be admitted to cover imperfect mixing and to promote air and fuel distribution. It is also important to verify boiler water levels. Combustion should never be established until adequate cooling water is in the tubes and steam drum.

To operate a boiler is aimed at maintaining desired primary and reheat steam temperatures and maximum boiler efficiency. To do so, the operator must be aware of the effect of all operating variables, and adjustments are always required.

Even the best control systems do not anticipate all of the factors affecting steam temperature. Despite the equipment installed for controlling superheater and reheater steam temperatures, certain conditions may produce abnormal steam temperatures. For instance, with a new coal-fired unit, it may be necessary to operate for a considerable time before normal furnace seasoning allows the unit to make predicted steam temperatures. " Normal furnace seasoning " is often defined as the condition of furnace-wall slag or ash deposits which remains after sootblower operation.

Low steam temperatures may also result from insufficient excess air, higher-than-design feedwater temperature, reheater inlet temperature lower than specified, an externally fouled superheater or reheater, leaking attemperator spray water, and poorly adjusted controls.

On the other hand, high steam temperature may result from an "over-seasoned" furnace, too high an excess-air ratio, feedwater temperature lower than specified, reheater inlet temperature higher than specified, irregular ignition or delayed combustion, and poorly adjusted control equipment.

An operating variable with a very great effect on steam temperature is the cleanliness of the radiant and convective heating surfaces. Although all modern coal-fired boilers are equipped with automatic sootblower systems, the judicious supplemental manual operation of certain blowers can improve overall unit operation. It can save valuable blowing medium and reduce required maintenance be minimizing the number of blowing cycles. To be most effective, a sootblower program requires periodic furnace observations. Based on such observations and performance results, selective sootblowing can lead to better steam temperature control and reduce the possibility of troublesome accumulations in the furnace and convection passes.

An effective operator should constantly strive to obtain maximum efficiency from a unit. The individual heat loss should be reduced by all means.

To operate a boiler most efficiently, therefore, the operator must have a reliable means of assessing the quantity of excess air leaving the boiler. In-situ oxygen recorders that measure the oxygen at the boiler or economizer outlet are the best information source. They must, however, be checked daily for proper calibration and maintained as necessary. The operator should maintain the required excess air by making sure the controls are in the correct mode or by manual bias of the fuel-to-air ratio.

On gas-or oil-fired units unburned-fuel loss is usually negligible, whereas unburned loss on coal-fired units can be appreciable. The boiler manufacturer will predict unburned-fuel loss and these values can usually be maintained with correct operation. There is no easy way to continuously monitor unburned carbon in the ash. Obtaining such values involves the time and manual effort of laboratory analysis of a flyash sample. The significant point is that the laboratory feed back the information to the operators. If values are consistently high, the plant operation department should develop a program to pinpoint what is causing the high unburns and how to improve the condition. Usually, high unburns can be traced to mixing process of the fuel and air in the furnace. Once the source is found, attention must be focused on how corrects it. For example, one cause of poor mixing of fuel and air could be inadequate windbox to furnace pressure. If this is so, monitoring pressure to keep it in line is easier than waiting for the periodic feedback of laboratory results.

Words and Expressions

smoother ['smuːðə] n. 路面平整机；滤波器
ingredient [ɪn'griːdɪənt] n. 原料；要素；组成部分
drum [drʌm] v. 击鼓；大力争取
furnace ['fɜːnɪs] n. 火炉；熔炉
deposit [dɪ'pɒzɪt] n. 沉淀物 v. 沉淀
sootblower [suːtb'ləuər] n. 吹灰；吹灰器
feedback ['fiːdbæk] n. 反馈；成果

6

Turbine

6.1 Steam Turbine

A turbine is a rotary engine which is driven by a stream of fluid (liquid or gas) directed on to the blades of the rotor. In a steam turbine this fluid is steam. Part of the heat and pressure energy of steam are changed into mechanical energy byimparting rotary motion to turbine blade wheels. In turbines the rotary motion is obtained by direct action of the steam on the blade wheels or rotors. The speedof the flow of the fluid, which in water turbines is produced by a fall in level, in steam turbines is produced by a fall in pressure of the steam from the boiler. The steam is expanded from a higher to a lower pressure in nozzles or in the blading, and then increases its speed at the expense or in the of its heat and pressure. The speed of the steam is then reduced by doing work on the moving blades.

The great advantages of the turbine are freedom from vibration and noise, smooth and uniform rotary force, and ability to handle large quantities of fluid-in this case steam. Its simplicity and reliability type of engine for driving pumps, blowers, and other equipment. In these cases the turbine's most efficient speed is usually much higher than that of the machine it is driving, so a speed reduction gear usually has to be used. Steam turbines donot work very efficiently in small sizes.

Very large steam turbines in conjunction with speed reduction gears are used fordriving ships; in fact, a steam turbine is the only practicable kind of engine for driving ships. It is in large electrical power stations that the steam turbine reaches its highest development, and some new power stations are being equipped with steam turbines producing more than 600 000 horsepower each.

The steam turbine consists of the following essential parts:

1. A casing usually divided at the horizontal centerline, with the halves bolted together for ease of assembly and disassembly, and containing the stationary blade system.

2. A rotor with the moving blades on wheels, and with bearing journals on the ends of the rotor.

3. A bearing box in the casing, supporting the shaft.

4. A governor and valve system for regulating the speed and power of the turbineby controlling the steam flow, and an oil system for lubrication of the bearingsand a set of safety devices.

5. A coupling of some sort to connect with the driven machine.

6. Pipe connection to a supply of steam at the inlet, and to an exhaust system atthe outlet of the casing.

Fig. 6.1 shows a simple form of impulse turbine. In this the steam issues from a stationary nozzle (or nozzles) which is curved so as to direct the jet on to a ring of blades attached to a rotating wheel or disc. These blades are shaped to 'catch' the steam from the nozzle smoothly, and they are curved so that they changethe direction of the jet and in so doing receive an impulse which pushes them forward.

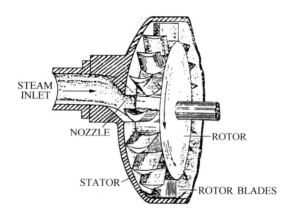

Fig. 6.1   Diagram of an impulse turbine

The steam, directed on to the blades, gives them an impulse which rotates the rotor

If, instead of using fixed nozzles and a separate wheel, we were to mount the nozzle itself on a wheel, the reaction of the issuing jet would drive it in the opposite direction to the impulse wheel. The very first steam turbine was a pure reaction turbine of this type, but for various reasons it is never used nowadays.

There is another kind of turbine (Fig. 6.2) which combines the principles of impulse and reaction but is usually referred to simply as a 'reaction' turbine. An essential characteristic of a nozzle is that the passage narrows from the inlet onwards, and consequently the fluid which enters at a relatively low speed must come out at a much higher speed. The increase in speed is produced by a drop of pressure, the pressure of the fluid being higher as it enters the nozzle than as it leaves. The casing in Fig. 6.2 carries a complete ring of nozzles which, as in the impulse turbine, are curved and direct the steam on to the moving blades at the most effective angle. The moving blades are also nozzles, similar to the stationary nozzles but facing the other way,

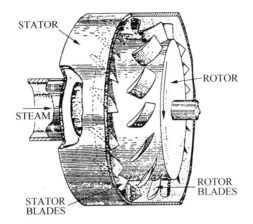

Fig. 6.2 Diagram of a reaction turbine
The stator blades form nozzles through which the steam is accelerated and directed on to the nozzles formed by the rotor blades

and in addition to catching and deflecting the steam issuing from the stationary nozzles, they also accelerate it, the drive coming half from an impulse and half from a reaction force. The jet speed in this type of turbine is half what it is in an impulse turbine having the same blade speed. In either case the steam leaves the moving blades more or less at right angles to the direction of motion of the blades.

The simplest type of steam turbine has one stage; that is, one row each of stationary and of moving blades. Such turbines are commonly used for power outputs of a few hundred horse-power at most, with moderate inlet pressures and temperatures, and for an atmospheric or higher pressure at the exhaust. Under these conditions it is possible to use the steam with adequate efficiency in a single stage.

To obtain as much power as possible from each pound of coal

burned in the boiler it is necessary to work with a high steam pressure and temperature at the inlet to the turbine and as low a pressure as possible at the exhaust. By condensing the exhaust steam in a separate condenser, using a large quantity of cooling water, a very low exhaust pressure can be maintained and the condensed steam pumped back to the boiler as pure feed water. If the steam were allowed to expand from boiler pressure to condenser pressure in one step, the jet velocity from the nozzle would be so great that it would be impossible to build a turbine to run fast enough to utilize such a high jet speed efficiently-indeed, a single stage steam turbine normally has a very low efficiency. For large power output, and for the high inlet pressures and temperatures and low exhaust pressures which are required for good thermal efficiency, both with impulse and reaction turbines, a single stage is not adequate. Steam under such conditions has high available energy and for its efficient utilization the turbine must have many stages in series. Also, under these conditions the exhaust volume flow becomes large, and it is necessary to have more than one exhaust stage; for example, a large turbine may have three are alternately rows of stationary blades carried in the casing and rows of blades attached to the rotor, arranged so that the steam is directed to enter each row of stationary and moving blades at the proper angle. The stationary blades are always nozzles, the rotor blades are also nozzles in the case of a reaction turbine but only guide channels in the case of an impulse turbine.

 The successive stages are normally arranged side by side along a horizontal axis, constituting what is called an "axial flow" turbine. The steam enters at one end and leaves at the other, or, if the flow is very big, the steam may enter at the middle and leave at both ends, an arrangement called "double flow". The casing consists of a bottom half, which usually carries the bearings that support the rotor, and a top half, which is bolted to the bottom half at the horizontal joint after the rotor has been placed in position.

When the stages are very numerous it has proved most practicable to use two or more casings or cylinders, usually arranged in line and with the shafts coupled together.

Modern turbines are supplied by the boiler with steam that is highly superheated. As the steam passes through the turbine, its pressure and temperature fall until at a certain stage all the superheat is lost, and thereafter drops of water areformed by condensation of some of the steam. These drops can damage the blades and reduce the turbine efficiency, and this is one reason why the steam, after passing through the high-pressure turbine, is sometimes re-superheated before entering the medium-pressure turbine.

Words and Expressions

rotary ['rəutəri] *a.* 旋转的,转动的
blade [bleid] *n.* 叶片,刀片
rotor ['rəutə] *n.* 转子,旋转部
blading ['bleidiŋ] *n.* 叶片(装置)
nozzle ['nɔzl] *n.* 喷管,喷嘴
reliability [rilaiə'biliti] *n.* 可靠性
blower ['bləuə] *n.* 鼓风机
lubricate [lu:bri'keit] *v.* 润滑
inlet ['inlet] *n.* 入口,插入物,注入
cylinder ['silində] *n.* 气缸,圆筒
superheat *n. v.* 过热
medium-pressure *a.* 中压的
by imparting to 通过把……给与
in conjunction with 与……相结合

in series   串联地,多级地
side by side   并排地

6.2 Gas Turbine

This is a form of internal combustion engine in which air, heated by burning fuel, expands, and in doing so is made to turn a specially shaped wheel (the turbine wheel) directly, instead of pushing pistons up and down as in the reciprocating engine.

Because of the continuous, smooth nature of its internal processes, the gas turbine, like the steam turbine, is almost completely free from vibration; and this, together with its essential simplicity, makes it more reliable and easier to maintain. It is lighter and less bulky than the piston engine, and it can be built in larger sizes to give higher powers from single power units. For all these reasons, the use of gas turbines is increasing for all forms of transport, on land, sea, and in the air. It may be wondered, in view of all these advantages, why the gas turbineengine was not introduced sooner, especially since the general idea of a gas turbine is not a new one. Indeed, the idea of using the energy in hot gases to turn a wheel directly is perhaps a more obvious one than the more complicated system employed in piston engines. In fact, the turbine principle is more difficult to apply in practice. The first small and relatively inefficient gas turbines were operated by the exhaust gases from piston engines, and these were used to drive superchargers. It was not until the 1930's that successful self-operating gas turbines were made, and used for aircraft propulsion. About the same time that aircraftturbines were being achieved, gas turbines had been developed forstationary use and as power units for railway locomotives.

The gas turbine consists essentially of an air compressor, a combustion chamber, and a turbine wheel.

Compressors Two basic types of compressors are used in gas turbines: axial and centrifugal. In a few special cases a combination type known as a mixed wheel, whichis partially centrifugal and partially axial, has been used. The axialflow compressor is the most widely used because of its ability to handle large volumes of air at high efficiency. For small gas turbines in the range of 500 hp. and less, the centrifugal replaces the axial.

Combustors Combustors, sometimes referred to as combustion chambers, for gas turbines take a wide variety of shapes and forms, for example, the annular, can-type orcannular. The gas turbine combustor components are fuel nozzle, combustion section and transition section to turbine inlet. Air for the combustion chamber is forced into the engine by a compressor. Fuel is mixed with the compressed air and burned in combustors. The heat energy thus released is changed by the turbine into totary energy. Because of the high initial temperature of the combustion products, excess air is used to cool the combustion products to the turbine inletdesign temperature.

Turbine wheels Two types of gas turbine wheels are used: radial-inflow, and axial-flow. Small gas turbines use the radialflow wheel. For large volume flows, axialturbine wheels are used almost exclusively. Although some of the turbines used in the small gas turbine plants are of the simple impulse type, most high performance turbines are neither pure impulse nor pure reaction. The high performance turbines are normally designed for varying amounts of reaction and impulse to give optimum performance.

The compressor and the turbine wheel are on the same shaft and rotate together. The hot gases from the combustion chamber strike the turbine blades, driving the shaft and thus rotating the compressor. Air from the atmosphere is sucked into theinlet ports of the compressor and flows forward through each blade stage (the axial-flow compressor). As the air pressure increases, its volume decreases untilmaximum compression is reached at the last stage. The highly compressed (and thehigh temperature) air is then discharged into the duct leading to the combustion chamber. This unit has one or more fuel nozzles, through which the fuel is sprayed to mix with the moving air. In starting, the fuel spray is ignited by using of spark plugs. Once ignited, the fuel-air mixture burns continuously, so that the ignition can be switched off.

Instead of the single combustion chamber, which is the annular form of the chamber, a number of separate chambers, known as can-type or cannular chambers, are often used. Thus in a typical aircraft gas turbine, eight to ten can-type chambers, each with its own fuel nozzle, are employed.

The products of combustion leave the chamber through a duct and fixed guides or nozzes to enter the turbine. Here the gases flow axially, falling in both temperature and pressure as they transmit most of their energy to the turbine wheel.

Fig. 6. 3 illustrates diagrammatically the basic principles of this type of engine, and makes clear the technical difficulties which delayed the development of successful gas turbines. (A) is the air intake through which air passes to the compressor(B) , and then into the combustion chamber(C) , at a high pressure and hotter than it was owing to the compression(to at least 50 1b. per square inch). Fuel is injected into the compressed air, and burned with high efficiency in the combustion chambers. The combustion raises the temperature to 850 ℃. or more, and this expands the air. The resultant gases at high pressure and temperature blow continuously on to the turbine wheel (D) which drives the compressor. After they leave D , the gases, still at

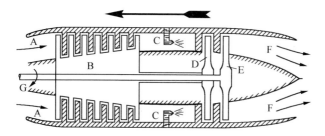

Fig. 6.3 Diagram of a Gas Turbine
A. Air intake. B. Compressor. C. Combustion chambers. D. Turbine wheel drivingcompressor. E Turbine wheel driving propeller. F. Tailpipe through which gases escape. G. Propeller shaft. The large arrow shows the direction of flight, the smaller ones the direction of air and burnt gases

a fairly high pressure and temperature and still expanding, can be used in two ways. On the gas turbine proper, and in turbo-prop aircraft engines, the issuing gases drive a further turbine wheel (or series of wheels) (E) , which is fixed to the power shaft. This shaft may drive a propeller, as in turbo-prop engines or, for example, a motorcar gearbox, as in a gas turbinecar.

In the pure jet engine, on the other hand, the issuing gases pass straight out intothe air through a tail pipe, forming a high-speed jet which pushes the engine forward on the reaction principle, like a rocket. In the ¿by-pass' jet aircraft engine there is a low-pressure and a high-pressure compressor. Some of the air from the first by-passes the second and the combustion chamber, giving a cooler, slower, heavier jet of air in the tail pipe, more suitable for slower jet aircraft.

The material of the turbine wheels is continuously exposed to the very hot gases, and the demands made on the metals used for the blading of a gas turbine are very heavy-even more than for a steam turbine. Another problem concerns theefficiency of the air compressor; if this is inefficient, it will absorb too muchpower itself, and so much of the available energy of the gases will be used up in the turbine wheel (D) that there will be little left to deliver as thrust, or as useful power from the second wheel (E). Gas turbines therefore, could not be developed until very efficient air compressors had been evolved, well as steels or other metals metals able to resist high temperatures.

For some purposes, the piston type of engine is still preferable to the gas turbine. Its fuel consumption is usually appreciably lower for a given power output, but the gas turbine is lighter. Also it is not easy to make satisfactory gas turbines of low power output, suitable, for example, for road vehicles although effortsare being made to solve this problem.

The gas turbine has special advantages for aircraft propulsion, owing to its lowweight and small size, and it has found in aviation its first important application and the greatest stimulus for its development. As an aero-engine it is used either for pure jet propulsion or to drive a conventional propeller.

Jet-propulsion engines are most efficient at high altitudes and high airspeeds and are particularly suited for high-performance military aircraft. Modern military jet-propulsion engines are capable of producing tremendous power. In emergencies this can be augmented still further with the aid of an afterburner, which adds heat to the gases just before they enter the exhaust nozzle. This afterburning increases their velocity and adds to the forward thrust or the engine.

Another gas-turbine application for aircraft is the turboprop. In this application the gas turbine has two purposes: it drives a conventional propeller, and it produces additional thrust by means of the reactive force of the jet leaving the exhaust nozzle of the engine.

The advantage of short takeoff inherent in propeller-driven aircraft is thus combined with the faster and higher flying capabilities of the conventional jet-propulsion engine.

Intermediate between the conventional jet-propulsion engine and the turboprop is a later development called the turbofan engine. It differs from the ordinary jet-propulsion engine in that a fan is located at the inlet that takes in a great deal more air than actually passes through the core of the engine. The fan compresses this air slightly and then delivers most of it though a bypass duct around the engine, where, it is accelerated and released with a higher velocity than it had at intake, thus adding to the thrust of the engine. The remainder of the air flows through the core of the engine, where it is compressed, heated and expanded through the turbine and exhaust nozzle as in a conventional jet.

The ratio of air bypassed through the duct surrounding the core of the engine tothat passing through the core is called the bypass ratio. This varies widely according to application. Bypass ratio as high as 8 to 1 are common in large turbofan engines. In general, high bypass ratios and high compression ratios result in improved fuel economy.

The turbofan engine has a number of advantages. The added thrust of the engine eliminates the need for carrying heavy additional loads of water sometimes employed for injection to increase the thrust of conventional engines during take off on warm days. When operating within the proper speed and altitude range, fuel savings of the order of 20 percent can be realized. These advantages have made this type of engine the favourite for commercial use on very large jet aircraft.

In the field of electric-power generation, the gas turbine, as compared with thediesel engine and steam turbine, are limited in capacity by the fact that the pressure involved is low, making it necessary to employ large turbines and compressors in order to handle the huge volumes of air required. For this reason no serious attempt has been made to design a gas-turbine-gas-power plant in the modern central-station to replace steam power plant in which single units as largeas 1 200 000 kilowatts have been built.

Three applications deserve special mention: (1) operation in combination with steam power plants as a means of increasing the overall efficiency; (2) for standbyand peakload service; and (3) for portable power plants. A promising combinedsteam-turbine-gas-turbine power plant is one in which high temperature exhaust gases from a conventional gas turbine are employed to supply oxygen to the furnace of a steam boiler in place of preheated combustion air. This combination is feasible because the gases exhausted from a gas turbine still contain about 80 percent of the oxygen in the air suppliedto the compressor inlet. Such an arrangement is capable of increasing substantially the overall efficiency of the plant. It also offers savings in size and weight of the boilers required, less building volume, quicker starting of the boiler, and elimination of the forced and induced draft fans normally required by the boiler.

Other ways in which the gas turbine can be employed to improve the efficiency ofa steam power plant are to use the exhaust gases for feedwater heating or for the generation of steam in an exhaust-heat boiler.

The gas turbine offers an attractive means for providing additional peak-load and standby power. It can often be installed for this purpose at lower cost than additional steam or hydroelectric capacity. Furthermore, it offers the advantages of virtually automatic operation, simplicity, small space requirements, and minimum maintenance. Another similar application is for end-of-the -line voltage-booster service on long distance transmission lines. A third application is for portable power plants. Here the gas turbine can be mounted on railroad cars or bargesfor emergency use.

Words and Expressions

piston ['pistən] n. 活塞
supercharge ['sju:pətʃa:dʒə] n. 增压器
propulsion [prə'pʌlʃən] n. 推进(装置),推力
locomotive ['ləukəməutiv] n. 机车 a. 运动的
chamber ['tʃeimbə] n. 室,容器
centrifugal [sen'trifjugəl] a. 离心的
combustor [kəm'bʌstə] n. 燃烧室
annular ['ænjulə] a. 环形的
optimum ['ɔptiməm] n. 最佳值 a. 最佳的
resultant [ri'zʌltənt] a. 总的,生成的 n. 合力,组合
gear-box n. 变速箱
by-pass n. 旁路,支流 a. 旁通 v. 分流
propeller [prə'pelə] n. 螺旋浆,推进器
turbofan n. 涡轮风扇(发动机)
kilowatt ['kiləwɔt] n. 千瓦(特)
peakload ['pi:k'ləud] n. 峰值负荷
straight out 直接地
is preferable to 优于
of the order of 大约,约为

6.3 Compressor

The most important way in which gases differ from liquids and solids is that they can easily be compressed, or squeezed to occupy a smaller volume. A machine fordoing this is known as a compressor, of which the ordinary bicycle pump is the simplest example. There are two main classes of compressor—reciprocating and rotary.

Reciprocating compressors are the type used in the liquefaction of gases, and also to provide a source of power for the familiar pneumatic road drill. They can compress a gas up to 30 000 1b per square inch and more, but they are not suitable for handling large volumes of air at pressures below 50 1b. per square inch.

The reciprocating compressor consists essentially of a cylinder, a piston(p), connecting rod(R), and crankshaft(cs) arranged much the same as in an internal combustion engine. Except at very high pressures, the valves in compressors are notworked mechanically, but are simply thin metal flaps opened and closed by the air itself. As the piston travels downward, it sucks open the inlet valve(v_1), andgas is drawn into the cylinder. On the return stroke the gas in the cylinder is forced out through the delivery valve(v_2), while the pressure in the cylinderholds the inlet valve closed.

The delivery pipe is smaller than the inlet pipe because the gas, being at a higher pressure, occupies a smaller volume. As gas gets hot when compressed, high-pressure compressors must be cooled, either by blowing air or by circulating cooling water in a jacket round the cylinder. A common arrangement is a two-cylindercompressor in which the gas delivered by the first cylinder is cooled before being passed to the second cylinder and further compressed. The gas takes up less room after it has been compressed by the first cylinder and so the second cylinder need not be so large.

The two most important types of rotary compressor are the blade type, and the "positive displacement" type. Until recently, blade— type compressors—of which the ordinary ventilating fan is a simple example—were used only for very low pressures, but now the compressors incorporated into the modern gas turbine can compress air up to 50 1b. per square inch and more. Blade compressors—both ventilating fans and compressors for gas turbines work on either the radial or axial flow principle; in each case the blades are surrounded by a casing in which the compressed air is collected.

With radial-flow compressors the air enters at the centre of the whirling blades and is flung outwards. For higher efficiencies and pressures, however, axialc-flow compressors are used. These work on the same principle as propellers—the blading "screws" the air up to the required pressure, and the air travels through the blades from end to end. They can handle much larger quantities of air for a given overall size of machine, but they must run at high speed and must, therefore, bevery carefully manufactured and balanced. The ordinary household electric fan isa simple form of axialflow compressor.

Positive displacement rotary compressors are so called because, as in a reciprocating compressor, the air is pushed through the machine mechanically. A type which is designed for supercharging internal combustion engines consists of a barrel-shaped casing, inside which a rotor with four vanes is mounted out of the centre with the barrel. Air enters at inlet port, is trapped by the vanes as the rotor rotates, and is compressed as the space between the rotor and casing diminishes. The compressed air is delivered at the outlet port.

Words and Expressions

squeeze ['skwi:z] v. 挤,压,使缩减
reciprocate [ri'siprəkeit] v. 往复移动
liquefaction [ˌlikwi'fækʃən] n. 液化(作用),熔解
pneumatic [nju:'mætik] a. 空气的,气体的,气动的
drill [dril] n. 钻床

crank-shaft   n. 曲轴
flap   [flæp]   n. 风门片
ventilate   ['ventileit]   v. 使通风,使换气
fling   [fliŋ]   v. 抛,猛冲
super-charge   v. 对……增压
vane   [vein]   n. 叶片,翼
take up   占据
out of the centre   偏心地

6.4 Gas Turbine Plants

Introduction

  A gas turbine plant (Fig. 6.4) consists of a turbo-compressor, combustion chamber (or heat exchanger) and turbine. The plant is started by rotating the compressor-turbine assembly by a starting motor or any other device. When the compressor develops enough pressure to support combustion of the fuel in the combustion chamber, the hot gases can themselves drive the gas turbine, and the plant becomes self-sustaining. The turbine should develop enough power to be able to drive the compressor and load (if any). The output of the plant is the difference between the turbine work and the compressor work. The actual output at the generator terminals will be much less than this.

  A majority of aircraft gas turbine plants use kerosene or gasoline where as other plants can use natural gas, bunker oil and blast furnace gas. Coal or gasifiedcoal can also be used in electric power generating gas turbine plants.

  If the gas turbine plant is used as an aircraft engine, the net output at the turbine shaft is used to drive a propeller in a turbo-prop engine, whereas in a turbo-jet engine the turbine output equals the

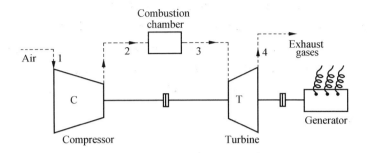

Fig. 6.4 A simple open circuit gas turbine plant

power required to drive the compressor. The output of such a plant is the energy in the exhaust gases which is used for jet propulsion.

The shaft power of a gas turbine plant can also be used for driving electric generators, draft fans, compressors and other industrial devices.

As will be discussed later, the combustion chamber in a large number of industrial applications is replaced by a heat exchanger.

Gas turbine plants can be compared with steam turbine plants; the chief distinguishing features of the gas turbine plants are their high inlet gas temperatures ($t_{max} > 1\ 500$ K) and lower pressures. The exhaust gas pressures of the gas turbine plants are nowhere near the considerably lows pressures (≈ 22.5 m bar) employed in the condensing steam plants. This explains why it is not necessary to employ large low pressure cylinders and multiple exhaust even in large terrestrial gas turbine plants. On the other hand, when compared with the reciprocating internal combustion engine, the gas turbine has the advantage of very high flow rate, light weight and mechanical simplicity.

Component efficiencies and inlet gas temperatures were critical for the successful development of the gas turbine plant. Therefore in the earlier stages of its development major attempts were made to improve turbine and compressor efficiencies and develop high temperature materials. At present, the component efficiencies are in excess of 85% and the turbine blade cooling has enabled the employment ofgas temperatures as high as 1 600 K at the inlet.

Open and Closed Circuit Plants

In the simple open circuit gas turbine plants (Fig. 6. 4) atmospheric air is continuously compressed in the compressor and delivered to the combustion chamber at a high pressure. The hot gases from the combustion chamber pass out to the atmosphere after expanding through the turbine. In this arrangementsince the working fluid is not restored (at station 1 in Fig. 6. 4) to its initial state, technically speaking such a plant does not execute a cycle.

A cycle can only be executed in the closed circuit gas turbine plant shown in Fig 6. 5. Here the same working fluid (air or any other gas) circulates through its various components. Heat cannot be supplied to the working fluid by internal combustion; instead, it is supplied externally by employing a heat exchanger which replaces the combustion chamber of the open circuit plant.

A pre-cooler is included between the turbine exit and the compressor entry. Thisdecreases the specific volume of the air or gas entering the compressor. The lower value of the specific volume reduces the compressor work ($\int v \mathrm{d}p$) and its size.

The closed circuit gas turbine plant with its separate external combustion system and precooler looks like a condensing steam plant.

Some advantages of the closed circuit gas turbine plant are given below.

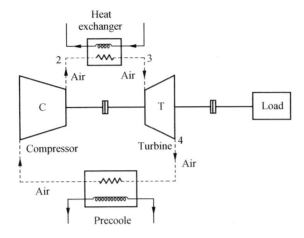

Fig. 6.5 A simple closed circuit gas turbine plant

1. Since the working fluid does not leave the plant, fluids with better thermodynamic properties other than air can be employed to derive some aero-thermodynamic advantages. For example, the velocity of sound is higher in helium which permitshigher peripheral speeds of the rotor. It is inert and has a higher specific heat and thermal conductivity, resulting in a smaller heat exchanger.

2. By employing high density working fluids, the plant size for a given power can be reduced. In large plants this is a great advantage in terms of mechanical design. A higher density also provides a higher heat transfer rate.

3. The air in a conventional open circuit plant brings its own impurities which cause additional problems of blade erosion and filtration. In a closed circuit plant blade erosion due to solid particles in the air as well as in the products ofcombustion is absent.

4. This arrangement provides better control of the plant.

5. The chief disadvantage of this plant is that heat is supplied

externally to the working fluid. This requires additional equipment besides being less efficient.

Words and Expressions

combustion [kəm'bʌsʃən] n. 燃烧,氧化
chamber ['tʃeimbə] n. 室,房间,箱
kerosene ['kerəsi:n] n. 煤油
gasoline ['gæsəli:n] n. 汽油
bunker ['bʌŋkə] n. 燃料舱,煤箱
terrestrial [ti'restriəl] a. 地球上的,陆地的
helium ['hi:ljəm] n. (化)氦
peripheral [pə'rifərəl] a. 周界的,边缘的
impurity [im'pjuəriti] n. 杂质
erosion [i'rəuʒən] n. 腐蚀,磨蚀
filtrate ['filtreit] v. 过滤

6.5 Classification of Steam Turbines

Steam turbines may be classified into different categories depending on their construction, the process by which heat drop is achieved, the initial and final conditions of steam used and their industrial usage as follows.

1. According to the number of pressure stages:

(1) Single-stage turbines with one or more velocity stages usually of small-power capacities;

(2) Multistage impulse and reaction turbines; they are made in a wide range of power capacities varying from small to large.

2. According to the direction of steam flow:

(1) Axial-turbines in which the steam flows in a direction parallel to the axis of the turbine;

(2) Radial-turbine in which the steam flows in a direction

perpendicular to theaxis of the turbine;one or more low-pressure stages in such turbines are madeaxial.

3. According to the number of cylinders(casings):

(1) Single-cylinder turbines;

(2) Double-cylinder turbines;

(3) Three-cylinder turbines;

(4) Four-cylinder turbines.

Multicylinder turbines which have their rotors mounted on one and the same shaftand coupled to a single generator are known as single shaft turbines; turbines with separate rotor shafts for each cylinder placed parallel to each other are known as multiaxial turbines.

4. According to the method of governing:

(1) Turbines with throttle governing;

(2) Turbines with nozzle governing;

(3) Turbines with bypass governing in which steam besides being fed to the firststage is also directly led to one, two or even three intermediate stages of theturbine.

(4) Turbines with sliding pressure governing in which steam pressure varies withthe speed or load of turbine;

5. According to the principle of steam turbine:

(1) Impulse turbines;

(2) Reaction turbines;

6. According to the heat drop process:

(1) Condensing turbines with regenerators: in these turbines steam at a pressureless than atmosphere is directed to a condenser; besides, steam is also extracted from intermediate stages for feed water heating. Small-capacity turbines of earlier designs often do not have regenerative feed heating.

(2) Condensing turbines with one or two intermediate stage extractions at specific pressures for industrial and heating purposes.

(3) Back pressure turbines, the exhausted steam from which is utilized for industrial or heating purposes.

(4) Topping turbines: these turbines are also of the back pressure type with thedifference that the exhausted steam from these turbines is further utilized in medium-and low-pressure condensing turbines. These turbines, in general, operate at high initial conditions of steam pressure and temperature, and are mostly used during extension of power station capacities, with a view to obtain better efficiencies.

(5) Back-pressure turbines with steam extraction from intermediate stages at specific pressures; turbines of this type are meant for supplying the consumer with steam of various pressure and temperature conditions.

(6) Low-pressure (exhaust-pressure) turbines in which the exhausted steam fromreciprocating steam engines, power hammers, presses, etc, is utilized for powergeneration purpose.

(7) Mixed-pressure turbines with two or three pressure stages, with supply of exhausted steam to its intermediate stages.

The turbines enumerated under " b " or " e " usually have extractions for regenerative feed-heat, in addition to the extraction of steam at specific pressures forother purposes.

7. According to the steam conditions at the inlet of turbines:

(1) Low-pressure turbines, using steam at pressures of 0. 12 to 0. 2 MPa.

(2) Medium-pressure turbines, using steam at pressures of up to 3. 9 MPa.

(3) High-pressure turbines, utilizing steam at pressures of 16. 8 MPa and higher and temperatures of 535 ℃ and higher.

(4) Turbines of supercritical pressures, using steam at pressures of 22.2 MPa and above and temperatures of 538 ℃ and above.

8. According to their usage in industry:

(1) Stationary turbines with constant speed of rotation primarily used for driving alternators.

(2) Stationary steam turbines with variable speed meant for driving turbo-blowers, air circulators, pumps, etc.

(3) Non-stationary turbines with variabe speed; turbines of this type are usually employed in steamers, ships and railway locomotives (turbo-locomotives).

All these different types of turbines described above depending on their speed of rotation are either coupled directly or through a reduction gearing to the driven machine.

Words and Expressions

initial condition of steam　蒸汽初参数
final condition of steam　蒸汽终参数
single-stage　单级
multistage　['mʌltisteidʒ]　*adj.* 多级
power capacity　容量,功率
axial-turbine　轴流式透平,轴流式汽轮机
radial-turbine　辐流式透平,辐流式汽轮机
parallel to　平行于
perpendicular to　垂直于
casing　['keisiŋ]　*n.* 汽缸,气缸,机匣,机壳
single-cylinder turbine　单缸汽轮机
multicylinder turbine　多缸汽轮机
singe shaft turbine　单轴汽轮机
multiaxial turbine　多轴汽轮机
throttle governing　节流调节

nozzle governing   喷嘴调节
bypass governing   旁路调节
sliding pressure governing   滑压调节
intermediate stage   中间级
heat drop process   热力过程
condensing turbine   凝汽式汽轮机
back pressure turbine   背压式汽轮机
topping turbine   前置式汽轮机
with a view of   为了……的目的
steam extraction   抽汽
power hammer   汽锤
enumerate   [i'nju:məreit]   vt. 数,计点,枚举,计算
railway locomotive   火车机车
reduction gearing   减速齿轮

6.6   Current Practice and Trends of Turbine

The earlier years of steamturbine history are replete with designs of unorthodoxmachines. Perhaps the most unusual departure from modern practice was the vertical turbine. It was arranged with its shaft disposed in a vertical direction, and many units of this type were built. Today the horizontal turbine is universally used. Another characteristic of earlier turbines was the frequent and generous use of the velocity-compounded stage, today called the two-row-wheel. This type of stage, consisting of a nozzle and two moving rows of buckets, with a turning vanebetween the moving rows, was inferior in efficiency but extremely flexible in its characteristics. Many turbines were built using several such stages in series. Modern turbines still use this type of stage for the widely varying requirementsof the first stage in a multistage turbine, though usualy only one such stage isused in a given machine.

Experience has shown that the multivalve, multistage horizontal turbine is by far the most acceptable from every standpoint, and we shall be concerned entirely with this type.

One of the most outstanding tendencies from early history to the present time has been to increase the speed of operation of turbines and generators. Whereas theearly units operated at 1 200 r/min in the large sizes, modern large turbinesare being constructed for the maximum permissible speed in a 60-cycle electrical system, that is, 3 600 r/min. The chief effect of the trend to higher speeds has been the reduction of weight of units, so that designers are able to cope with higherpressures and temperatures, because of the reduced diameters which accompany thehigher speeds. Since the peripheral velocities of the elements in the turbine generators are no less than they were in the older slow-speed machines, thestresses are not reduced.

Capacities of larges units are lower at the higher speeds than at the lower speeds, because they are economically limited by the size of the last-stage bucket which can be built. The economic capacity of a steam turbine is roughly proportional to the projected area of the active length of the last-stage bucket. At twice the speed, the diameters are approximately 1/2 as large, and the bucket heights are approximately 1/2 as great, so that the area is approximately 1/4 as great. For this reason, the permissible rating of 3 600 r/min units is roughly 1/4 the permissible rating in 1 800 r/min units. Of course, one may double the capacity of a given turbine by using a "double-flow" exhaust, but this same arrangementcould also be used in the slower-speed type. It will later be seenthat the economic size of turbine becomes larger as the initial steam conditions become higher, so that, since the 3 600 r/min turbine may properly be credited with permitting higher steam conditions, its maximum rating per last stage is considerably greater than 1/4 the maximum rating of an 1 800 r/min machine.

Both pressures and temperatures have steadily increased from the earliest days of steam turbines. Most of the increases in temperature have been permitted by thediscovery of better steel alloys and better knowledge of the materials used in turbines. Outstanding among these is molybdenum, which has permitted construction of turbines up to 950 °F, and higher, with no unusual problems. It may safely be said that progress beyond the 750 °F level was made possible solely by the use of molybdenum in turbine steel.

The data in Table 6.1 are interesting because they indicate how relatively recent is our progress into the higher pressure and temperature range.

Table 6.1 Progress in pressure and Temperature

Pressure	First year of use	Temperature	First year of use
540 psig	1924	750 °F	1926
1 200 psig	1926	825 °F	1933
2 300 psig	1941	900 °F	1936
		950 °F	1938
		1 050 °F	1948

The data in Tabel 6.2 indicate the extremely rapid trend to high temperatures and pressures which has occurred over two successive four-year periods, as indicated by the orders of one major manufacturer.

Table 6.2

Year(inclusive)	Initial conditions	Kilowatts as per cent of total
1940 ~ 1943	1 200 psi and higher	32
	800 ~ 900 psi	40
	900 ~ 1 000 psi	76

Table 6.2

Year (inclusive)	Initial conditions	Kilowatts as per cent of total
1944 ~ 1947	1 200 psi and higher	36
	800 ~ 900 psi	45
	900 ~ 1 000 °F	86

Increase in units for over 800 psi from 72% to 81%.

Increase in units for 900 °F and higher from 76% to 86%.

In the 1920's, a trend to an initial pressure of about 400 psig and initial temperature of 750 °F became evident. This was soon superseded by a new pressure and temperature level in the larger central stations, which may be generalized at about 600 psi-825 °F. The next plateau at which steam conditions leveled off was approximately 850 psi-900 °F, with some competition from the 1 200 psi-900 °F steam conditions. Almost universal adoption of these higher pressures and temperatures in new plants led to the formulation of preferred-standard steam conditions.

Words and Expressions

replete ［ri′pli:t］ *a.* 充满的
unorthodox ［′ʌn′ɔ:θədɔks］ *a.* 非正统的,异端的
horizontal ［ˌhɔri′zɔntl］ *a.* 水平的,卧式的
multistage ［′mʌltisteidʒ］ *a.* 多级的
peripheral ［pə′rifərəl］ *a.* 周界的,边缘的
alloy ［′ælɔi］ *n.* 合金
molybdenum ［mɔ′libdinəm］ *n.* 钼
plateau ［′plætəu］ *n.* 平稳段,平稳状态

6.7 The Modern Steam Power Plant

A power plant, of whatever variety, consists of three essential elements: the heat source, the heat utilizer, and the waste heat reservoir or refrigerator. To generatepower or produce useful work it is required that heat be supplied to a working fluid, from the heat source. The utilizer is required to convert a portion of theheat supplied to the working fluid into useful power. Since, by the second law ofthermodynamics, not all the heat can be converted to useful power, a refrigerator is required to dispose of the remainder of the heat.

Fig. 6.6 is a diagram of a modern steam plant, showing most of the essential elements. It may be divided into two main halves. One half consists of the boiler (or heat source) and its auxiliaries; the other, the turbine cycle, consists of turbine, generator, condenser, pumps and feedwater heaters. The turbine cycle, which includes not only the heat utilizer but also the refrigerator, will occupy the major part of our attention in this text.

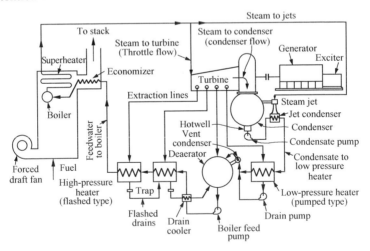

Fig. 6.6 Flow diagram of a typical steam power plant

Considering first the boiler half of the cycle, feedwater is supplied through an economizer to the boiler drum. The economizer reclaims part of the heat in thestack gases and transfers it to the feedwater, thus decreasing the heat to be supplied in the boiler while reducing the temperature of the stack gases. In the boiler drum, the water is boiled and converted to dry and saturated steam, which enters the superheater where the heat of superheat is added. The major part of the steam leaving the superheater is taken to the steam turbine. In many plants some of the steam is bled off for use in a steam-jet air-ejector, discussed below. Steam passing through the steam turbine produces mechanical power on the turbineshaft, which drives the alternator, where electrical energy is generated for distribution. In passing through the turbine in the modern regenerative cycle, someof the steam is bled from the turbine at a series of three or four openings (more or less), for use in feedwater heaters. Approximately 70 to 75% of the steam supplied to the turbine at the throttle continues all the way through the turbine to the exhaust hood, whence it passes to the condenser.

In the condenser, which is a large surface-type heat exchanger, the steam is condensed, by transferring its latent heat to circulating water taken from a nearby river or lake. The circulating water is supplied to the condenser by circulating water pumps, either motor or steamturbine driven. Since tremendous quantities of steam pass into the condenser, it is unavoidable that a certain proportion of non-condensable gases accompanies it. In order that a very low pressure, approximating a perfect vacuum, may be maintained in the condenser, these "noncondensables" must be removed from the shell of the condenser, these "noncondensables" must be removed from the shell of the condenser. Usually they are removed by means of a steam-jet air-ejector, consisting principally of a nozzle through which steam passes at high velocity and in which the non-condensable vapors are entrained. The steam passing through the nozzle (motive steam) and the non-condensable gases mechanically entrained in it are then taken to a heat-transfer device knownas an after-condenser, where the steam is condensed at atmospheric pressure andthe non-condensable vapors are vented to atmosphere. The steam-jet air-ejector, built in either one or two stages, is essentially a compressor for raising thepressure of the non-condensable vapors from an almost perfect vacuum to atmospheric pressure, to dispose of them.

The main steam, having been condensed in the condenser, is now in the form of liquid water at a very low pressure and approximately saturation temperature. This water drains by gravity to the bottom of the condenser, where it enters a hotwell. Usually the level of the water in the hotwell is maintained by a control appliedto the hotwell pump. The hotwell pump removes the water from the hotwell and pumps it through the lower part of the feedwater heating system to another pump, theboiler feed pump. The water discharged from the hotwell pump is taken first to a low-pressure heater in which heat is supplied by the lowest pressure extraction. The low-pressue heater shown in Fig. 6.6 is equipped with a drain pump, the duty of which is to remove the drains (formed by the condensing steam) from the heater and to pump them into the main condensate line, beyond the beater. This type ofheater is known as a pumped heater.

From the low-pressure heater the condensate passes to a deaerating heater. The deaerating heater, a direct contact type, serves as a means of boiling the condensate to eliminate any entrained oxygen. Removal of oxygen in the deaerating heateris based on the principle that solubility of non-condensable gases in water isgreatly reduced as the temperature of the water approaches the boiling point. Steam extracted from the turbine supplies the heat required to raise to the boilingpoint the temperature of the condensate entering the deaerator. The non-condensable gases discharged from the surface of the water must be removed. Normally thedeaerator is operated at a pressure higher than atmospheric, so that these gasesmay be vented through a vent condenser. Usual practice is to cool the vent condenser with incoming condensate, to cool the non-condensable gases, and simultaneously to condense the steam, some of which unavoidably escapes from the deaerator with the gases. By proper design of the vent condenser, the steam may be condensed and permitted to drain back into the deaerator, while the non-condensable gases are vented to atmosphere through an orifice.

Occasionally in the original design it may be planned that the deaerator operateat pressures below atmospheric. Even when the fullload design pressure is considerably higher than atmospheric, it is found that at the lighter loads the pressure becomes subatmospheric. It is then essential that the non-condensables continue to be removed from the deaerator, and a steam-jet ejector is necessary for accomplishing this result. The expense and complication in operation occasioned by such an installation make it undesirable. For this reason it is common practice to provide for the shifting of extraction stages at light loads so that the deaerator steam supply is furnished by the next-hight loads so that the deaerator steam supply is furnished by the next-higher extraction point. A simple arrangement is to install a crossover pipe containing a controlling valve, with a check valve in the lower-pressure extraction line before its junction with this crossover pipe. In such an installation opening of the valve in the crossover line automatically supplies higher-pressure steam to the deaerator, and the check valve closes, preventing backflow to the lower extraction stage.

In many power plants a surge tank containing reserve stored water is connected in parallel with the deaerator. The function of the surge tank is to serve as an emergency supply of distilled water, in the event of failure of other sources, or as a reservoir for excess water during load changes, etc. Normally the storage capacity of the deaerator is sufficient to operate the power plant for several minutes, but most designers consider it wise to augment this storage capacity with alarge surge tank.

In the majority of large power plants the boiler-feed pump is connected to the discharge of the deaerator. Since the water in the deaerator is at its boiling point, it is essential that the boiler-feed pump be located a considerable distance (usually 20 ft or more) below the deaerator, to avoid flashing of the water in the boiler-feed pump suction. Water leaving the deaerator goes to the boiler-feed pump suction and is pumped into the next higher heater. In Fig. 6.6 this heater is shown as a drain cooler heater, that is, a heater the drains from which pass through a heat exchanger (drain cooler) , giving up heat to the incoming condensate. After leaving this heater, the condensate goes to the top or high-pressure heater, in which the condensate is heated to the final feedwater temperature. In Fig. 6.6 the top heater is shown as a flashed heater, so called because its drains are permitted to pass through a controlling orifice or trap to the next-lower heater where part of the saturated water flashes into steam. This arrangements eliminates the use ofdrain pumps and drain coolers, but it causes a considerable thermodynamic loss. The final feedwater temperature leaving the top heater is in the order of 300 to450 °F in large modern power plants, and occasionally higher.

Illustrated in Fig. 6.6 are examples of the four types of heater, namely the flashedheater, the drain-cooler heater, the deaerating or contact heater, and the pumped heater.

To provide the uninitiated reader with a few data which give a perspective of the quantities involved in a modern power plant, the following typical data are cited. In modern large steam-turbine practice the pressure at the turbine inlet istypically from 800 to 1 200 psig. Occasionally pressures lower than these are used in the larger turbines (30 000 kW and higher), but today they are the exception rater than the rule. These pressures have been arrived at by power-plant designers, through long practice, as being the ones that give the greatest return on the investment under average conditions.

Temperatures at the inlet to large modern steam turbines range from 825 to 1 050 °F, these temperatures also having been established by usage as those that yield the greatest return on the investment, all things considered. Exhaust pressures for steam turbines in central stations are determined to a large extent by the cooling-water temperature available. These exhaust pressures range from 3/4 in. Hg in the northern parts of the United States to approximately 2.5 in. Hg in the southern parts, or higher-particularly where cooling towers are required because ofinadequate water supply. A reasonable national average seems to be about 1.5 in. Hg.

Condensate-pump discharge pressures normally range from 50 to 150 psig. Boiler-feed pump discharge pressures are normally from 10 to 25% higher than the drum pressure in the boiler. Pressure drops in the extraction lines between turbines and heaters are usually about 5% of the pressure existing at the turbines. Pressuredrops between the superheater discharge and the turbine inlet are normally from 5 to 10% of the pressure at the superheater discharge. Deaerating heater pressures range from subatmospheric values to approximately 55 or 60 psig, 30 ~ 40 psig representing a reasonable average full-load value.

The number of feedwater heaters used in modern power plants varies from as few as one in the smaller plants having cheap fuel to as many as 8 or 10 in the larger plants having expensive fuel or where the designer is seeking the lowest possible fuel consumption. Although the higher number of heaters gives better thermal performance, in many plants the fixed charges on the more expensive heater installation make a large number of heaters prohibitive. The choice is always an interesting economic problem and quite easily solved.

In a steam turbine arranged for regenerative feedwater heating, the throttle steam rate of the turbine is normally about 15% higher than in a plant arranged for "straight-condensing" operation (without extraction for feedwater heating). Inthe regenerative cycle the condenser flow is normally about 70% to 75% of the throttle flow, 25% to 30% of the throttle flow having been extracted for supply of the feedwater heaters.

Stack gas temperatures from modern boilers range from approximately 300 to 600 °F, the tendency being in the direction of the lower figure, which is necessary toobtain high boiler efficiency. Stack gas temperature may be reduced by means of either air-preheaters of feedwater economizers. A large number of feedwater-heating stages with a high discharge temperature from the high-pressure heater precludes the use of an extensive economizer. In such installations it is necessary toresort to an air-preheater to recover some of the heat in the stack gases. While air-preheat temperature is limited to the lower values in a stoker installation, modern pulverized fuel installations have been designed which use very high air-preheat temperatures, of the order of 500 ~ 600 °F, with higher values distinctly feasible.

Words and Expressions

utilizer ['juːtilaizə] n. 利用装置
reservoir ['rezəvwaː] n. 蓄水池
refrigerator [ri'fridʒəreitə] n. 冷藏器, 冷藏间

thermo-dynamics　　n. 热力学
auxiliary　　[ɔːɡˈziljəri]　　n. (复)辅助设备
feed-water　　n. 给水
economizer　　[iˈkɔnəmaizə]　　n. 省煤器
stack-gas　　n. 排放的烟气
saturate　　[ˈsætʃəreit]　　v. 使饱和
superheater　　n. 过热器
alternator　　[ˈɔːltəneitə]　　n. 交流发电机
throttle　　[ˈθrɔtl]　　n. 节流阀　v. 节流
hood　　[hud]　　n. 帽
whence　　[hwens]　　ad. 从何处
vacuum　　[ˈvækjuəm]　　n. 真空(度)
entrain　　[inˈtrein]　　v. 带走,夹带,卷吸
hotwell　　n. 温泉
deaerate　　[diːˈeiəreit]　　v. 使除去气体
vent　　[vent]　　v. 排放出　n. 出口
orifice　　[ˈɔrifis]　　n. 孔,口,喷管
cross-over　　n. 交叉
surge-tank　　n. 备用箱
augment　　[ɔːɡˈment]　　v. 增加
air-preheater　　n. 空气预热器
preclude　　[priˈkluːd]　　v. 预防,排除
pulverize　　[ˈpʌlvəraiz]　　v. 研磨,使成粉末
bleed off　　放出

6.8　Wind Turbines

Wind is air in motion. Windmills or wind turbines convert the kinetic energy of wind into useful work.

It is believed that the annual wind energy available on earth is about 13×10^{12} kW h. This is equivalent to a total installed capacity of about 15×10^5 MW or 1 500 power stations each of 1 000 MW capacity. While the power that could be tapped out from the vast sea of wind may be comparable with hydropower, it should be remembered that it is available in a highly diluted form. Therefore, while dams are built to exploit and regulate hydropower, there is no such parallelon the wind power scene.

Wind had been used as a source of power in sailing ships for many centuries. Theforce that acted on ship's sail was later employed to turn a wheel like the water wheel which already existed. The winddriven wheel first appeared in Persia in the seventh century A. D. By tenth century A. D. , windmills were used for pumping water for irrigation and by thirteenth century A. D. for corn grinding.

The corn grinding mill was a two-storey structure; the mill stone was located inthe upper storey and the lower storey consisted of a sail rotor. It consisted ofsix or twelve fabric sails which rotated the mill by the action of the wind. Shutters on the sails regulated the rotor speed. In 1592 A. D. the windmill was used to drivemechanical saws in Holland. A large Dutch windmill of the eighteenth century with a 30. 5 m sail span developed about 7. 5 kW at a wind velocity of 32 kmph.

The energy of flowing water and wind was the only natural source of mechanical power before the advent of steam and internal combustion engines. Therefore windmills and watermills were the first prime movers which were used to do small jobs such as corn grinding and water pumping. It is generally believed that the windmill made its appearance much later than the watermill.

The watermills had to be located on the banks of streams. Therefore, they sufferedfrom the disadvantage of limited location. In this respect windmills had greaterfreedom of location. If sufficient wind velocities were available over reasonable periods, more important factors in choosing a site for the windmill would be the transportation of corn for grinding and the site for water pumping.

In both wind and water turbine plants the working fluid and its energy are freely available. Though there are no fuel costs involved, other expenditures in harnessing these forms of energy are not negligible. The capital cost of some wind power plants can be prohibitive. As in other power plants, the cost per unit of energygenerated decreases as the size of the wind turbine increases.

Medium-sized ($100 \sim 200$ kW, $d \simeq 20$ m) wind turbines are suitable for electricpower requirements of isolated areas in hills and small islands where other sourcesof power may be non-existent of difficult to install and operate. The use of some of an energy storage system can take care of the random nature of the wind energy.

Large wind power plants of capacities of a couple of megawatts can be connected to the main network fed by thermal and hydrostations. In such a system wind energy can be utilized for saving fuel and water.

Compared to other well-established sources of energy, the wind energy at presentappears to be insignificant as far as the contribution to the total energy requirement is concerned. However, at a time when mankind is facing an energy crisis every source, however small, should be tapped.

Elements of a wind power plant

A windmill or turbine is an extended turbomachine operating at comparatively lower speeds. A wind turbine power plant consists of principally the propeller or rotor, step-up gear, and electric generator and the tail vane, all mounted on a tower or mast. The actual design will depend upon the size of the plant and its application.

Various elements of a wind turbine power plant are described here briefly.

Rotor

The shape, size and number of blades in a wind turbine rotor depend on whether itis a horizontal or vertical axis machine. The number of blades generally varies from two to twelve. A high speed rotor requires fewer blades to extract the energy from the wind steam, whereas a slow machine requires a relatively larger numberof blades.

In horizontal axis machines two-bladed rotors are known to have greater vibration problems compared to three blades.

In wind turbine rotors blades are subjected to high and alternating stresses. Therefore, the blades must have sufficient strength and be light. Thus the strength-to-density ratio of the material used is an important factor.

Wood is widely used for small high-speed machines. It has the required strength-density ratio.

Various metals and their alloys also used. Small blades are cast. Plastic materials are now also making inroads into the manufacture of wind machines. They have high strength-density ratio, offer great ease in manufacture and are also weather resistant.

Step-up gear

On account of the great difference in rotational speeds of the wind turbine rotor(which is generally low) and the machine that is drives, a step-up gear for obtaining the required high speed is generally employed between the driving and driven shafts. This invariably takes the form of a gearing arrangement consisting ofone or more gear trains. The entire gearing arrangement must have high efficiency and reliability coupled with light weight.

Belts and chains have not been employed as widely as the gearing.

Speed-regulating mechanism

From aerodynamic considerations, it is desirable to operate a wind turbine at a constant blade-to-wind speed ratio. However, in many applications a mechanism to maintain the speed of the wind turbine constant at varying wind velocities and loads is required.

A propeller type of pump and a hydraulic brake (water paddle for producing hot water) are excellent speed governors themselves. Speed regulation can be obtained for both fixed and variable pitch blades.

The mechanism for variable pitch blades is the same as that used in Kaplan hydroturbines or aircraft propellers. The variable pitch mechanism enables the rotor to operate most efficiently at varying wind velocities and in feathering during gusts.

The centrifugal force acting on the blades at speeds higher than the design is also employed to change the blade pitch. This can also be achieved by a fly-ball governor.

Electric generator

Besides driving pumps and corn grinding mills, wind turbines are now being increasingly used for driving electric generators or "aerogenerators" as they are sometimes called. These aerogenerators are both direct and alternating current machines and are available from a capacity of a few watts to hundreds of kilowatts.

The direct current machines operate in a considerable speed range, whereas the alternating current generator with constant frequency requires constant speed.

For small isolated communities, some kind of energy storage is always required. This is best met by do generators feeding a battery of accumulators during low load and high wind periods.

To minimize weight, aerogenerators must operate at high speeds which depend on the type of the wind turbine (Blade-to-wind speed ratio) and the weight of the step-up gear.

When the speed of the wind turbine is low, multi-pole synchronous alternators are used. But the large number of poles increases the weight of the aerogenerators. However, such a machine is acceptable if it eliminates the speed-up gear by using higher blade-to-wind speed ratios.

When an alternator is directly coupled to an ac network, its speed is nearly constant. Such a generator can be designed for sufficient overload capacity to absorbthe wind energy available at high wind velocities.

Orientation mechanism

A horizontal axis wind turbine requires a mechanism which turns the rotor into the wind stream. The working of the vertical axis machines does not depend on the wind direction and, therefore, an orientation mechanism is not required.

In primitive windmills the rotor was turned manually into the wind direction by apole hanging from the tail. Modern wind turbines have sophisticated automatic mechanisms to obtain the orientation as and when required.

The simplest and most widely used method to orient small windmills in the wind direction is by employing a wind vane.

Another method is to employ an automatic direction finding and orienting mechanism. This is relatively faster.

A fan-tail whose axis of rotation is normal to the axis of the main rotor is also employed to turn the windmill into the wind stream. The cross wind drives the auxiliary rotor which in turn rotates the windmill into the wind through reduction gears. This is a slow mechanism.

Tower

All windmills have to be mounted on a stand or a tower above the ground level. Tower heights of over 250 m have been employed for obtaining high wind velocities and mounting large wind turbine rotors. Increasing the tower height besides increasing the capital cost also increases the maintenance cost. Therefore the gain in the power output due to high wind velocity at a given altitude must be accurately estimated to justify the high costs. Economic and vibration problems are major factors in the design of towers for large wind turbines.

An angle iron tower of a four-sided pyramidal shape is commonly used. A similar structure constructed from metal pipings is also used. Towers have also been constructed from wood, brick and concrete.

Words and Expressions

kinetic ['kai'netik] *a.* 动力的
hydropower ['haidrə,pauə] *n.* 水力发出的电力
dilute [dai'lju:t] *v.* 稀释,冲淡
megawatt ['megəwɔt] *n.* 兆瓦(特)
inroad ['inroud] *v.* 袭击 *n.* 损害
aero-generator *n.* 空气发电机
auxiliary [ɔ:g'ziljəri] *a.* 辅助的
pyramidal [,pirə'mikəl] *a.* 金字塔形的,角锥状的
piping ['paipiŋ] *n.* 笛声,尖叫声
synchronous ['siŋkrənəs] *a.* 同步的

6.9 The Principle of Steam Turbine

A heat engine is one that converts heat energy into mechanical energy. So the steam turbine is classed as a heat engine, as are the steam and internal-combustion engines. The turbine makes use of the fact that steam when issuing from a small opening attains a high velocity. The velocity attained during expansion depends upon the initial and final heat content of the steam. This difference in heatcontent represents the heat energy converted into kinetic energy (energy due tovelocity) during the process. The kinetic energy or work available in the steamleaving a nozzle is equal to the work that the steam could have done had it been allowed to expand (with the same heat loss) behind a piston in a cylinder.

The fact that any moving substance possesses energy, or the ability to do work, is shown by many everyday examples. A stream of water discharged from a fire hose may break a window glass if directed against it. When the speed of an automobile is reduced by the use of brakes, an appreciable amount of heat is generated. In like manner the steam turbine permits the steam to expand and attain high velocity. It then converts this velocity energy into mechanical energy. There are two general principles by which this can be accomplished. In the case of the fire hose, as the stream of water issued from the nozzle, its velocity was increased, and owing to this impulse it struck the window glass with considerable force. A turbine that makes use of the impulsive force of high-velocity steam is knownas an "impulse turbine". While the water issuing from the nozzle of the fire hose is increased in velocity, a reactionary force is exerted on the nozzle. This reactionary force is opposite in direction to the flow of the water. A turbine that makes use of the reaction force produced by the flow steam through a nozzleis a "reaction turbine". Practically in all commercial turbines a combinationof impulse and reactive forces is utilized. Both impulse and reaction blading on the same shaft utilize the steam more efficiently than does one alone.

Impulse-turbine nozzles organize the steam so that it flows in well-formed high-speed jets. Moving buckets (blades) absorb the jet's

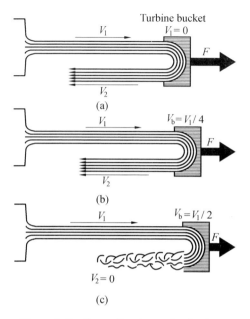

Figure 6.7 Steam flow in moving buckets

kinetic energy and convert it to mechanical work in a rotating shaft (Fig. 6.7). When the bucket is locked, the jet enters and leaves with equal speed and develops maximum force F but no mechanical work is done. As the bucket is allowed to speed up, the jet moves more slowly and force F shrinks. Fig. 6.8 shows how both force and work done vary with the blade speed. The steam jet does maximum work when the bucket speed is just one-half of the steam speed. In this condition, the moving bucket leaves behind it a trail of inert steam, since all kinetic energy is converted to work. The starting force or torque of this ideal turbine is double the torque at its most efficient speed.

For practical reasons, most impulse turbines mount their buckets on the rims of disks (wheels), and nozzles feed steam from one side (Fig. 6.9). Pressurizedsteam from the nozzle box flows through parallel

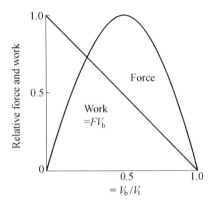

Figure 6.8   Curves of the reactive force and work with bucket speed

converging nozzles formed by vanes or foils. Steam leaves as a broad high-speed jet to flow through the slowermoving-bucket passages, which turn the steam flow to an axial direction as theyabsorb its kinetic energy. The steam leaves with lower internal energy and speed.

Steam pressure and speed vary through the true impulse stage. When the impulse stages are pressure-compounded, which are called Rateau stages, pressure drop occurs in steps and exhausted steam from one-stage flows through following similarimpulse stages, where it expands to a lower pressure. If the impulse stages arevelocity-compounded, which are called Curtiss stages, steam velocity is absorbed in a series of constant-pressure steps.

In the reaction stage (Fig. 6.10) , steam enters the fixed-blade passages; it leaves as a steam jet that fills the entire rotor periphery. Steam flows between moving blades that form moving nozzles. There it drops in pressure, and its speedrises relative to the blades, which creates the reactive force that does work. Despite the rising relative speed, the overall effect reduces the absolute steamspeed through one stage. When the enthalpy drop is about equal in moving and stationary blades, it is called a 50 percent reaction stage.

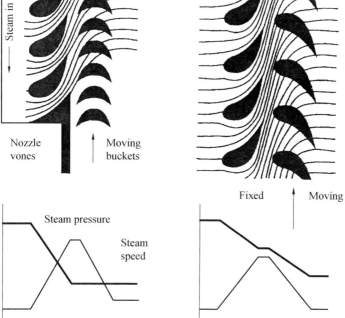

Fig. 6. 9   Steam flow in an impulse stage

Fig. 6. 10   Steam flow in a reaction stage

Fig. 6. 11 shows a velocity-compounded control stage followed by two reactionstages. The high-speed steam jet gives up only part of its kinetic energy in thefirst row of moving buckets. Then come reversing blades that redirect the slowed-up steam into the second row of moving buckets, where most of its remaining kinetic energy is absorbed. Steam then enters the series of reaction stages.

In practice, so-called impulse-stage turbines use about 5% to 10% reaction in their design. This means there is a small steam pressure drop through the moving-blade passages. These buckets,

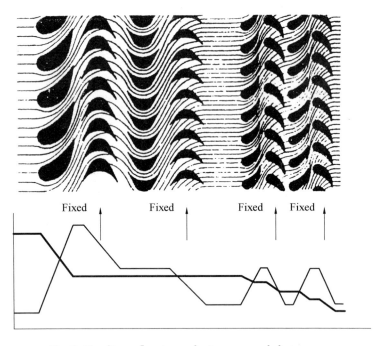

Fig. 6.11 Steam flow in a velocity-compounded stage

instead of taking the symmetrical shape, have a longer tail to form a slightly converging passage at the exit.

Words and Expressions

heat engine 热机
steam engine 蒸汽机
internal-combustion engine 内燃机
issue from 从……喷出,从……流出
heat content 热值
kinetic energy 动能
heat loss 热损
piston ['pistən] n. 活塞
cylinder ['silində] n. 气缸,汽缸

nozzle ['nɔzl] n. 喷嘴,喷管,燃烧器
discharge from 从……排出,从……流出
fire hose 消防水龙头
brake [breik] n. 制动器,刹车
impulsive force 冲击力
impulse turbine 冲击式透平,冲击式汽轮机
reactionary force 反击力
reaction turbine 反击式透平,反击式汽轮机
commercial turbine 商业透平,商业汽轮机
balding ['bɔːldiŋ] adj. 叶片,叶栅
jet [dʒet] . 汽流,射流,喷气式发动机,喷气式飞机
moving bucket/blade 动叶
rotating shaft 转轴
shrink [ʃriŋk] vt. 收缩,减小,热套
rim of disk/wheel 轮缘
converging nozzle 渐缩喷嘴
vane [vein] n. 叶片,轮叶,刀片,节气阀
foil [fɔil] n. 叶形饰,翼,薄片
leave behind 遗留,把……丢在后面,超过
nozzle box 喷嘴室
Rateau stages 托拉级,压力级
pressure drop 压降
Curtiss stage 柯蒂斯级,复速级
velocity-compounded stage 复速级
enthalpy drop 焓降
control stage 调节级
give up 释放,放弃,中断
reversing blade 转向导叶片
symmetrical [si'metrikəl] adj. 对称的

7

Environmental Protection, Corrosion and Others

7.1 Ash Removal and Disposal

The problems of ash removal and disposal are significant principally in the case of solid fuels. The amount of ash in fuel oil is small and usually is a problemprimarily inside the furnace and boiler setting. However, mechanical dust collectors are occasionally used.

With the early methods of burning coal on grates using natural draft, most of the coal ash remained on the grate and was ultimately discharged into a hopper fordisposal. With more modern stokers, such as the spreader stoker, part of the burning is accomplished in suspension and this results in a greater carry-over of particulate matter in the flue gas.

With pulverized-coal firing, all the burning is accomplished in suspension with the result that about 80% of the ash remains in the flue gases in the case of a dry-ash pulverized coal-fired unit. This may be reduced to about 50% with a slag-tap unit with pulverized-coal firing.

With Cyclone-Furnace firing, the fly-ash loading in the flue gases is reduced to 20% to 30% of the ash in the coal. The problem of particulate carry-over in the flue gases is thus reduced by a factor of 3 or 4 for Cyclone Furnace firing as compared with a dry-ash pulverized coal-fired unit. This is important from the standpoint of the cost of equipment required to achieve a given particulate content in the stack gases.

Ash removal from the furnace

Stoker-fired units and dry-ash pulverized-coal-fired units are designed so that the ash settles in hoppers from which it is removed for disposal. Some possible uses for this slag are as land fill, road-base material, granular material forroofing, aggregate for use in concrete blocks and preformed concrete, asphaltmixmaterial, cinders for icy reads, insulation, and grit for sandblasting. Most of these uses apply also to ash removed in dry form from stoker-and pulverized-coal-fired furnaces.

Particulate removal

To meet the objective of a clear stack, some form of particulate-removal equipment is now generally required to remove the fly ash from flue gases from units where fuels are burned in suspension. Several types of particulate-removal equipment are available. These may be classified as electrostatic precipitators, mechanical dust collectors, fabric filters and wet scrubbers. Fly ash removed by equipmentof these types may be used for most of the applications listed for ash removed as slag.

Electrostatic precipitators

Electrostatic precipitators produce an electric charge on the particles to be collected and then propel the charged particles by electrostatic forces to the collecting electrodes. The precipitator operation involves 4 basic steps:

1. An intense, discharging field is maintained between the discharge electrode and the collecting electrodes.

2. The carrier gases are ionized by the intense, discharging field. These gas ions, in turn, charge the entrained particles.

3. The negatively charged particles, still in the presence of an electrostatic field, are attracted to the positively (grounded) charged collecting electrodes.

4. The collected dust is discharged by rapping into storage hoppers.

The collection efficiency of the electrostatic precipitator is related to the time of particle exposure to the electrostatic field, the strength of the field, and the resistivity of the dust particle. An efficiency of 99% is obtained at a costgenerally favorable in comparison with other types of equipment. Hence, as of 1970, a very high percentage of particulate-removal units installed in commercial boiler plants are electrostatic precipitators.

Mechanical collectors

The operation of mechanical collectors depends on exerting centrifugal force on the particles to be collected by introducing the dust-laden gas stream tangentially into the body of the collector. The particulate matter is thrown to the outside wall of the collector where it is removed. Mechanical collectors operate most effectively in the particle-size range above about 10 microns. Below 10 microns, the collection efficiency drops considerably below 90%. As efficiency requirements continue to increase, the use of mechanical collectors is expected to decline.

Fabric filters

Fabric filters operate by trapping dust by impingement on the fine filters comprising the fabric. As the collection of dust continues, an accumulation of dust particles adheres to the fabric surface. The fabric filter obtains its maximum efficiency during this period of dust buildup. After a fixed operating period, the bags must be cleaned. Immediately after cleaning, the filtering efficiency is reduced until the buildup of collected dust takes place.

The fabric filter can be applied in any process area where dry collection is desired and where the temperature and humidity of the gases to be handled do not impose limitations. At efficiencies of 99% and less, the fabric filter is generally not competitive with the electrostatic precipitator for boiler application. However, for particulate matter, efficiencies above 99% can be achieved with fabric filters, and applications in congested areas may increase.

Wet scrubbers

Wet scrubbers remove dust from a gas stream by collecting it with a suitable liquid. (see Fig. 7.1)

A good wet scrubber is one that can effect the most intimate contact between thegas stream and liquid for the purpose of transferring the suspended particulatematter from the gas to the liquid. Collection efficiency, dust-particle size, and pressure drop are closely related in the operation of a wet scrubber. The required operating

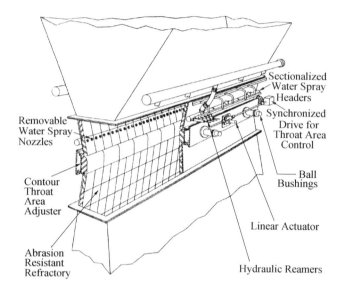

Fig. 7.1 Veturi-type wet scrubber

pressure drop varies inversely as the dust-particle size for a given collection efficiency; or a given dust-particle size, for a given collection efficiency; or for a given dust-particle size, collection efficiency increases as operating pressure drop increases.

Unlike other particulate collection equipment, the wet scrubber employs a liquid stream to collect particulate matter. For this reason, it can usually perform additional process functions besides dust collection. Gas absorption, chemical reaction, and heat transfer are some of these. Simultaneous removal of dust and gaseous pollutants by use of a suitable scrubbing liquid can be accomplished with a wet scrubber.

Words and Expressions

ash [æʃ] n. 灰

suspension [səs'penʃən] n. 悬浮,暂停
disposal [dis'pəuzəl] n. 丢掉,处理,布置
scrubber ['skrʌbə] n. 刷子,刷洗工具,擦洗者
precipitator [pri'sipiteitə] n. 除尘器,聚尘器
ionize ['aiənaiz] v. 使离子化 vi. 电离
rap [ræp] v. 叩击,敲击
tangential [tæn'dʒenʃəl] a. 正切的,切线方向的
decline [di'klain] v. 拒绝,倾斜,跌落
trap [træp] v. 用陷阱捕捉,诱捕
humidity [hju:'miditi] n. 湿气,潮湿,湿度

7.2 Oil-ash Corrosion

High-temperature corrosion

The sodium-vanadium complexes, usually found in oil-ash deposits, are corrosive when molten. The corrosion mechanism is probably one of accelerated oxidation of metal brought about by oxygen transfer to its surface by the constituents in the molten ash, accompanied by the removal by the ash of the normal protective oxide coating on the metal surface.

Corrosion can also be caused by sulfate attack, particularly when sodium(or someother) chloride is also present in the fuel oil, and this may occur at metal temperatures as low as 1 000 °F. This type of corrosion is more apt to be encountered on boilers burning a low-vanadium fuel oil but containing several hundred ppm of sodium chloride. Even when the chloride content of the fuel oil is negligible, sulfate corrosion may still be severe when reducing or alternating oxidizing-reducing conditions prevail around the tubes.

A measurable corrosion rate can be observed over a wide range of metal and gas temperatures, depending on the amount and composition of the oil-ash deposit.

The effect of the sodium level in the fuel oil is not quite so clearcut because combustion conditions and the chloride content of the fuel oil may be controlling. The sodium content does, however, definitely affect the minimum metal temperature at which corrosion will be significant.

At the present time there does not appear to be any alloy that is immune to oil-ash corrosion. In general, the higher the chromium content of the alloy the moreresistant it is to attack. This is the main reason for the use of 18 Cr-8Ni alloys for high-temperature superheater tubes. High chromium contents, greater than 30%, give added corrosion resistance but at the expense of physical properties; 25Cr-20Ni has been used as a tube cladding but even this alloy has not provided complete protection. The presence of nickel in high-temperature alloys is needed for strength. High-nickel alloys may be fairly resistant to oil-ash attackunder oxidizing conditions but they are liable to sulfide attack brought about by local reducing conditions or by the presence of chloride in the ash deposit. Since it is difficult to avoid such conditions entirely, high-nickel content of alloys may be of limited value. In any event, the higher material cost must be justified by longer life, which is not always predictable.

Low-temperature corrosion

In oil-fired boilers the problem of low-temperature corrosion resulting from the formation and condensation of sulfuric acid from the flue gases is similar tothat previously described for coal firing.

Oil-fired boilers are more susceptible to low-temperature corrosion than are most coal-fired units for two reasons:

1. the vanadium in the oil-ash deposits is a good catalyst for the conversion of SO_2 to SO_3 and

2. there is a smaller quantity of ash in the flue gases. Ash particles in the flue gas reduce the amount of SO_3 vapor in the gas. Since oil has considerably less ash than coal, significant differences would be expected. Furthermore, coal ash is more basic than oil ash and tends to neutralize any acid deposited; oil ash generally lacks this capability.

Under certain conditions, oil-fired boilers may emit acidic particulates from their stacks that stain or etchpainted surfaces in the neighborhood of the plant. The acidic deposits or smuts are generally caused by metallic surfaces (air heaters, flues and stacks) operating well below the acid dew point of the flue gases orby soot which has absorbed sulfuric acid vapor in its passage through the boiler. Methods that can be used to prevent acid-smut emission include:

1. Minimize SO_3 formation in the flue gases,

2. Neutralize SO_3 in flue gases,

3. Maintain all surfaces in contact with the flue gases above about 250 °F.

4. Completely burn fuel oil to eliminate soot particles.

Methods of control

The methods of control that have been used or proposed to control fouling and corrosion in oil-fired boilers are summarized, but in every instance economics governs their applicability. There is no doubt that reducing the amountof ash and sulfur entering the furnace is the surest means of control, and that minimizing the effects of the ash constituents, once they havedeposited on the tubes, is the least reliable. Since the severity of fouling and corrosion depends not only on the fuel-oil characteristics but also on boiler design and operating variables, a generalized solution to these problems cannot be prescribed.

Fuel oil supply

Although fuel selection and blending are practiced to some extent in this country, it is done to provide safe and reliable handling and storage at the user's plant rather than to avoid fouling difficulties. Since the threshold limits of sodium, sulfur and vanadium are not accurately defined for either fouling or corrosion, utilization of these means of control cannot be fully exploited.

Processes are available for both the desulfurization and de-ashing of fuel oils. Water washing of residual fuel oil has been successfully applied to a few marine-type boilers, but it is doubtful that it will be widelyused because only sodium and sediment, mainly rust and sand, are removed by the process. Use of low-sulfur, low-ash crudes and desulfurized fuel oil is expected to increase.

Fuel oil additives

The practice of water washing out of service and, to a limited extent, in service has been beneficial in overcoming some of the troubles experienced with present oil fuels. In addition, continued study of the problem has revealed another approach that is effective where the fuel-oil ash is most troublesome. In brief, the method involves adding to the fuel or furnace small amounts of materials that change the character of the ash sufficiently to permit its removal by steam or air sootblowers or air lances.

Additives are effective in reducing the troubles associated with superheater fouling, high-temperature ash corrosion, and low-temperature sulfuric acid corrosion. Most effective are alumina, dolomite and magnesia. Kaolin is also a source of alumina.

The reduction of fouling and high-temperature corrosion is accomplished basically by producing a highmelting-point ash deposit that is powder or friable and easily removed by sootblowers or lances. When the ash is dry, corrosion is considerably reduced.

Low-temperature sulfuric-acid corrosion is reduced by the formation of refractory sulfates by reaction with the SO_3 gas in the flue-gas stream. By thus removing the SO_3 gas, the dew point of the flue gases is sufficiently reduced to protect the metal surfaces. The sulfate compounds formed are relatively dry and easily removed by the normal cleaning equipment.

In general, the amount of additive used should be about equal to the ash content of the fuel oil. In some instances, slightly different proportions may be requiredfor best results, especially for high-temperature corrosion reduction, in whichit is generally accepted that the additive should be used in weight ratios of 2or 3 to 1, based on the vanadium content of the oil.

Several methods have been successfully used to introduce the additive materials into the furnace. The one in general use consists of metering a controlled amount of an additive oil slurry into the burner supply line. The additive material should be pulverized to 100% through a 325 mesh screen (44 microns) for good dispersion and minimum atomizer wear.

For a boiler fired by a high-pressure return-flow oil system, it has been found advantageous to introduce the additive powders by blowing them into the furnace at the desired locations. The powder has to be 100% through a 325-mesh screenfor good dispersion.

A third, and more recent method, is to introduce the additive as a water slurry through specially adapted sootblowers or lances. This method offers the advantage of applying the additive in exactly the location desired, with a possible reduction in the quantity required. Some caution should be observed with this system to prevent possible thermal shock (quench-cracking) damage to the hot tubes. The presence of chlorides in the water slurry, from either the water or the additive material, could possibly produce stress-corrosion cracking of austenitic tubing andshould be considered.

The choice of the particular additive material depends on its availability and cost to the individual plant and the method of application chosen. For example, alumina causes greater sprayer-plate wear than other materials when used in an oilslury.

The quantity of deposit formed is, of course, an important consideration for each individual unit from the aspect of cleaning. A comparison of the amounts of deposit formed with different additives shows that dolomite produces the greatest quantity because of its sulfating ability, alumina and kaolin form the least, and magnesia is intermediate. However, when adequate cleaning facilities are available, the deposits are easily removed, and the quantities formed should not be a problem.

Excess-air control

As mentioned previously the problems encountered in the combustion of residual fuels-high-temperature deposits(fouling) , high-temperature corrosion, and low-temperature sulfuric-acid corrosion-all arise from the presence of vanadium and sulfur in their highest states of oxidation. By reducing the excess air from 7% to 1% or 2% , it is possible to avoid the formation of fully oxidized vanadium and sulfur compounds and, thereby, reduce boiler fouling and corrosion problems.

In a series of tests on an experimental boiler, it was found that the maximum corrosion rate of type 304 stainless steel superheater alloy held at 1 250 °F in 2100 °F flue gas was reduced more than 75% when the excess air was reduced form anaverage of 7% to a level of 1% to 2%. Moreover, the ash deposits that formed onthe superheater bank were soft and powdery, in contrast to hard, dense deposits thatadhered tenaciously to the tubes when the excess air was around 7%. Also, the rate of ash buildup was only half as great. Operation at the 1% to 2% excess air level practically eliminated low-temperatures corrosion of carbon steel at all metal temperatures above the water dew point of the flue gases. However, much of the beneficial effects of low excess-air combustion are lost if the excess air at the burner fluctuates even for short periods of time to a level of about 5%. Carbon loss values for low excess air were approximately 0.5%, which is generally acceptable for electric utility and industrial practice.

A number of large industrial boilers both in this country and in Europe have been operating with low excess air for several years. As a result, the benefits in reducing low-temperature corrosion are well established for units with steamtemperatures of 1 000 °F or less. However the benefits on high-temperature slagging and corrosion arenot wholly conclusive. In any event, great care must be exercised to distribute the air and fuel oil equally to the burners, and combustion conditions must be continuously monitored to assure that combustion of the fuel is complete before the combustion gases enter the convection tube banks.

Words and Expressions

corrosion [kə'rəuʒən] *n.* 腐蚀,腐蚀作用
sodium-vanadium 钠-钒
molten ['məultən] *a.* 熔化的,熔铸的

chloride ['klɔːraid] n. 氯化物,漂白粉
acidic [ə'sidik] a. 酸性的
neutralize ['njuːtrəlaiz] v. 使中立,中和,取消
govern ['gʌvən] v. 治理,统治,支配
desulfurization [diːˌsʌlfərai'zeiʃən] n. 脱硫,去硫
slurry ['sləːri] n. 泥浆,水泥浆
kaolin ['keiəlin] n. 瓷土,高岭土
dense [dens] a. 密的,稠密的,浓厚的
fluctuate ['flʌktjueit] vi. 波动 vt. 使波动,变动

7.3 Control of Pollutant Gases

Air pollution control

The control of atmospheric pollution is one part of a prime present-day problem-environmental control. The by-products from boiler furnaces are by no means the major factor in producing air pollution. In the larger cities, other factors, particularly the automobile and industrial or manufacturing processes, produce the larger share of air pollution. Generally power plant stacks contribute only about 15% of the total weight of atmospheric contaminants emitted from all sources.

While air pollution has been increasingly present since the beginning of the industrial revolution, it is particularly in the last 25 years that the total release of pollutants from all sources has signaled a national air pollution problemof increasing proportions, indicating the necessity for remedial measures. Even though the combustion products from boiler furnaces constitute a small part of total air pollutants, the growth of industry indicates an increasing need for remedial measures. Some of these measures are currently available and in general use.

Others are in the development stage and are expected to become available within the next few years. These developments are being spurred by an aroused public interest and an increasing amount of legislation.

It is important to note that there are substantial costs associated with equipment to remove particulates and gaseous pollutants from stack gases, and these costs must ultimately be borne by the consumer. In the case of the electric power industry, the costs of equipment to reduce air pollution necessarily increase power generation costs, and hence the kilowatt-hour cost to the consumer. The costs of this equipment can vary from $6 to $35 per kW of installed capacity, depending on the type and scope of equipment, and must be recognized as part of the price for maintaining a good atmospheric environment. Gaseous pollutants are more difficult to remove than particulate matter. Even though all forms of gaseous pollutants have not been identified, oxides of sulfur and nitrogen are recognized as being harmful.

Sulfur oxides

Sulfur oxides are produced in significant quantity by the combustion of most coals and fuel oils. The amount of sulfur oxides produced in gas-fired units is insignificant. However the demand for natural gas for domestic fuel makes it less available for steam generation

Sulfur oxides can be controlled by removing sulfur from the fuel prior to its use, or by removing the sulfur oxides from the combustion gases before they are released to the stack. Several systems to reduce the emission of gaseous sulfur compounds are under development or in pilot-plant operation. Meanwhile several governmental agencies have promulgated regulations limiting the fuels burned in congested areas to those containing a certain maximum sulfur content, typically 1% or less.

Some plants which have been burning fuel oil are meeting these requirements by using low-sulfur oil at a premium price. In some cases the sulfur-content limit is met by blending low-sulfur oils with less expensive higher-sulfur oils. Alsoa number of coal-burning plants are being converted to oil, or to oil and gas firing.

In the case of coal, transportation costs are such an important factor that the coals which can be burned in a particular locality are generally limited to thosethat are mined within a distance of 150 to 200 miles or those that can be transported by water. The economics of removing sulfur from the higher sulfur coals appears less encouraging than removing sulfur oxides from the gaseous products of combustion. Hence there is an increasing incentive to develop methods for the removal of sulfur oxides from flue gases.

Since sulfur dioxide (SO_2) represents 98% of sulfur oxide pollutants, the principal interest attaches to the removal of sulfur dioxide. As of 1970, four principal approaches are being investigated:

1. Addition of materials such as limestone or dolomite in the combustion furnace.

2. Wet scrubbing of flue gases without sulfur recovery.

3. Wet scrubbing of flue gases with sulfur recovery.

4. Dry Sorbent systems.

Limestone addition

In this system an additive, such as limestone, is injected intothe furnace of the steam generator. Once in the furnace the carbonate is calcined by hot combustion gases to form calcium oxide, which combines with the sulfur dioxide and oxygen to form calcium sulfate. The calcium sulfate can be removed subsequently in a dry state by more conventional particulate-removal systems. However, SO_2 removal efficiencies are low with this method, commonly ranging from 20% to 35%.

When limestone is used as the additive, successful results are obtained when theadditive system is combined with aqueous scrubbing, but equally good results canbe obtained with aqueous scrubbing alone.

Wet scrubbing system without sulfur recovery

A wet scrubbing system without sulfur recovery is shown diagramma-tically in Fig. 7. 2. A limestone slurry is used as the scrubbing fluid to remove up to 85% of the sulfur oxides and about 99% of the particulates from the flue gas. This system requires a minimum capital expenditure; however, large quantities of refuse must be disposed of and operating costs are high.

Magnesium-oxide system with sulfur recovery

A magnesium-oxide wet-scrubbing system with sulfur recovery is

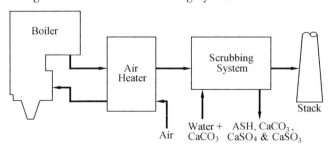

Fig. 7. 2 Wet-scrubbing system without sulfur recovery

shown in Fig. 7. 3. Magnesia solutions or slurries are used to remove up to 95% of the sulfur oxides and 99% of the particulates from the flue gas. The scrubbing effluent is regenerated to recover MgO for reuse. A salable sulfur product is produced.

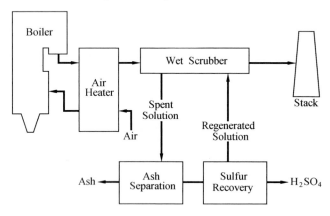

Fig. 7. 3   Wet-scrubbing system with sulfur recovery

Dry sorbent systems

Although a longer range development, systems using a dry sorbent for sulfur-oxide removal promise equal or lower costs without the disadvantage of wet scrubbing. The heart of these systems is a fixed sorbent bed containing material to adsorb the sulfur oxides. This material may be char, activated carbon, or alumina impregnated with copper. The sorbent bed is located ahead or after the air heater, depending on the gas temperature which is most suitable for the sorbent material used. The sorbent material is regenerated, and sulfur, usually as acid, is reclaimed as a byproduct. Efficiencies of 90% and perhaps higherappear to be practicable. Although a precipitator is required for particulate removal, capital requirements are projected as equal to those of the magnesium-oxide wet-scrubbing system.

Oxides of nitrogen

The oxides of nitrogen also contribute to air pollution and much effort is beingdirected toward their control, particularly in large urban areas. The reaction leading to the formation of oxides of nitrogen proceeds rapidly at combustion temperatures in excess of 3 000 °F. To help reduce this type emission, flame temperatures are moderated by two-stage combustion or recirculation of flue gas through the burners.

Words and Expressions

contaminant [kən'tæmənənt] n. 污染物,沾染物
emit [i'mit] v. 放射,发出,发行
remedial [ri'mi:diəl] v. 补救的,改正的
legislation [ˌledʒis'leiʃən] n. 法规,立法
scrub [skrʌb] v. 用力擦洗
limestone ['ləimstəun] n. 石灰石
reuse ['ri:'ju:z] v. n. 再使用
sorbent ['sɔ:bənt] n. 吸收剂,吸着剂
alumina [ə'lju:minə] n. 氯化铝,矾土
impregnate ['impregneit] v. 使充满
urban ['ə:bən] a. 都市的,城市居民

7.4 Fans

A fan moves a quantity of air or gas by adding sufficient energy to the stream toinitiate motion and overcome all resistance to flow. The fan consists of a bladed rotor, or impeller, which does the actual work, and usually a housing to collectand direct the air or gas discharged by the impeller. The power required dependsupon the volume of air or gas moved in unit time, the pressure difference acrossthe fan and the efficiency of the fan and its drives.

Power may be expressed as shaft horsepower, input horsepower to motor terminals, if motor driven, or theoretical horsepower computed by thermodynamic methods. Each has its own significance. As far as the fan is concerned, the important factors are the power input to the shaft and the power dictated by thermodynamic calculations.

Stacks seldom provide sufficient natural draft to cover the requirements of modern boiler units. The 200 foot high stack of the previous example with a 490 °F average gas temperature will develop a theoretical natural draft of approximately 1.15 in. of water, whereas resistances to gas and air flow may be as high as 50 inches. These higher draft loss systems require the use of mechanical draft equipment and a wide variety of fan designs and types is available to meet this need.

The forced draft fan

Bolers operating with both forced and induced draft use the forced draft fan to push air through the combustion air supply system into the furnace. The fan must have a discharge pressure high enough to equal the total resistance of air ducts, air heater, burners or fuel bed and any other resistance between the fan discharge and the furnace. This makes the furnace the point of balanced draft or zero pressure. Volume output of the forced draft fan must equal the total quantity of air required for combustion plus air heater leakage. In many boiler installations, greater reliability is obtained by division of the total fan capacity between twofans operating in parallel. If one fan is out of service, the other usually can carry 60 percent or more of full boiler load, depending on how the fans are sized.

To establish the required characteristics of the forced draft fan, the system resistance from fan to furnace is calculated for the actual weight of air required for combustion plus the expected leakage from the air side of the air heater. It is usual boiler design practice to base all calculations on 80 °F air temperature entering the fan. The results are the net requirements which are then adjusted totest block specifications by the safety factors previously discussed.

For pressurized units without an induced draft fan, the forced draft fan is sizedfor the entire system to the stack entrance.

A forced draft fan for boiler service operates under far more stringent conditions than the ordinary ventilating fan and selection should consider the followinggeneral requirements:

Reliability. Modern boilers must operate continuously for long periods (up to 18 months in some instances) without shutdown for repairs or maintenance. Thus the fan must have a rugged rotor and housing and conservatively loaded bearings. The fan must also be well balanced, and the blades so shaped that they will not collect dirt and disturb this balance.

Efficiency. High efficiency over a wide range of output is necessary because boilers operate under varying load conditions.

Pressure. Fan pressure should vary uniformly with output over the capacity range. This facilitates damper control and assures minimum disturbance of air flow when minor adjustments to the fuel-burning equipment change the system resistance.

Capacity. When two or more fans operate in parallel, the pressure-output curves should have characteristics similar to the straight blade or backward-curved blade fans in order to share the load equally near the shutoff point.

Horsepower. Motor driven fans require self-limiting horsepower characteristics, so that the driving motor can not overload. This means that the horsepower should reach a peak and then drop off near the fullload fan output.

In general, backward-curved centrifugal designs meet most forced draft fan requirements. Small boiler units, however, may use a single propeller-type fan mounted directly on the burner windbox. This fan saves space and the cost is low.

The induced draft fan

Units designed to operate with balanced furnace draft or without a forced draft fan require induced draft to move the gaseous products of combustion over convection heating surfaces and through the gas passages between the furnace and stack. Where it is not practical or economical to design for natural draft, induced draft fans discharging essentially at atmospheric pressure are used to provide the necessary negative static pressure.

The gas weight used to calculate net induced draft requirements is the weight of combustion product gas at maximum boiler load plus any air leakage into the boiler setting from the surroundings and from the air side to the gas side of the air heater. Net gas temperatures are based on the calculated unit performance at maximum load. Induced draft fan test block specifications of gas weight, negative static pressure and gas temperature are obtained by adjusting from net values by margins similar to those used for forced draft fans.

An induced draft fan has the same basic requirements as a forced draft fan except that it handles higher temperature gas which may contain erosive ash. Flat, forward-curved and occasionally backward-curved blades are used. If backward-curved blades are used curvature is usually less than found in forced draft fans. Using a lesser curvature results in a lower tip speed for the same head, which diminishes the erosive effect of ash particles, and, because of its shape, less dirt clings to the back of the blades. A flat-bladed centrifugal fan of lower speed maybe selected to handle particularly dirty or erosive gases. Excessive maintenancefrom erosion is sometimes avoided by protecting casing and blades with replaceable wear strips. Bearings, usually water-cooled, have radiation shields on the shaft between rotor and bearings, to avoid overheating.

Gas recirculating fans used variously for controlling steam temperature, furnaceheat absorption and slagging of heating surfaces, are generally located to extract gas at the economizer outlet and inject it into the furnace at locations depending on the intended function. This multiple purpose is also an important consideration in properly sizing and specifying gas recirculating fans. This selection may be dictated by the high static pressure required for tempering furnace temperatures at full load on the boiler unit, or by high volume requirement at partialloads for steam temperature control.

Even though gas recirculating fans have the same basic requirements as induced draft fans, the designer or engineer must consider additional factors. Since the gasrecirculating fan operates at higher gas temperatures, intermittent service may cause thermal shock or unbalance. When the fan is not in service, suitable protection in the form of tight shut-off dampers and sealing air must be provided to prevent the backflow of hot furnace gas and a turning gear is often used on largefans to rotate the rotor slowly to avoid distortion.

Words and Expressions

fan　　　　[fæn]　　　　　n. 风机,扇子
impeller　　[im′pelə]　　　n. 推进器,叶轮,叶轮激动器
leakage　　[′li:kidʒ]　　　n. 漏出,泄漏,漏风
entrance　　[′entrəns]　　　n. 入口,进入
ventilate　　[′ventileit]　　v. 使通风,安装通风设备
damper　　[′dæmpə]　　　n. 节气闸
negative　　[′negətiv]　　　a. 负的
margin　　[′ma:dʒin]　　　n. 系度,亲裕
erosive　　[i′rəusiv]　　　v. 腐蚀性的,侵蚀的
cling　　　[kliŋ]　　　　vi. 粘住,依附,坚持
inject　　　[in′dʒekt]　　　n. 引入,注入
distortion　[dis′tɔ:ʃən]　　n. 扭曲,变形

7.5　Stokers

Mechanical stokers, as an improvement over hand firing, were developed early in the history of the steam boiler. Today many small and medium size boilers are firedwith stokers, and several types of stokers are available. All are designed to feed fuel onto a grate within the furnace and to remove the ash residue. Higher rates of combustion are possible than with hand firing, and the continuous process ofstoker firing permits good control and high efficiency.

A successful stoker installation requires the selection of the correct type and size for the fuel to be used and the desired capacity. Also, the associated boilerunit should have the necessary instruments for the proper control of the stoker. The grate area required for a given stoker type and capacity is determined fromallowable rates established by experience. Table 7.1 lists allowable fuel burning rates (Btu/sq ft, hr) for various types of stokers, based on using coals suitedto the stoker type in each case.

Table 7.1 Maximum allowable fuel burning rates

Type of Stoker	Btu/sq ft, hr
Spreader-stationary and dumping grate	450 000
Spreader-traveling grate	750 000
Spreader-vibrating grate	400 000
Underfeed-single or double retort	425 000
Underfeed-multiple retort	600 000
Water-cooled vibrating grate	400 000
Chain grate and traveling grate	500 000

For a boiler of a given steam capacity, these maximum fuel burning rates determine the plan area for a stokerfired furnace. As boiler unit size is increased, practical considerations limit stoker size and, consequently, the maximum rate of steamgeneration with this method of firing. Because of the greater flexibility in furnace design with pulverized-coal and Cyclone-Furnace firing and the trend toward larger boiler units, the present market for stokers is less than in former years. The practical steamoutput limit of boilers equipped with mechanical stokers is about 400 000 lb/hr, although many engineers limit the application of stokersto lower steam capacities. However, within their capacity range, mechanical stokers are an important and valued element of modern equipment for the production of steam or hot water. When applicable, stokers are often preferred over pulverizers because of their greater operating range, capability of burning a wide range of solid fuels, and lower power requirements.

Almost any coal can be burned successfully on some type of stoker. In addition, many by-products and waste fuels, such as coke breeze, wood wastes, pulpwood bark and bagasse can be used either as a base or auxiliary fuel.

Mechanical stokers can be classified in four main groups, based on the method of introducing fuel to the furnace:

1. Spreader stokers.
2. Underfeed stokers.
3. Water-cooled vibrating-grate stokers.
4. Chain-grate and traveling-grate stokers.

Among these several types, the spreader stoker is the most generally used in thecapacity range from 75 000 to 400 000 1b of steam per hr, because it responds rapidly to load swings and can burn a wide range of fuels.

Underfeed stokers of the single-retort, ram-feed, side-ash-discharge type are used principally for heating and for small industrial units of less than 30 000 1b of steam per hr capacity. Larger size underfeed stokers of multiple-retort, rear-ash-discharge type have been largely displaced by spreader stokers and by the water-cooled vibrating-grate stokers in the intermediate range. Chain and traveling-grate stokers, while still used in some areas, are gradually being displaced by the spreader and vibrating-grate types.

Spreader stokers

The spreader stoker is capable of burning a wide range of coals, from high-rank . Eastern bituminous to lignite or brown coal and a variety of by-product waste fuels.

As the name implies, the spreader stoker projects fuel into the furnace over the fire with a uniform spreading action, permitting suspension burning of the fine fuel particles. (Fig. 7.4). The heavier pieces, that cannot be supported in the gas flow, fall to the grate for combustion in a thin fast-burning bed. This method of firing provides

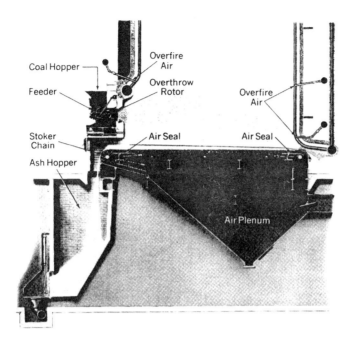

Fig. 7.4 Traveling-grate spreader stoker with front ash discharge

extreme sensitivity to load fluctuations as ignition is almost instantaneous on increase of firing rate and the thin fuel bed can be burned out rapidly when desired.

The modern spreader stoker installation consists of feeder-distributor units inwidths and numbers as required to distribute the fuel uniformly over the width of the grate, specifically designed air-metering grates, forced draft fans for both undergrate and overfire air, dust collecting and reinjecting equipment, and combustion controls to coordinate fuel and air supply with load demand.

Spreader mechanism

Fig. 7.5 illustrates a fuel feeder-distributor unit of the variable stroke, reciprocating-feed-plate type. The reciprocating-feed plate

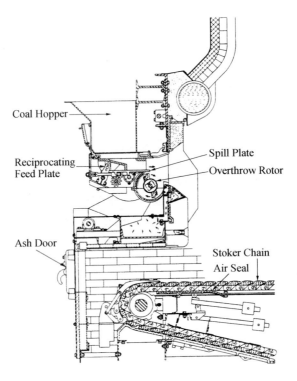

Fig. 7.5   Reciprocating-feeder distributor and overthrow rotor for spreader stokers

moves coal from the supply hopper over an adjustable spill plate to fall onto an overthrow rotor. This rotor is equipped with curved blades for uniform coal distribution over the furnace area.

While the details of the several means used to feed and distribute the coal may vary with different manufacturers, the overthrow rotor design illustrated hasthewidest usage. The object in all cases is to provide a continuous well-distributed supply of fuel at a variable rate as required by the load demand.

Words and Expressions

stoker ['stəukə] n. 加煤机,抛煤机
flexibility [ˌfleksə'biliti] n. 适应性,易曲性
vibrating-grate 振动炉排
permit [pə'mit] v. 许可,容许 n. 许可证
uniformly ['juːnifɔːmli] adv. 一律地,一样地
illustrate ['iləstreit] v. 显示,加插图,说明

7.6　Flue Gas Desulfunzation

Background

The first commercial application of flue gas desulfurization(FGD) to power plant sulfur oxide control was in the United Kingdom in the early 1930s. The BatterseaA Power Plant (228 MW) of the London Power Company, London, UK, began flue-gas washing in 1933. The process utilized wet scrubbing with Thames River water providing most of the alkaline absorbent. The spent absorbent was discharged back intothe Thames after settling and oxidation. The FGD system operated successfully at up to 95% SO_2 removal efficiency until the Battersea A Power Plant closed down in 1975. A similar FGD system operated on the Battersea B Power Plant(245 MW) between 1949 and 1969, when FGD operation was temporarily suspended because of adverse effects on the Thames water quality.

The ICI Howden process, also developed in England, was developed to avoid discharged scrubber effluent into the Thames. A solid sludge was produced and barged to sea for dumping. This process was applied to the Swansea Power Plant in 1935 and the Fulham Power Plant in 1937. These systems operated successfully until early World War II when they were shut down.

The next FGD unit was installed at the Electrolytic Zinc company in Tasmania in 1949. Tidal water was used there as the absorbent for SO_2 from smelter gas.

In 1952 the first unit of the new oil-fired Bankside Power Station in London, UK, was commissioned. This FGD system is an improved version of the Battersea system, using water from the Thames. This system is still operating at up to 98% removal efficiency and with a present capacity of 240 MW.

The 1950s and 1960s were a time of laboratory and pilot plant investigations of new processes. During the 1950s the Tennessee Valley Authority(USA) investigated lime/limestone systems, both dry and wet, and dilute acid processes; in Germany the first major carbon adsorption processes were developed. During the 1960s themagnesium oxide, copper oxide, and sulfite scrubbing processes were investigated among others.

Lime/limestone processes were installed in 1964 on an iron ore sintering plant in Russia and on a large sulfuric acid plant in Japan in 1966.

In 1966 Combustion Engineering developed a dry limestone injection process, whichwas installed at five boilers in the United States by 1972. Because of major problems associated with dry limestone injection including plugging(especially of the boiler tubes), low sulfur dioxide removal, and reduced particulate collectionin the electrostatic precipitators, these systems proved inadequate. The five installations are now either closed down or converted to other control systems.

Japan has at present the largest installed capacity of FGD systems. Most of these systems were built between 1975 and 1977. Systems based on lime/limestone predominate. As of December 1977, the United States had 27 operating utility units treating about 35×10^6 Nm^3/h (normal conditions are 0 ℃ and 1 bar), 34 units under construction to treat 50×10^6 Nm^3/h, and 20 units are planned to treat 34×10^6 Nm^3/h; in addition 25 industrial boilers were operational or under construction with a capacity of about 5×10^6 Nm^3/h. In the Federal Republic of Germany, approximately 775 000 Nm^3/h of flue gas are being treated by lime and carbon adsorption processes, and in Norway 155 000 Nm^3/h are treated by seawater scrubbers on oil-fired boiler.

Process Categories

FGD process can most conveniently and usefully be categorized by the manner in which the sulfur compounds removed from the flue gases are eventually produced for disposal. In this way three main categories result:

(1) Throwaway processes, in which the eventual product is disposed of entirely as waste. Disposal can include landfill, ponding, discharge to water course or ocean, or discharge to a worked-out mine.

The processes in this category involve wet scrubbing of the flue gases for absorption, followed by various methods for neutralizing the acidity, separating the sulfur compounds from the scrubbing liquor, and usually recycling at least part of the scrubbing liquor.

(2) Gypsum processes, which are designed to produce gypsum of sufficient qualityeither for use as an alternative to natural gypsum or as well-defined waste product with good disposal characteristics.

As with the throwaway processes, this category involves wet scrubbing for absorption followed by various methods of neutralizing lime or limestone and recovering the sulfur compound. An oxidation step is included to insure recovery of the sulfur compounds in the form of gypsum.

(3) Regenerative processes, which are designed specifically to regenerate the primary reactants and concentrate the sulfur dioxide that has been removed from the flue gases. Further chemical processing can then convert the concentrated SO_2, into sulfuric acid or elemental sulfur, or physical processing into liquefied sulfur dioxide. The surveyed processes in this category contain both wet scrubbingand dry adsorption processes.

Status of Operating FGD Systems

There are now 144 known FGD systems operating on fossil-fueled combustion sources. Of these, 74 are operating on power utility boilers, representing about 70×10^5 m³/h of flue gas capacity from about 20 GW generation. The remainder is operating on industrial combustion sources, principally boiler plants, but alsoon iron- ore sinter plants and petroleum refinery plants.

In the NATO-CCMS Process Status Reports, 35 FGD systems were surveyed. Althoughit was originally desired to include only the large, commercially available installations with adequate operating experience, it was necessary to include data on some smaller scale operation and some that had been installed originally for demonstration purposes in order to provide sufficient comparability between the various processes.

Throwaway Processes: This category includes the three processes that produce a calcium sulfite/sulfate sludge and also the seawater scrubbing process. The sludge processes are becoming the most widely used FGD systems; 30 systems are in operation and 53 are planned or under construction. They have been used successfully on both coal and oil-fired plants with a wide range of fuel sulfur contents and are reported to have high SO_2 removal efficiencies, whereas plant availabilities are variable.

Double Alkali Process: It is a further development designed to overcome the scaling, plugging, arid erosion problems that have been generally associated with lime or limestone systems. Double alkali systems are presently used mainly with small to medium-sized boilers where the extra process equipment can be offset by lower maintenance coasts.

Gypsum Processes: These processes are designed to produce a quality of gypsum that may be used in place of natural gypsum in such markets as plaster or plaster wallboard, or as a setting retarder in cement manufacture. It is expected that if sufficient markets are not available for gypsum, it will be disposed of as a solid waste. Gypsum has better setting characteristics than sludges containing calcium sulfite from the throwaway processes.

Words and Expressions

scrub [skrʌb] vt. 擦洗,洗涤
alkaline absorbent 碱性吸收剂
SO_2 removal efficiency 脱硫效率
ICI 帝国化学公司
solid sludge 污泥,泥渣
lime/limestone 石灰/石灰石
magnesium oxide 氧化镁
copper oxide 氧化铜
sulfite ['sʌlfait] n. 亚硫酸
electrostatic precipitators 静电除尘器
predominate [pri'dɔmineit] vi. 支配,统治
worked-out 用过的,废弃的
neutralizing the acidity 中和酸

gypsum   ['dʒipsəm]   n. 石膏
recover   [ri'kʌvə]   vt. 回收
concentrate   ['kɔnsentreit]   vt. 浓缩,冷凝
sulfur dioxide   二氧化硫
NATO   北大西洋公约组织(即北约)
calcium sulfite   亚硫酸钙
calcium sulfate   硫酸钙
under construction   正在建设中
sulfur contents   含硫量
plaster   ['plaːstə]   n. 熟石膏,烧石膏
retarder   [ri'taːdə]   n. 抑制剂,控制剂,阻滞剂

7.7 Steam Separation

Separation and solids removal

In a modern drum boiler, the separation of steam from the mixture delivered by the steam-water risers (Fig. 7.6) usually takes place in two steps. The primary separation removes nearly all the water from the mixture, so that, in effect, no steam is recirculated to the heating tubes. However, the steam may still contain solid contaminants which must be removed or reduced in amount before the steam is sufficiently pure for use in high-pressure turbines. This step is called secondary separation or "steam scrubbing". Both steps are usually accomplished in one steam drum.

Part of the contamination of the steam is caused by dissolved solids contained in tiny water droplets that may remain after primary separation. The rest of the contamination appears to be silica, either in solution in steam or in vaporized form. This type of contaminant cannot be mechanically removed by primary separation. Washing or scrubbing

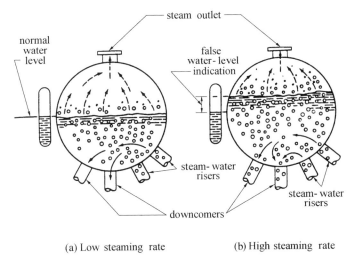

Fig. 7.6 Effect of rate of steam generation on steam separation in a boiler drum without separation devices

is necessary for its dilution or removal.

Gross impurities in the steam may be caused by periods of abnormally high water level from operational upsets, during which the separating equipment is submerged, allowing the water to be carried over in gulps. This action is called "priming". Another type of gross carry-over can occur if the boiler water producesexcessive foam in the drum. With high concentration of solids in the boiler water, this "foaming" may be severe enough to render the separating devices ineffective. Foaming and priming are comparatively rare occurrences in the modern boiler with proper water-level regulation and control of boiler-water quality by chemical methods.

Factors affecting steam separation

Separation of steam form the mixture discharged into the drum from steam-water risers is related to both design and operating factors, which may be listed as follows

Design factors

1. Design pressure
2. Drum size, length and diameter
3. Rate of steam generation
4. Circulation radio-water circulated to heated tubes divided by steam generated
5. Type and arrangement of mechanical separators
6. Feedwater supply and steam discharge equipment and arrangement
7. Arrangement of downcomer and riser circuits in the steam drum

Operating factors

1. Operating pressure
2. Boiler load (steam flow)
3. Type of steam load
4. Chemical analysis of boiler water
5. Water level carried

In steam drums without separation devices, where separation is by gravity only, the manner in which some of the above items affect separation is indicated in simplified form in Fig. 7.6 and Fig. 7.7.

For a low rate of steam generation (up to about 3 ft/sec velocity of steam leaving the water surface) there is sufficient time for the steam bubbles to separate from the mixture by gravity without being drawn into the downcomers and without carrying entrained water droplets into the steam outlet (see Fig. 7.6(a)). However, for this same arrangement at a higher rate of steam generation (Fig. 7.6(b)) the time is insufficient to attain either of these desirable results. Moreover, the dense upward traffic of steam bubbles in the mixture may cause a

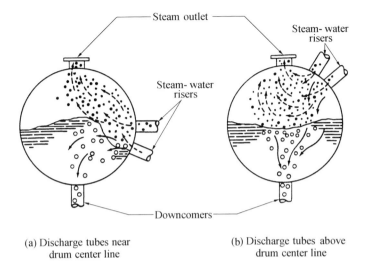

(a) Discharge tubes near drum center line

(b) Discharge tubes above drum center line

Fig. 7.7 Effect of location of discharge from risers on steam separation in a boiler drum without separation devices

false water level, as indicated.

The effect of the location of the riser circuits in relation to the water level is illustrated in diagrams (a) and (b) , Fig. 7. 7. Neither arrangement is likely to yield desirable results in a drum where gravity alone is used for separation.

Separation by the action of gravity alone is possible if the velocity of either the mixture or the steam bubbles within the mixture is sufficiently low, but the arrangement will probably be uneconomical. For gravity separation in a single drum, the steam generated per sq. ft of disengaging surface must be kept extremely low. A single drum under these conditions is generally uneconomical except for small low-duty boilers. By using multiple drums of reasonable size in series, some what higher steam outputs per ft length of drum are possible with gravity separation.

Operating pressure has an effect on the natural tendency of steam and water to separate. The relationship between pressure and the differential in the densities of water and steam is indicative of this effect. In the separation of steam from water, the limiting velocity of a water particle conveyed in steam and the force of gravity both vary directly with the differential in the densities of the water and the steam. Hence, as the density differential diminishes with increase in operating pressure, so does the force of gravity available for separation. The effect of increasing operating pressure (above 300 psi for comparison) on steam flow per unit of flow area, on steam velocity above the drum water level, and on the force of gravity for separation is shown in Fig. 7.8. It will be noted that the percentage drop in gravity-separating force closely follows the drop in limiting velocity.

As steam pressure increases, the density of steam increases, and the size of steam bubbles in the mixture decreases. Consequently, the velocity of the mixture leaving the riser circuits is reduced. This permits a higher capacity per ft length of a given diameter drum, or the use of a small drum.

Words and Expressions

silica ['silikə] n. 硅土,氧化硅
dilution [dai'luːʃən] n. 冲淡,稀释物
foam [fəum] vi. 起泡沫,充满 vt. 使起泡沫
discharge [dis'tʃaːdʒ] v. 排出,发射 n. 发射,放电量
list [list] n. 目录 v. 列表
indicate ['indikeit] v. 指示,表示,说明
bubble ['bʌbl] n. 气泡,泡沫 v. vi. 起泡,沸腾
tendency ['tendənsi] n. 趋势,倾向

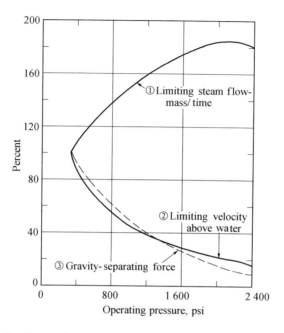

Fig. 7.8 Effect of increase in operating pressure (above 300 psi for comparison on ① limiting steam flow per unit of flow area, ② limiting velocity above water, and ③ gravity-separating force-steam and water

7.8 Pulverizers

Design fundamentals

1. **Feeding** In direct-firing systems the fuel rate must be capable of automatic control by the boiler load demand. Pulverizer air flow must be proportioned to fuel rate to provide the air required for drying, the correct primary-air-coal ratio, and the velocity required for transporting the fuel to the burners.

B & W uses a control that maintains a predetermined variable air-fuel ratio over the entire operating range of the pulverizer. Air flow is measured by an orifice or a pitot tube in the duct supplying air to the pulverizer and fuel flow is measured by feeder speed, a gravimetric feeder, or by the static pressure differential across the pulverizer grinding zone.

2. **Drying** In order to pulverize and circulate fuel pneumatically within a pulverizer, enough of the moisture must be removed to leave the fuel dry and dusty. Formost commercially available coal, preheated air to the pulverizer is required. Drying is accomplished quickly as the coal is being circulated and ground. The use of preheated air permits control of the temperature of the fuel-air mixture to the burners for the most stable ignition.

3. **Grinding** The pulverizer must do adequate work on each passage of the materialthrough the grinding zone and without the production of excessive superfines. This is best accomplished by internal recirculation of coarse material. The pulverizer should maintain its grinding ability over thelife cycle of the grinding elements and be able to reject foreign matter that enters with the feed. These objectives should be attained without excessive wear and power consumption.

The grinding elements of B & W pulverizers are spring loaded to provide the necessary grinding force throughout the life of the elements. Shallow cupped rings furnish adequate grinding surface, allow rapid material flow, and facilitate the discharge of foreign material.

4. **Circulating** Circulation of coal within a pulverizer is required (1) to promote rapid drying by mixing the incoming feed with dry material in the pulverizer, (2) to keep the grinding elements loaded at all times, and (3) to remove pulverized material from the grinding elements.

Rapid circulation is maintained in B & W pulverizers by utilizing the pulverizerair in combination with centrifugal force and gravity to move the material as desired.

5. *Classifying* It is not feasible to grind all the coal to the desired fineness in a single passage through the grinding elements. Therefore a device called a "classifier" is provided. Coal pulverized to the proper fineness leaves the pulverizer and goes to the burners. Oversize coal is separated out by the classifier and returned to the grinding zone.

If separation is not discriminative, oversize particles will go to the furnace and cause unburned combustible loss. Separation must be effective over the entire operating range, and the classifier must be adjustable for product size, since the required fineness is not the same for all applications.

The stationary, multiple-inlet-cyclone-type classifier used in the B & W pulverizer meets these requirements. The shrouded discharge prevents reentrainment of oversize particles. Fineness varies inversely with rating so that the highest fineness is obtained at the lowest load. The movable inlet vanes permit adjusting the classifier for the fineness desired.

6. *Transporting* The velocity in pulverizer discharge lines mustbe sufficiently high to prevent settling and drifting of coal. At the burners the air-coal mixture must be uniform and the velocity suitable.

The B & W system, by a variable controlled air-coal relationship, increases the air-coal ratio at lower loads and decreases it at higher loads to provide a maximum load range. The uniform discharge from the classifier and the symmetrical take-off of burner lines from the pulverizer assure equal distribution of coal to each burner.

Pulverizer requirements

1. Rapid response to load change and adaptability to automatic

control.

2. Continuous service for long operating periods.

3. Maintenance of prescribed performance throughout the life of pulverizer grinding elements.

4. A wide variety of coals should be acceptable.

5. Ease of maintenance with the minimum number and variety of parts, and space adequate for access.

6. Minimum building volume required.

The rank of coal can its end use govern the fineness to which coal must be ground. The data of Table 7.2 are helpful in this specification.

Table 7.2 Required pulverized fuel fineness percent through 200 U.S. sieve*

Type of Furnace	ASTM Classification of coals by rank					
	Fixed carbon, %			Fixed carbon below 69%		
	97.9-86 (Petroleum coke)	85.9-78	77.9-69	Btu/lb above 13 000	Btu/lb 12 900-11 000	Btu/lb below 11 000
Marine boiler	—	85	80	80	75	—
Water-cooled	80	75	70	70	65**	60**
Cement kiln	90	85	80	80	80	—
Metallurgical	(As determined by process, generally from 80% to 90%)					

* The 200-mesh screen (sieve) has 200 openings per linear inch or 40 000 openings per square inch. For U.S. and ASTM sieve series, the nominal aperture for 200 mesh is 0.0029 in. or 0.074 mm. The ASTM designation for 200 mesh is 74 microns.

** Extremely high ash content coals will require higher fineness than indicated.

Selecting pulverizer equipment

A number of factors must be considered when selecting pulverizer equipment. If selection anticipates the use of a variety of coals, the pulverizer should be sizedfor the coal that gives the highest "base capacity". Base capacity is the desired capacity divided by the capacity factor. The latter is a function of the grindability of the coal and the fineness required.

The extent of drying in a given pulverizer dependsupon its design and the methodused to introduce preheated air into the grinding zone. Raw coal with very high surface mositure, over 15%, can be efficiently dried when fed into the grinding zone of a pulverizer designed for a high internal circulating load, i. e. , a high ratio of coal recirculated to coal feed. As the recirculated material is dry, the more of it there is, the less effect the wet feed has on the performance of the mill.

As a practical matter, temperature is the only variable for controlling the heat input for drying, since the weight of primary air is usually a fixed quantity at any given output.

The percentage of volatile matter in the fuel has a direct bearing on the probability of premature ignition of the primary-air-fuel mixture at the burners. Thegenerally accepted safe values for exit fuel-air temperatures are given in Table 7. 3.

Table 7.3 Prevalent pulverizer exit primary-air-fueltemperature

Fuel	Exit Temp, F
Lignite	120-140
High-volatile bituminous	150
Low-volatile bituminous	150-175
Anthracite	200
Petroleum coke	200-250

The temperature of the primary air entering the pulverizer may run 650 °F or more, depending on the amount of surface moisture and the type of pulverizer.

Fine grinding of coal is necessary to assure complete combustion of the carbon for maximum efficiency and to minimize the deposit of ash and carbon on the heatabsorbing surfaces. This applies not only in the firing of steam boilers but also in other applications where close temperature control and the avoidance of carbon contamination are important. Chemical and metallurgical processes using pulverized coal as a source of thermal or chemical energy generally require very finelyground coal to assure the optimum reaction in a limited combustion zone and often under difficult firing conditions.

Fineness is expressed as the percentage of the product passing through various sizes of sieves, graded from. No. 16 to No. 325 in the ASTM designation. Coal classification by rank and the end use of the product determine the fineness to which coal should be ground.

The range through which the equipment will operate must be considered in selecting pulverizing equipment for direct firing. The range through which a single pulverizer can operate is an inherent feature of the pulverizer. For B & W pulverizers it is about 3 to 1. However, the range for safe operation depends on the type and number of burners, type of fuel, and whether the furnace is "hot" or "cold".

When B & W pulverizers are operated at fractional loads, the fineness of the product increases automaticaly as the air flow is decreased. This is beneficial to low-load operation as it assists in ignition and flame stability.

Words and Expressions

orifice　　[ˈɔrifis]　　n. 口,洞,孔
gravimetric　　[ɡrəviˈmetrik]　　a. 重量分析的,重量的
promote　　[prəˈməut]　　v. 升级,促进,发起
drift　　[ˈdrift]　　n. 吹积物　v. 吹积,漂流
symmetricical　　[siˈmetrikəl]　　v. a. 对称的,整齐的

prescribe [pri'kraib] v. 限定,限制
metallurgical [ˌmetə'lɔːdʒikəl] a. 冶金的 n. 冶金学者
index ['indeks] n. 索引,指针,路标 v. 指示

7.9 Prevention of Scaling in Boilers

The term scale describes a continuous, adherent layer of foreign material formedon the water side of a surface through which heat is exchanged. By adding certain chemicals the growth of scales can be inhibited and the insoluble particles can be dispersed in the recirculating water and removed by blowdown. Should the particles come out of suspension, however, they can accumulate as sludges in quiet sections of a boiler. Deposit is a rather general term applied to more-or-lessloose accumulations often found in less turbulent sections of boilers and water-treating systems. Scales are objectionable because of their insulating effect. In a boiler tube, for instance, they cause overheating and eventual failure of the metal. Deposits often cause plugging in critical areas such as waterwalls, waterwall headers, in blowdown lines, and in gauge glasses.

Types of Scale

Many different mineral structures have been identified in boiler scales by the methods of x-ray diffraction, electron diffraction, and polarizing microscopy, Examples of silicate scales are: acmite, $Na_2O \cdot Fe_2O_3 \cdot 4SiO_2$; analcite, $Na_2O \cdot 3Al_2O_3 \cdot 4SiO_2 \cdot 2H_2O$; serpentine, $3MgO \cdot SiO_2 \cdot 2H_2O$; sodalite, $Na_2O \cdot 3Al_2O \cdot 6SiO_2 \cdot 2NaCl$; and xonotlite, $5CaO \cdot 5SiO_2 \cdot H_2O$. When phosphate is used for internal treatment, ferric, phosphate, $FePO_4$, basicmagnesiumphosphate, $Mg_3(PO_4)_2 \cdot Mg(OH)_2$, and hydroxyapatite, $Ca_{10}(PO_4)_6(OH)_2$, may also be encountered, as well as the more common anhydrite, $CaSO_4$, and aragonite, $CaCO_3$. As noted before, the presence of these and other scales impedes the circulation of water and reduces heat transfer, both of which cause overheating and failure of tubes.

Mechanism of Scale Formation

Scales and deposits form because the compounds of which they are composed are insoluble under the conditions prevailing in the boiler. Two factors combine to make calcium salts especially troublesome: certain anhydrous calcium salts, notably the sulfate, decrease in solubility as temperature and pressure increase, whereas increasing temperature shifts the equilibrium of the following reaction to the right, causing $CaCO_3$ to precipitate:

$$Ca^{2+} + 2HCO_3^- =\!=\!= CaCO_3 + H_2CO_3 \qquad (7.1)$$

In addition, hydrolysis of excess bicarbonate increases the concentration of hydroxyl ion, precipitating $Mg(OH)_2$, the solubility product of which is 5.5×10^{-12}. The solubility of $CaSO_4$ decreases rapidly with increasing temperature, producing an extremely hard, adherent coating on boiler tubes, especially in locations where heat flux is high. The compositions of several scales containing aluminum, magnesium, calcium, and silicate are given above. Analcite and acmite, which form at high temperature, are invariably found beneath sludges of hydroxyapatite or serpentine, or under porous deposits of iron oxides. Occasionally other extremely, insoluble iron or magnesium silicates are also encountered, and now and then aquartz, SiO_2 appear, usually originating from colloidal silica, finely divided silt, or sand in the feed water.

Accumulations in boiler drums are most often in the form of mud or sludge. When oil is present as a contamination in boiler water, loose scales may form, particularly in water-wall tubes. Oil serves as a nucleus and binder for scaling at hot spots, although these scales are often merely baked mud that is easily dislodged by hammering the tubes. The " oil balls " found in steam drums and water-wallheaders are typical formations in turbulent sections; they are especially common in steam drums, where they are formed by the rolling motion of water.

Chemical Treatments

Obviously, the most effective method for preventing scaling is to eliminate scale-forming elements from the feed water, or to transform them by some means into, an innocuous form. The methods for doing this are conveniently classified as external and internal treatments.

Chemical Softening. The treatments of water that are accomplished outside of theboiler are referred to as preboiler, or external treatments. The processes for removing calcium and magnesium ions from water are called softening, and are signal importance in preventing scales. It is apparent from the equation:

$$Ca^{2+} + 2HCO_3^- = CaCO_3 + H_2CO_3 \qquad (7.2)$$

That calcium is precipitated if carbonic acid is neutralized by adding an alkaline reagent. If an excess of alkali is added, magnesium hydroxide also precipitates and the total hardness of the water is reduced. Lime is the alkaline reagent most often used because its cost is low and it is relatively easy to handle; theprocess is called lime softening.

Softening by Cation Exchange. The removal of calcium and magnesium ions by cation exchange is commonly called zeolite softening, from the reaction characteristic of the mineral zeolites. The latter are hydrous sodium aluminum silicates in which the sodium is labile and exchangeable for calcium and magnesium ions flowing over through the mineral. The exchange reaction is:

$$Na_2Z+Ca^{2+}=\!=\!=CaZ+2Na^2 \qquad (7.3)$$

In this type of treatment the cation exchange resin is in the acid form, while the anion exchange resin, which removes negative ions, is in the hydroxide form.

Precipitants. The amount of hardness that can be tolerated in feed water decreases as the pressure of the boiler increase, but in any case calcium and magnesiumare prevented by adding phosphate to the boiler water; this precipitated both calcium and magnesium in a soft dispersed form. The precipitate formed by calciumand orthophosphate is usually represented as the normal phosphate. $Ca_3(PO_4)_2$. Attempts to precipitate this salt in the laboratory, however invariably produce hydroxyapatite, the formula of which can be written in various ways including $Ca_{10}(PO_4)_6(OH)_2$, $3Ca_3(PO_4)_2 \cdot Ca(OH)_2$, and $Ca_5(PO_4)_3OH$. A consideration of the solubility products $[Ca^{2+}][CO_3^{2+}]=4.8\times10^{-9}$, $[Ca^{2+}]^3[PO_4]^2=1.3\times10^{-12}$, and $[Ca^{2+}]^2[PO_4][OH^-]=3\times10^{-58}$ indicates that the basic salt forms in boiler water. Magnesium forms similar salts such as than $Mg(OH)_2$.

Magnesium salts are sometimes added to boilers operated at low pressure to precipitate magnesium silicate. This salt separates as a flocculent precipitate that can be removed by blowdown. Also, soda ash, Na_2CO_3, is used in low-pressureboilers fed with water containing 20~75 mg/L of hardness to precipitate $CaCO_3$ and $Mg(OH)_2$.

Words and Expressions

come out of 有……结果
diffraction [di'frækʃən] n. 衍射
polarize ['pəuləraiz] v. 偏振,极化
acmite ['ækmait] n. 锥辉石

analcite　　　[ə'nælsait]　　n. 方沸石
serpentine　　['sə:pəntain]　　adj. 蛇纹石
sodalite　　['səudəlait]　　n. 方钠石
xonotlite　　['zəunət,lait]　　n. 硬硅钙石
hydroxyapatite　　[hai,drɔksi'æpətait]　　n. 含氧酸磷灰石
anhydrite　　[æn'haidrait]　　n. 酸酶
aragonite　　[ə'rægənait]　　n. 散文石
anhydrous　　[æn'haidrəs]　　adj. 无水的
hydrolysis　　[hai'drɔlisis]　　n. 水解
hydroxyl　　[hai'drɔksil]　　n. 氢氧
binder　　['baində]　　n. 黏合
innocuous　　[i'nɔkjuəs]　　adj. 无害(毒的)
zeolite　　['zi:əlait]　　n. 沸石
orthophosphate　　[,ɔ:θəu'fɔsfeit]　　n. 亚磷酸盐

7.10　Air Pollution

　　A great deal of energy is needed to run the factories of modern industrial nations. Automobiles, trains, planes, and buses need energy, too. Nearly all of this energy is produced in the same way—by burning fuels. The burning produces wastes. Some of the wastes get into the air, causing air pollution.

　　Government officials in the United states estimate that 200 000 000 tons of these wastes enter the air each year—1 ton for each person in the country!

　　A curtain of smog often hangs over big cities. It irritates the eyes and chests. The word "smog" is a combination of the words "smoke" and "fog", but "smog" itself is a mixture of many more ingredients. It begins with some of the pollution from burning: carbon monoxide, and oxides of nitrogen and sulfur are among them. Some of the pollutants react with one another to form new irritating substances. Energy is needed for the reactions, and it is supplied by the light of the sun. The resulting mixture is photochemical smog. ("Photo" means light.) It can be deadly.

In London, Tokyo, New York and other cities, a weather condition called a temperature inversion allows smog to hang over the city for several days at a time. Many people become ill, and the death rate among elderly people and people with lung disorders climbs rapidly.

At least half of the pollutants in the air come from the engines of motor vehicles. As they burn fuel, they give off carbon monoxide as a waste. Carbon monoxide is a colorless, odorless gas, and a deadly poison. The amount of carbon monoxide that an engine gives off can be reduced by special devices designed to make the engine burn the fuel more efficiently.

Automobile manufacturers are working on experimental cars run by electricity or other means that will reduce pollution. City governments in various parts of theworld have begun to close certain streets to automobile traffic, hoping to lowerpollution levels. Many city planners believe that cities, or at least their central areas, should be kept free of automobiles.

Motor vehicles are not the only air polluters. Coal and oil, used to heat homes and factories and to generate electricity, contain small amounts of sulfur. When thefuels are burned, sulfur dioxide, a poisonous gas, is produced. It is irritatingto the lungs. Some cities have passed laws that allow coal and oil to be burned only if their sulfur content is low.

Most electricity is generated by steam turbines. About half of the sulfur dioxidein the air comes from burning fuel to make steam. Nuclear power plants do not burn fuel, so there is no air pollution of the ordinary kind. But the radioactive materials in these plants could present a danger in an accident. Also, there is a problem in disposing of the radioactive wastes in a way that will not endanger the environment.

Another type of pollution, called thermal (heat) pollution, is caused by both thefuel-burning and nuclear plants. Both need huge amounts of cold water, which is warmed as it cools the steam. When it is returned to the river, the warm water maystimulate the growth of weeds. It may also kill fish and their eggs, or interferewith their growth.

Physicists are studying new ways of generating electricity that may be less damaging to the environment. In the meantime, many power plants are being modernizedto give off less polluting material. Also, engineers try to design and locate new power plants to do minimum damage to the environment.

Words and Expressions

smog [smɔg] n. 烟雾
irritate ['iriteit] v. 激怒,使急躁,使兴奋
ingredient [in'gri:diənt] n. 成分,组成部分,原料,要素
monoxide [mə'nɔksaid] n. 一氧化物
photochemical [ˌfəutəu'kemikəl] a. 光化学的
inversion [in'və:ʃən] n. 逆温,逆增
lung [lʌŋ] n. 肺
disorder [dis'ɔ:də] n. (身心,机能的)失调,轻病
odo(u)rless ['əudəlis] a. 没有香气(气味)的
poison ['pɔizn] n. 毒,毒物 v. 毒害,毒死
engine ['endʒin] n. 发动机
radioactive [ˌreidiəu'æktiv] a. 放射性的
fuel-burning a. 燃料燃烧的

7.11　Pressure Measurement

Instruments and methods for measuring pressure, temperature, flow and the quality and purity of steam are essential in the operation of a steam generating unit. Serving to assure safe, economical and reliable operation of the equipment, they range from the simplest manual devices to the measuring devices used to actuate thecomplete automatic control of boilers and all associated equipment.

Test instrumentation, often of a portable nature, is employed in the performance testing of equipment to determine flow, pressures and temperatures required to satisfy the user and the equipment supplier that the conditions of design and operation have been met. Requirements for these instruments are summarized in the *ASME Performance Test Codes*. These instruments require skilled technical operators, careful handling, and frequent calibration. They are generally not suitable forlong-term continuous commercial operation.

Commercial instruments are those permanently installed and are expected to give satisfactory accuracy for extended periods. The emphasis is on dependability andrepeatability. This often demands some compromise in absolute accuracy. However, the accuracy of commercial instruments is being improved, and they are being used increasingly for test purposes.

The pressure gage is probably the earliest instrument used in boiler operation. Today more than one hundred years after the first "water-tube-safety boiler", the use of a pressure gage for determining steam drum pressure is still a requirement, even though modern controls and interlocks make overpressuring of a boiler virtually impossible. The Bourdon tube gage(Fig. 7.9)illustrates a type of gage which has been used for many years for pressure indication. Although improvements have been made in construction and accuracy, the basic principle has notchanged.

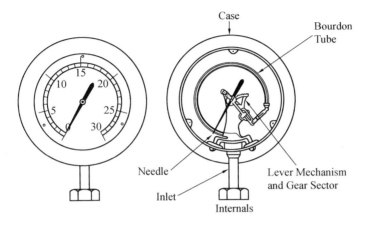

Fig. 7. 9 Bourdon gage

Pressure-measuring instruments take various forms, depending on the magnitude ofthe pressure, the accuracy desired and other conditions.

Manometers, which may contain a wide variety of fluids, depending on the pressure, are capable of high accuracy with careful use. The fluids used vary from those lighter than water for low pressures to mercury for relatively high pressures. Fig. 7. 10 illustrates an inclined manometer for reading small differentials at low pressure. Differential diaphragm gages using a magnetic linkage are now coming into use for low-pressure measurement. Fig. 7. 11 shows a high-pressure mercury manometer. Manometers are considered an accurate means of pressure or pressure-differential measurement and are acceptable for *ASME Performance Test Code* purposes. For greater precision in measuring small pressure differentials, such as theaccurate reading of flow orifice differentials, hook gages or micro-manometers

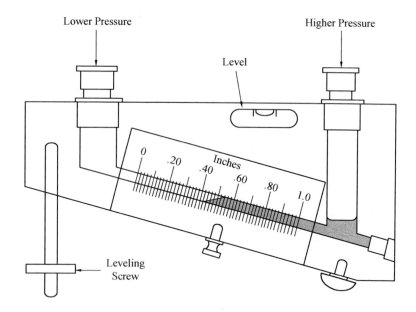

Fig. 7.10 Inclined differential manometer(*Dwyer Instruments,Inc*).

may be used. A hook gage is illustrated in Fig. 7.12.

Bourdon tube gages are available for the measurement of a wide range of static pressures in varying degrees of precision and accuracy. The precision and accuracynecessary are determined by the requirements of the application. Pressure gagesused as operating guides need not be of high precision and normally have scale subdivisions about 1% of full-scale range. For certain test procedures, such as hydrostatic testing of pressure parts and boiler efficiency tests, a higher degree of precision is required. Gages with scale subdivisions of 0.1% of full-scale range are available and should be used for these purposes. For efficiency testing, where temperatures and pressures should be known with high precision for accurate determination of

Environmental Protection, Corrosion and Others 281

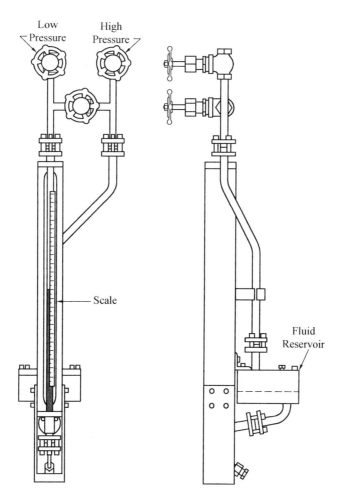

Fig. 7.11 High-pressure mercury manometer(*Meriam Instrument Company*).

enthalpy of steam and water, dead-weight gages are preferable toBourdon gages for pressure measurement.

Diaphragm-type gages are used for the measurement of

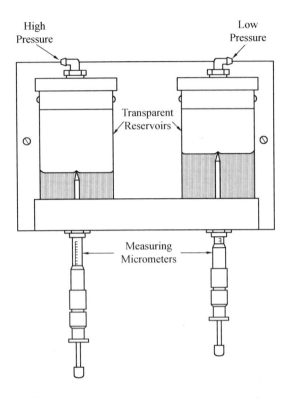

Fig. 7.12　Hook gage(*Dwyer Instruments, Inc.*).

differential pressures. Fig. 7. 13 illustrates a typical slack-diaphragm pressure gage for reading small differentials in inches of water where total pressure does not exceed about one psig. For high static pressures, opposed bellows gages (Fig. 7. 14) read a wide rangeof differential pressures. They are suitable for reading fluid pressure drops through boiler circuits and can be used to measure differentials from 2 to 1 000 psiat pressures up to 6 000 psi.

　　More sophisticated devices for the measurement of pressures and differential pressures are now on the market. These are generally

Environmental Protection, Corrosion and Others 283

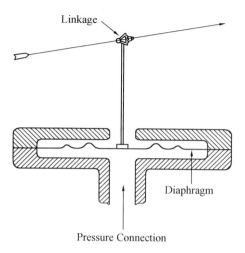

Fig. 7.13   Slack-diaphragm pressure gage.

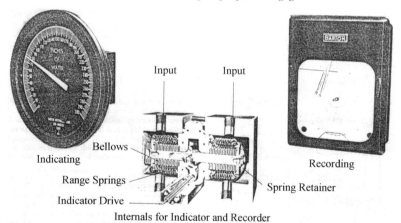

Fig. 7.14   Opposed bellows gage (*ITT BARTON*, a unit of *International Telephone and Telegraph Corporation*).

described as transducers and are based on a variety of principles. Some examples are transducers using a straingage mounted on a diaphragm, or those using a crystal which undergoes a change inelectrical resistance as the element is deformed. Since such elements necessitate elaborate and frequent calibration they are not normally used as basic instruments for operating guides or test equipment. However, with their rapidly increasing reliability and ease of application, pressure transducers are finding wider application.

Pressure readings

In recording and reporting pressure readings, suitable correction to gage readings must be made for water leg, where it exists, and for converting to absolute pressure by the addition of atmospheric pressure, if required. Water leg is merely theadded pressure imposed on the gage not contributed by the actual pressure, but by an effective leg of condensate or water standing above the gage. Fig. 7. 15 illustrates the application of water-leg correction to a pressure-gage reading. Forpractical usage it is sufficient to reset the gage to zero with pressure off the system and the water leg completely filled.

Pressure drops across various types of devices such as orifices, nozzles, or pitottubes provide a means of measuring flow and are described in a later section ofthis chapter.

Instrument connections for pressure measurement

The guiding principles governing the location of connections to the pressure source for measuring devices are in general the same regardless of the magnitude ofthe pressure, the type of measuring device, or the fluid being measured.

Pressure connections, or taps, in piping, flues or ducts, should be located in a position which avoids errors due to impact or eddies, thus assuring that a true static pressure is being measured. The connecting lines should be as short and directas possible and free of leaks. For

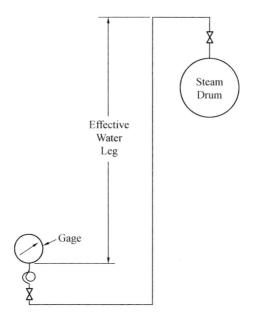

Fig. 7.15 Application of water-leg correction to pressure-gage reading.

differential-pressure readings it is preferable to use a differential-pressure-measuring device rather than to take the difference between the readings on two instruments.

Words and Expressions

measurement ['meʒəmənt] n. 量度,测量
instrument ['instrumənt] n. 仪器,器具
associate [ə'səuʃit] vt & vi. (使)发生联系,(使)联合 n. 伙伴,同事
intertocks [ˌintə'lɔks] n. 联动装置
manometer [mə'nɔmitə] n. 压力计
diaphragm ['daiəfræm] n. 膈,隔膜,光圈
precision [pri'siʒən] n. 精确度,准确(性)
sophisticated [sə'fistikeitid] adj. 精密的,尖端的

7.12 Clean Coal Technologies

Coal is well known to be a dirty fuel, so it is necessary to develop "clean coal" techniques in order to comply with more and more stringent environmental legislation.

The first approach consists in reducing emissions from existing Pulverized Coal (PC) installations by developing depolluting devices that act on combustion in the furnace (primary process) and/or that treat flue gas leaving the furnace (secondary process).

The second approach consists in designing entirely new technologies, all based on fluidized bed combustion, which enables to set coal combustion conditions favorable to simultaneous NO_x and SO_x depollution in the furnace. In addition, coal gasification is considered.

So, the Clean Coal Technologies to be considered in this study are the following:

1. Primary and Secondary Depolluting Systems for Existing Units;
2. Pulverized Coal with Flue Gas Treatment (PC+FGT);
3. Atmospheric Circulating Fluidized Bed Combustion (ACFBC);
4. Pressurized Bubbling Fluidized Bed Combustion (PBFBC);
5. Pressurized Circulating Fluidized Bed Combustion (PCFBC);
6. Integrated Gasification Combined Cycle (IGCC);
7. Hybrid Cycle Applied to Circulating Fluidized Beds (HC: HC-ACFBC and HC-PCFBC).

Clean Coal, Technologies for Existing Units

· Primary Processes

Denitrification Devices. Burners are more and more designed to limit nitrogen oxide formation during combustion. These burners, known as "low-NO_x", rely on the concept of air injection staging and of fuel distribution modification. The principle is to avoid too high flame temperatures and to reduce oxygen excess in the furnace, which favors nitrogen oxide formation. Another primary process consists in staging the combustion air in the furnace and is known as Over Fire Air (OFA). An additional process consists in staging the fuel injection into the furnace and is known as "reburning".

Desulphurization Devices. The primary desulphurization processes consist in injecting lime or limestone as a fine powder into the furnace in order to absorb the generated sulphur dioxide. If necessary, slaked lime and water are injected into the flue gas in order to improve the desulphurization efficiency. These processes can be used because of their low cost even if their efficiency is moderate: about 40% to 70%.

· Secondary Processes

Denitrification Devices. The reduction of NO_x emissions can be also achieved by means of catalytic or non-catalytic chemical processes. The most used secondary process (95% of installed systems) is the Selective Catalytic Reduction. Gaseous ammonia is mixed with combustion gas at the boiler outlet before the air-heater. The mixture gets then across a reactor containing catalysts to give N_2 and water. The temperature range of operation is 350 ~ 430 ℃.

Desulphurization Devices. For the recent installations, the SO_2 emissions are generally reduced by wet limestone/gypsum Flue Gas Desulphurization (FGD) systems. Sulphur dioxide is removed from combustion gas in the form of gypsum ($CaSO_4$), essentially through a wet process using a solution of carbonate, sulphite and sulphate of calcium in-suspension.

Atmospheric Circulating Fluidized Bed Combustion

The principle of Atmospheric Circulating Fluidized Bed Combustion (ACFBC) power plant consists in producing steam at high temperature and pressure from the heat generated by the complete coal combustion in a fluidized bed furnace. Pressure in the furnace is about atmospheric pressure and fluidizing velocity is high. Solid particles leaving therefore the furnace are collected and recirculated into the furnace. This recirculating of solid matters in the furnace enables an efficient coal combustion kept at about 850 ℃ (in order to favour sulphur dioxide retention by limestone and to minimize nitrogen oxide formation). Electricity is delivered by an alternator associated with a steam turbine where the steam generated by the process is expanded.

Pressurized Bubbling Fluidized Bed Combustion

In a Pressurized Bubbling Fluidized Bed Combustion (PBFBC) power plant, the boiler is operating under pressure; between 1.0×10^6 Pa and 1.6×10^6 Pa, and thebed fluidizing velocity is low. So the fluidized bed presents a free solid surface distinct from the gaseous phase above. At this fluidizing velocity, gas bubbles are getting through the bed to its surface, and it is called as "Bubbling Bed". Electricity is delivered by two generators, the first one associated with a steam turbine where the steam generated by the process is expanded, the secondone with a gas turbine where flue gas is expanded. The PBFBC technology involves a combined cycle.

Pressurized Circulating Fluidized Bed Combustion

In a Pressurized Circulating Fluidized Bed Combustion (PCFBC) power plant, the boiler is operating under pressure, between 1.0×10^6 Pa, and 1.6×10^6 Pa, and the bed fluidizing velocity is high, similar to ACFBC. The PCFBC properties due to the Circulating Fluidized Bed are the same as those of ACFBC. The only difference is that the PCFBC furnace operates under pressure.

Integrated Gasification in a Combined Cycle

In IGCC, gas obtained from coal gasification is cleaned up in order to eliminatein particular dust and sulphur compounds, prior to being burnt, generally in a gas turbine, to generate electricity. A heat recovery boiler allows to recover part of the sensible heat of flue gas by producing steam. This steam is also used to drive a steam turbine to generate electricity also.

The new techniques of coal or oil residue gasification offer today the possibility to generate electricity in combined cycle with high efficiency. The IGCC technology presents many variants. They can be notably distinguished not only by thegasified type (fixed bed, fluidized bed), but also by the oxidizer used (air oroxygen) and by the gas cleaning system.

Words and Expressions

Clean Coal Technology(CCT)　洁净煤技术
emission　[i'miʃən]　*n.* 发出,排出物
Pulverized Coal(PC)　煤粉
flue gas　烟道内烟气
fluidized bed combustion　流化床燃烧
coal gasification　煤气化
Circulating Fluidized Bed(CFB)　循环流化床
Bubbling Fluidized Bed(BFB)　鼓泡流化床
Integrated Gasification Combined Cycle(IGCC)　整体煤气化(蒸汽一燃气)联合循环
Hybrid cycle　混合循环
denitrification device　除氮装置
burner　['bəːnə]　*n.* 燃烧器
air injection staging　空气分段送入
nitrogen oxide　氮氧化物
Over Fire Air(OFA)　过燃风
desulphurization devices　除硫装置
lime　[laim]　*n.* 石灰

limestone ['laimstəun] n. 石灰石
sulphur dioxide 二氧化硫
slaked lime 熟石灰
Selective Catalytic Reduction(SCR) 选择性催化剂脱氮装置
gaseous ammonia 氨气
catalyst ['kætəlist] n. 催化剂
carbonate ['kaːbəneit] vt. 碳酸盐
sulphite ['sʌlfait] n. 亚硫酸盐
sulphate ['sʌlfeit] n. 硫酸盐
calcium ['kælsiəm] n. 钙
suspension [səs'penʃən] n. 悬浮
alternator ['ɔːltə(ː)neitə] n. 交流发电机
deliver [di'livə] vt. 释放,发出
sensible heat 显热
gasifier ['gæsifaiə] n. 气化床
oxidizer ['ɔksidaizə(r)] n. 氧化剂

参考译文

流体黏度(1.1)

在流体的所有特性中，黏度是我们研究流体流动时所需要考虑的最主要内容。黏度的本质、特征及绝对黏度和运动黏度的量纲与转换因子将在本节中被讨论。黏度是流体能够抵抗剪切力所依靠的特征，牛顿黏滞定律表明，对于给定的角变形，流体所受到的切应力与其黏度成正比。糖浆和焦油是高黏性液体，而水和空气的黏度却很小。

气体的黏度随着温度的升高而增加，但液体的黏度却随着温度的升高而减小，因此温度的变化可以通过测定黏度而获知。流体抵抗剪切力依靠的是它的内聚力和分子动量的转移速率。对于液体来说，其分子间距远小于气体，故有着比气体更大的内聚力。

在液体中，由于内聚力随温度升高而下降，所以内聚力对于其黏性占有支配作用；对于气体，它的内聚力很小，其绝大部分抵抗切应力的能力是由分子动量的转移所体现。

下面以一个粗略的例子来说明动量转移所引起的表观切应力，考虑两个理想载有海绵的小车在两平行轨道上行驶，如图 1.1 所示。假设每个小车上有水箱和水泵，并且喷嘴与车轨成直角。首先让 A 车固定，让 B 车向右运动，水从喷嘴中射出击打 A 车并被海绵吸收。A 车将因为吸收了平行于轨道方向的动量而开始运动，从而引发 A 与 B 之间的表观切应力。A 先以相同的速率将水喷回 B，它的作用结果将使 B 慢下来并获得与反向同等大小的表观切应力。当 A 和 B 都固定或以相同速度运动时，喷水将不会产生表观切应力在任何一个小车上。

在流体中，存在着分子间穿越假想层的现象。当一个层相对相邻层运动时，分子动量将从一层转移到另外一层，因此产生了表观切应力，从而导致其对层间相对运动的抵抗，使得流体相邻层之间的速度趋向于相等，这在某种程度上类似于图 1.1。衡量层相对于相邻层之间运动的量就是 du/dy。

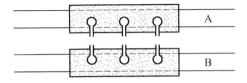

图 1.1　说明动量转移的例子

气体中分子的热运动所引起的表观切应力远大于内聚力的作用,并且由于分子的热运动剧烈程度随温度升高而增加,所以气体的黏度也随之增加。

常压下黏度仅随温度变化,而与压强无关。高压强下,气体与流体的黏度随压强的变化不确定。

尽管黏度依旧存在,但因为整个流体内部 du/dy 处处为零,所以流体静止或者相邻层之间无相对运动而流动时,将不出现表观切应力。由于静止液体只有法向应力和压力存在,即流体的任何一部分都只受重力和垂直面的力,表观切应力并不出现在静止的流体中,因此在研究流体静力学的时候,将不考虑表观切应力,这将大大简化流体静力学的研究。

黏度的量纲由牛顿黏滞定律所决定,解出黏度 μ,并引入量纲 F、L、T,分别表示力、长度和时间,所以表明 μ 的量纲是 $FL^{-2}T$。由于力的量纲是由牛顿第二定律得到的,$F = M \cdot LT^{-2}$,所以黏度的量纲可以表示为 $ML^{-1}T^{-1}$。

黏度的 SI 单位为牛顿秒/平方米或者牛顿/(米・秒),没有命名。黏度的美制单位(也是没有专门命名的)是磅秒/平方英尺或者斯勒格/(英寸・秒)(它们是一样的)。常用的黏度单位是厘米-克-秒单位制,称为泊,即 1 达因・秒/平方厘米或者 1 克/(厘米・秒)。因此,SI 单位比泊单位大 10 倍。

通常所提到的黏度 μ 通常是指绝对黏度或者动力黏度(同一概念的不同叫法),以避免与运动黏度 v(绝对黏度与质量密度的比值)混淆。

$$v = \frac{\mu}{\rho} \tag{1.1}$$

动力黏度在应用中会常常出现,例如流动流体中的无量纲雷诺数,VL/v,(其中 V 表示流体主体的速度,L 表示流体主体的长度尺寸)。v 的量纲是 L^2T^{-1},动力黏度的 SI 单位是 1 m^2/s,其美制单位是 1 ft^2/s。

在 SI 单位制中,要从 v 转换至 μ,需要用 v 除以 ρ,密度以千克/立方米为单位。在美制单位中,μ 的值可以以 ν 乘以质量密度来获得,单位是斯勒格/立方英尺。从斯(其单位为 cm^2/s)到泊的转换,就要乘以质量密度,以克/立方厘米为单位,数值上等于比重。

黏度几乎完全与压强无关而只与温度有关,液体及在给定压强下气体的动力黏度只是温度的函数。

流体的连续性假设、密度和比体积(1.2)

很明显,流体及所有物质的内部分子之间都有空隙。在流体力学中,宏观流体是由大量分子组成,其物理量(如压力、速度和密度)的表示是流体分子行动的统计平均和大多数流体分子的行为。1753 年,连续介质首次由欧拉在宏观流体模型中提出,这是流体真正地被认为是没有间隙的连续介质,被称为连续性流体的流动或连续性流体的基本假设。

作为用来处理与流体流动有关的数学和分析基础,有必要将流体的真实分子结构用假设的连续介质来代替,称为连续性假设。例如,在空间中一点的速度对于分子结构(的模型)来说是模糊不清的,除非有一分子精确占据该点,否则速度总是为零,但这并不意味着相邻点的速度为零。如果我们将一点的速度考虑为该点周围空间内所有分子的平均速度或者质量速度,将可避免这一难以想象的局面。假定这一周围球体空间的半径值远大于分子平均间距,如果每立方厘米中有 n 个分子,那么分子平均间距为 $n^{-1/3}$ 厘米。分子理论应用于计算流体性质(例如黏性)时必须联系分子运动,然而连续性方程用于计算的结果可以作为分子理论的特殊情况来计算。

在诸如海平面上 50 英里气压处的稀薄气体,流体在阀体或管道中流动时,其分子运动自由程或者气体特征长度是用来判断流动方式的依据,低速运动时的流动方式称为气体动力学模式;另外一种方式称为层流,即大量分子高速运动称为自由分子流。本节只研究气体动力学方式的运动。

质量密度、比容、黏度和加速度都是在大量连续性的流体中成立的假定(它们是一常量)。

流体的密度 ρ 定义为其单位体积的质量,即

$$\rho = \frac{m}{V} \tag{1.2}$$

为定义流体在某一点的密度,用小块体积 ΔV(包围着该点)的流体的质

量 Δm 除以体积，其极限值变成 ε^3，然而 ε 相比于分子间距里仍然大得多。例如，水在标准大气压和 4 ℃（39.2 ℉）时，$\rho=1.94$（slug·s）/ft^3，或者 1 000 kg/m^3。

比体积 v_s 是（质量）密度 ρ 的倒数，即流体单位质量所占的体积，因此

$$v_s = \frac{1}{\rho} \tag{1.3}$$

热力学的基本概念(2.1)

热力学的应用大部分都要求对系统及它的环境定义。热力系统定义为空间的某一区域或某一封闭面包围的物质质量，环境包括系统外面的一切物体，系统和环境由系统分界面分隔。这些分界面可以是运动的或固定不变的，可以是真实的也可以是假想的。

两个主要概念在任何热力系统中都适用，即能量和熵。熵计量某一给定系统分子的无序（程度），系统越混乱，它的熵就越大。相反，有序或不混乱的结构是一个低熵系统。

能量是产生某一效果的能力，并且可以分成储存能和瞬时能两类。储存型能量包括：

热（内）能 u ——由于分子运动和/或分子之间的作用力，系统所具有的能量。

势能 $P.E.$ ——由于分子间存在的吸引力或系统的高度，系统所具有的能量

$$P.E. = mgz \tag{2.1}$$

式中 m ——质量；

g ——当地重力加速度；

z ——相对于水平参考面的高度。

动能 $K.E.$ ——由于分子速度，系统所具有的能量

$$K.E. = mv^2/2 \tag{2.2}$$

式中 m ——质量；

v ——穿过系统边界的流体速度。

化学能 E_c ——由于组成分子的原子的排列，系统所具有的能量。

核（原子）能 E_a ——由于使质子和中子构成原子核的内聚力作用，系统

所具有的能量。

瞬时能包括：

热能 Q ——系统由于温度不同,穿过边界传递的能量总是朝着温度降低的方向。

功量——系统由于压力(或任何种类的力)不同,穿过边界传递的能量,它总是朝着压力降低的方向;如果该系统产生的总的效果能归纳成重物的升高,那么只有功量穿过边界。机械功或轴功 W,是由机械如透平、空气压缩机或内燃机传递或吸收的能量。

流动功是进入或跨越系统边界的能量,这是由于在系统外某处的泵送过程发生流体进入该系统而引起的。它作为系统外边界面处的流体为迫使或推动相邻流体进入系统而作的功更容易理解。当流体离开系统时也会产生流动功。

$$流动功(每单位质量) = pV \qquad (2.3)$$

式中 p——压力;

V——比热容或单位质量排开的体积。

系统的参数是任何可观察到的系统特性。系统的状态通过列出它的参数来确定。最常见的热力学参数是:温度(T)、压力(p)、比热容(V)或密度(ρ)。另外,热力学参数还包括熵、储存能和焓。

热力学参数常常结合起来形成新的参数。焓(h)(参数结合得出的结果)定义为

$$h = u + pV \qquad (2.4)$$

式中 u——内能;

p——压力;

V——比热容。

给定状态的每一参数只有一个确定值,并且任一参数在给定状态下总保持同一值,不管物质是怎样到达这一状态的。

过程即状态的变化,定义为系统参数的任何变化。过程可以通过指定初、终平衡态,路径(如果是可辨认的)及过程中穿过系统边界发生的相互作用来描述。循环是一个过程,或更经常地是指一系列过程,在这些过程中系统的初、终态相同。因而,在循环结束时,所有参数都有与它们在初态时相同的数值。

纯物质具有均匀不变的化学成分。它能以多相存在,但所在的相中化学

成分是相同的。

如果物质以饱和温度下的气态存在,则称为饱和蒸汽(有时用干饱和蒸汽这个术语来强调其干度为100%)。当蒸汽温度比其饱和温度高时,为过热蒸汽,过热蒸汽的压力和温度是独立参数,因为当压力保持不变时其温度可以增加。气体是高度过热的蒸汽。

导 热(2.4)

导热可以认为是通过物质分子间逐渐进行的能量交换而在物体(或物体联合体)内从高温区到低温区传递热量。在导热过程中,没有产生分子的具体的位移。然而,就金属来说,自由电子的运动大大有助于导热。

导热的基本定律归功于傅里叶。该定律可表示如下:考虑稳态的单向热流通过一固体,如图2.2(见原文)所示,取一横截面积为 A 的固体的厚片,该厚片垂直于热流路径。设厚片的厚度为 dx,厚片两端间的温差为 dt。傅里叶从试验中得出了如下关系

$$Q = -kA \frac{dt}{dx} \qquad (2.5)$$

式中　Q——单位时间的热流量;

　　　k——比例系数,称为导热系数;

　　　dt/dx——热流方向上温度随距离的变化率。

在国际单位制中,导热系数表示为

$$W/m^2 \div K/m = W/(m \cdot K)$$

大量的试验研究已得出了许多物质的导热系数值和温度对这些导热系数的影响。注意,任何金属的导热系数与任何气体的导热系数相比都是非常高的。已发表的金属导热系数值仅对指定纯度的金属才是正确的。尤其对那些具有最高导热系数值的金属,掺入少量其他金属就会引起导热系数的明显变化。

最佳的绝热固体应将其绝热性能归功于材料小孔内所含的空气或其他气体。这些小孔使热量经过长而弯曲的路径流经固体。另外,固体材料可得到的横截面积比投影面积小得多。实验证据表明,在使物质具有绝热值(性能)方面,许多单个小气孔要比有相同总体积的连接起来的一串气孔有效得多。任何给定的绝热材料,其导热系数都可能有很大的变化,因为导热系数

取决于材料的密度、体积、小气孔的数量和吸湿量。

通过实验确定固体的导热系数,有几种可以接受的方法。只要适当注意,对成分已知的给定固体就可以得到相当准确的导热系数值。然而,要确定气体、蒸气或液体的导热系数值却要困难得多,因为要从中去掉通过对流所传递的热量(与导热同时发生)几乎是不可能的,况且还没有包括准确测量其他因素的困难。因为这些原因,已发表的流体导热系数值都有大约10%~25%的误差。图 2.3(见原文)表示了在简单墙体中的热传导。假设墙体的宽度和高度要比墙体的厚度大得多,从而可以认为热流是单向的。墙体的一面维持均匀温度 t_1,另一面保持在温度 t_2。通过墙体的热量可以通过方程(2.5)积分得到。

考察附录中给出的各种物质的导热系数表明,对许多物质,其导热系数在相当大的温度范围内可以认为是恒定值。而且,对大多数物质,在信息可以得到的温度范围内,其导热系数是温度的线性函数。这样可以用导热系数的算术平均值 k_m 作为真实的导热系数。对简单墙体,方程(2.5)可积分如下

$$Q = \frac{k_m A}{x}(t_1 - t_2) \qquad (2.6)$$

根据方程(2.6),热流速率正比于热流面积、引起热流的温差和 k_m/x 项。该项称为导热率。

当导热系数不随温度线性变化时,平均导热系数 k_m 就不容易确定。在这种情况下,就需要在方程(2.5)中把导热系数表示为温度的函数,然后进行积分。

液体燃料和固体燃料的燃烧(3.5)

液体燃料(石油、重油)燃烧时的点火温度,特别是燃烧温度,要高于包含在液体燃料成分内的各单独组成的沸腾温度,所以首先靠加热使燃料表面进行蒸发,而后燃料蒸气同空气混合,加热到着火温度并燃烧,在离开液体表面一定距离处(0.5~1 mm 或更大)才形成火焰。

图 3.2(见原文)示出一滴液体燃料在不流动空气中燃烧时环绕着液滴形成向周围介质扩散的蒸气云。迎面有空气中氧的扩散,结果在离开液滴 r_{st} 处,可燃气体和氧之间达到了化学反应的配比。环绕液滴形成的球形燃料蒸

气的燃烧前沿就在这里,$r_{st}=(4\sim10)r_d$(这里的 r_d 是液滴直径),r_{st} 和液滴尺寸与燃烧区的关系极大,在 $r<r_{st}$ 的区域内,主要是燃料蒸汽,而它的浓度随着与液体表面的距离增加而减小。在 $r>r_{st}$ 区域内,含有向燃烧区扩散的氧与燃烧产物形成的混合物。在反应区,燃烧温度达到最高值,然后它的两侧降低,而且越靠近液滴,温度降低得越剧烈,这是由于消耗热量来加热燃料蒸气的缘故。

因此,液体燃烧中液滴燃烧的速度取决于液滴从表面蒸发的速度、在燃烧区里化学反应的速度以及氧气向燃烧区扩散的速度。正如前面所述,在气态介质中的反应速度是很高的且不会限制总的燃烧速度。通过球形表面扩散的氧气量与其直径的平方成正比,所以燃烧区离开液滴表面不远处,氧气的供给量就显著增加(在氧气不足的情况下),因此,液体燃料的燃烧速度主要决定于它的蒸发情况。为了提高液体燃料的燃烧速度,必须保证在燃料燃烧前把它喷得很细,以增加其总的蒸发表面积。此外,随着液滴尺寸的减少,它从单位表面积蒸发的强度增加。悬浮在空气中的液体燃料油滴的特点是雷诺数很小,$Re<4$,在这种情况下,通过球形表面的热流仅决定于通过边界层的导热系数 λ,而边界层的厚度又远大于液滴的直径,此时,放热系数 α 可用 Sokolsky 公式来表示

$$Nu = \alpha d/\lambda = 2 \qquad (3.5)$$

因此,
$$\alpha = 2\lambda/d = \lambda/r \qquad (3.6)$$

式中的 Nu 为努谢尔特数。

由式(3.6)可知,液滴同周围介质的热交换随着它的尺寸减少而增加,同时,液滴质量也在减少。结果是,液滴蒸发的时间正比于它的初始直径的平方。

固体燃料的燃烧 当煤粉在炉膛中与空气混合后,首先要经过燃烧预备阶段(图3.3,I,见原文),这个过程包括剩余水分的蒸发和挥发分的分离。煤粉被加热到一定温度(400~600℃)时,挥发分在十分之几秒的时间内发生了巨大变化,然后挥发分被点着,因此,环绕煤粉粒处的温度迅速提高,煤粉加热变快。挥发分的强烈燃烧持续0.2~0.5 s,许多煤种(如褐煤、油页岩、泥煤)的挥发分燃烧后产生的热量足以将煤粉加热到着火点。当某些煤种所含挥发分较低时,煤粉必须通过外部因素另外加热,最后阶段是煤粉在800~1 000℃的温度下燃烧,这是一个不同种类组成的过程。它的反应速度决定于反应物表面氧的供给。煤粉燃烧的时间占总时间的大部分(1/2~1/

3),总时间约为 1~2.5 s,它决定于煤种和颗粒的大小。

碳和氧的反应机理如下:氧从烟气中被吸收到煤粉表面,和碳发生化学反应生成复杂的碳-氧化合物 C_xO_y,然后它又分解成 CO 和 CO_2,在 1 200℃ 左右的反应可表示为

$$4C+3O_2 = 2CO+2CO_2 \tag{3.7}$$

实验表明,主要产物的比率,即 CO/CO_2,随着煤粉温度的提高而迅速变大。例如,1 700℃ 左右时反应可表示为

$$3C+2O_2 = 2CO+CO_2 \tag{3.8}$$

这里 CO/CO_2 的比率为 2。

主要的反应产物不断地从煤粉表面向周围移动,在这个过程中,一氧化碳遇到反向扩散的氧,并与之反应生成二氧化碳,导致在近煤粉表面处供给氧的浓度大减,而 CO_2 的浓度提高。在较高的燃烧温度下,一氧化碳可能消耗所有的供给氧,结果,氧气不能到达煤粉表面(图 3.4(b),见原文)。在这种情况下,吸热反应将在煤粉表面发生,即 CO_2 将转变成 CO。

因此,碳粒表面的不同燃烧可以包括 4 个接连的反应,其中两个是主要的

$$C+O_2 = CO_2+q_1$$
$$2C+O_2 = 2CO+2q_2$$

另外两个反应是次要的

$$2CO+O_2 = 2CO_2+2q_3$$
$$C+CO_2 = CO-q_4$$

这里的 q 是反应的热,单位为 MJ/mol。

第一个反应的热效应 $q_1=q_2+q_3$,$q_4=0.57q_3$。后面的等式表示即使吸热反应发生时,燃烧反应的温度仍能保持很高,这是由于容积中的反应放出更多的能量。

分析这些反应可知,碳表面的燃烧以部分气化的形式发生(形成的 CO 和容积中后期燃烧的气体),这个过程促进了碳粒的燃尽。

核燃料(3.6)

除了太阳能以外,传统的主要热能源是矿物燃料(例如木柴、煤、油和

气)的燃烧。第二次世界大战期间,当美国曼哈顿工程(Manhatten Project)研制出原子弹时,惹人注目地出现了一种新能源,一般把它叫做"原子"能。从那以后,军舰推进和民用动力计划都成功地将原子核裂变作为一种实用的热能源加以利用。这种能源,严格地说来应该叫做"核"能,是通过裂变使原子核里的某些物质转换成能量的,可根据爱因斯坦的质能方程进行计算

$$E = mc^2 \quad (3.9)$$

式中　E——能量;
　　　m——质量;
　　　c——光速。

用于生产蒸汽时,核能的各种实际应用都是利用裂变过程。一个重原子核分裂成两大块碎片,每块碎片都是一个轻原子核。分裂时,还释放出大量的能量。此外,还释放中子,这些中子可用于使别的原子裂变,从而形成"链式反应"。对链式反应加以控制,使它能保持连续不断地产生热能。

铀

铀是核动力工业的基本原料。它是稍带放射性的重化学元素,原子序数92,它是自然界里出现的非痕量的最重的元素。

在化学方面,铀是反应性强的金属,主要有 3 个化学价:+3,+4 和+6。它有 3 个晶相,在 2 070 ℉时熔化。在 α 相中,它比较有延展性,并可用标准的金属加工技术制造。因为铀的小颗粒或碎片极易自燃,所以在加工和储存碎片时要求有特别的预防措施,例如使用冷却剂或惰性气体。

天然铀是三种同位素的混合物:铀$_{234}$(0.01%),铀$_{235}$(0.71%)和铀$_{238}$(99.28%)。铀$_{234}$量小,意义不大。铀$_{235}$是可裂变同位素,铀$_{238}$一般叫作增殖同位素。

铀的这三种天然同位素都具有放射性,放出 α 粒子。然而,它们的半衰期足够长,因此在处理天然铀时,需采取的预防措施很少。铀是化学毒物,人不得摄入。在处理铀的区域,空气中的铀含量必须保持在规定的容许值以下。

铀$_{235}$裂变是它的原子核吸收了中子的结果。1 g 铀$_{235}$裂变时,释放的热量大约相当于 1 兆瓦日(24 000 kW·h 或 82 000 000 Btu)。当 1 短吨铀$_{235}$裂变时,释放的热量相当于 220 亿 kW·h 或 750 000 亿 Btu,这相当于储藏在大约 300 万 t 煤里的热量。

各种能级的中子都能使铀$_{235}$裂变,并能维持链式反应。铀$_{235}$是一种可裂变物质,意即可被"慢"(低能量或热)中子裂变。

铀$_{238}$不能维持链式核反应,但高能中子可使其裂变到一定程度。当暴露给中子时(就像在核反应堆里那样),铀$_{238}$原子核在俘获中子以后,最终将转换成钚$_{239}$——一种新元素的可裂变同位素。钚$_{239}$能维持链式反应,裂变时,每克钚$_{239}$释放的热量约等于每克铀$_{235}$裂变时释放的热量。由于具有这种能够嬗变成裂变物质的能力,因此铀$_{238}$叫增殖物质。

铀因其两种主要的同位素铀$_{235}$和铀$_{238}$而成为核动力工业的基本原料。前者是在自然界发现的唯一的一种大量存在的裂变物质;后者是能产生可裂变钚的增殖物质。因为铀$_{238}$的储量是铀$_{235}$的 140 倍,因此作为能源来说,它的最终潜力是很大的。

另一种可转换元素钍,可用来生产动力,但需要用铀来将钍转换成裂变物质。

铀的利用

产生蒸汽用的矿物燃料需要连续不断地给料才能很好地燃烧。与矿物燃料不同,核燃料的使用是成批地进行的。它以名叫"燃料组件"的预制组件形式装入原子炉(或称反应堆)。这些燃料棒组件由装在合金包壳管里的氧化铀芯块组成。"包壳"一词并不是说一种金属覆盖于另一种金属之外,而是简单地指核燃料外罩,它用于防止腐蚀和防止裂变产物释放到冷却剂中去。对于使用这种燃料组件的大型动力堆,它的每个燃料组件可长达 14 ft 或更长一些,横截面可达 8 in^2 或更大。在压水反应堆里,燃料棒必须设计成能承受高达 2 500 psi 的差压,那是在燃料组件使用初期由包壳管外的系统压力引起的。燃料管还必须承受燃料寿命期间累积的气体裂变产物所造成的内部压力。

下面是对产生蒸汽时使用的燃料(无论是核燃料或矿物燃料)的基本要求:

1. 控制反应堆或锅炉里的释热率;
2. 将燃料产生的热量传到水中去用以产生蒸汽;
3. 运行人员的防护,控制反应副产品;
4. 经济地使用燃料的设计。

液态副产品燃料(3.7)

沥青和焦油

石油和煤炭干馏出来的液体和半液体残余物质叫做沥青和焦油。这些残余物质的大部分都适合用作锅炉燃料。有些残余物质如同煤油一样便于处理和容易燃烧,而其它一些残余物质则会带来许多麻烦。为了证实某些沥青和焦油是否适合作为一给定设备的燃料,下列各项内容即是重要的:

水分 如果燃料中含有水分,就必须进行良好的乳化,防止燃料进入燃烧器时成为未蒸发的液滴。假如供给燃烧器的连续进料流程呈现瞬间中断,火焰即会熄灭。在重新供给燃料的同时,如果重新点燃燃烧器的时间延迟,炉膛就有可能发生爆炸。因此,如果未被蒸发的水滴将火焰瞬间熄灭的话,那末燃料供应中未被蒸发的水滴将是一场灾难。含水量高达35%的沥青和焦油亦可以在设计合适的设备中燃烧。

闪点和着火点 闪点的定义是,在一给定的条件下,液体燃料被充分地蒸发到一经点火就闪现瞬间火焰的最低温度。着火点的定义是,在给定的条件下,液体燃料被充分蒸发到一经点火就能连续燃烧的最低温度。许多液体燃料是由两种或两种以上不同液体组成的混合物。其中也许一种成分的闪点和着火点低,而另一种成分的闪点和着火点高。这样,低闪点的组成成分在燃烧器处燃烧掉了,而高闪点和高着火点的成分则在此燃烧,一般是有光亮的火焰,火焰呈暗黄色。实际上,如果燃烧器的紊流太小,或者燃烧产物从强燃烧区经过时因移动太快而熄灭,那末燃烧就会不完全,造成高的未燃尽可燃物质的损失。所以,正像闪点温度能用以确定燃料的贮存中是否包含着可能的危险一样,着火点则确定其是否适合在锅炉中燃烧。着火点高达600 °F的燃料也可以在设计正确的锅炉中燃烧。

黏度 实际上,所有的沥青和焦油都可以按燃烧油的同样方法进行燃烧。沥青和焦油在燃烧器内的雾化器中变成雾状分散物,然后蒸发、燃烧。对于大部分雾化器来说,为了能产生细微的颗粒,燃烧油的黏度必须正确,不得超过180赛波特通用秒数(SUS),尽管燃烧器在炉膛内的布置合适,也可以使用黏度高达1 000赛波特通用秒数(SUS)的燃料。

悬浮物质 这些燃料中都含有悬浮物质。如果含有悬浮物质的燃料进入燃烧器,就会产生下列情况:

1. 雾化器会出现不正常的沾污,需要经常地清洗。
2. 燃烧器部件的磨损率过大。
3. 整个设备内会出现未燃碳的沉淀,或者烟囱中会有有害物质排出。

因此,这种燃料在送入燃烧器以前应用滤网过滤。

相容性 当一些燃料如果同一般性燃料油接触时,就会结合成硬块状物质。如果这种情况发生在管道里或容器内就会造成麻烦。这种燃料混合物不能从容器内泵出,而且如果管道堵塞,则经常需要将设备完全解体进行清洗,燃烧器的运行也会是不稳定和有问题的。因此,大量的沥青和焦油与燃料油混合之前,必须先在实验室进行这种燃料在贮存温度下和泵送温度下的实验,以确定这两种燃料的相容性。

空气调节(4.1)

空气调节

空气调节(简称空调)是把室外空气与被调节空间结合起来,同时进行空气的调节和分配的过程。该过程能在同一时间内控制和维持所需空间的温度、湿度、空气流动、空气洁净度、声级和压差这些参数在预定的范围内,并且能够满足居住者的健康和舒适要求,满足产品加工要求,或两方面兼而有之。

首字母缩写 HVAC & R 代表加热、通风、空调和制冷过程。它相当于把这些过程通过函数组合成一个名词,即空气调节。

空调系统

空调或空调系统包括安排在各种过程中的组件和设备,这些过程包括连续加热和冷却过程、加湿或除湿过程、清洁和净化过程、减弱不良设备噪声的过程、运输处理过的室外空气和空气与被调节空间再循环的过程、控制和维护室内或封闭的环境的优化能源利用的过程。

建筑空调系统的类型可以分为以下几类:

①机构建筑,如医院和疗养院;
②商业建筑,如办公室、商店和购物中心;
③住宅建筑,包括独栋和多栋三层或更少层数的低层建筑;
④制造业建筑,如生产和储存产品的建筑。

空调系统的类型

在机构、商业和住宅建筑中,空调系统主要给居住者提供健康、舒适的环境,它们通常被称为舒适性空调系统。在制造业建筑中,空调系统创造产品加工的条件,给工人提供健康、舒适的环境,或满足工艺要求,它们被称为工艺性空调系统。

根据它们的大小、结构和操作特点,空调系统可分为下面几种。

● 个人空间系统或个人系统。一个单独的空调系统通常采用单个的、独立的、封装的空间空气调节器(安装在一个窗口或通过墙)或采用为一个单独的房间服务的独立的室内和室外单元。"独立的、封装的"是指工厂把组件组装在一个成套的设备中,准备好随时使用。

● 空间调节系统或空间系统。这些系统包括在以上被调节的空间中体现的空调设备的冷却、加热和过滤过程。室外空气由一个单独的室外通风系统提供。

● 统一封装的系统或封装系统。这些系统安装一个自包含、组装、封装的单位或两个分割单元:一个室内空气处理器(通常有一个风管系统)与一个包含制冷压缩机和冷凝器的户外压缩冷凝机组。在封装系统中,空气主要由一个被称为 DX 线圈的制冷剂直接蒸发冷却线圈冷却,用气体炉、电加热或热泵效应加热,热泵与制冷循环相反。

● 中央加热冷却循环系统或中央系统。在一个空气处理单元中,中央系统用通过中央工厂冷却和加热的、空气处理过的冷水或热水。从能量交换角度来讲,水的热容大约是空气的 3 400 倍。中央系统是通过组装和安装建立的组合系统。

封装系统是空气系统、制冷系统、供暖系统和控制系统几部分组合起来的。中央系统和空间调节系统包括以下几个方面。

● 空气系统。空气系统也被称为空气处理系统或空调的空气部分或空调系统,其功能是调节和分配空气,并根据需求控制室内环境。空气系统的主要设备是空气处理单元或空气处理器,这两者都包括风扇、线圈、过滤器、减震器、增湿器(可选)、供应和返回管道系统、供应渠道和返回入口和控制部分。

• 水系统。水系统包括冷却水系统、热水系统和冷凝器水系统。水系统包括水泵、管道工作及配件。水系统有时被称为中央或空间调节系统的水部分。

• 中央制冷系统和供暖系统。在中央系统中心部分的制冷系统通常包括室外冷凝装置的冷却器组件。制冷系统也被称为制冷的中央系统。在中央系统中心部分的锅炉及配件组成了供暖系统,在屋顶封装系统的空气处理器通常是作为加热系统的直燃式煤气炉。

• 控制系统。控制系统通常由传感器、基于微处理器的直接数字控制器、控制装置、控制元素、个人电脑和通信网络组成。

空调循环(4.2)

空调循环包括几个被有序连接起来的空调过程。空调循环决定了空调系统的运行性能。空调的工作物质可能是冷冻水或热水、制冷剂、干燥剂等。

每种类型的空气系统都有自己的空调循环。空调循环湿度分析是确定其运行的特点和在不同的系统中组成的湿空气状态的一个重要工具,包括供应空气的体积流量、线圈的负载、加湿和除湿能力。

根据循环性能,空调循环可以分为两类:

• 开式循环:湿空气在结束状态时不恢复至原来的状态。所有室外空气的空调循环是一个开放周期。

• 封闭循环:湿空气在结束状态时恢复至其原始状态。空调循环中的封闭循环是将循环风和室外空气混合后,提供出去,部分回风再循环,再次与室外空气混合作为送风。

根据室外天气和室内工作条件,空调循环的工作模式可以列为以下几种模式:

• 夏季模式:室外和室内的操作参数是在夏天工况下。

• 冬季模式:室外和室内的操作参数是在冬季工况下。

• 节能模式:所有的室外空气或一定量的超过居住者所需的最小新风量的室外空气被作为冷却剂带进空气处理单元或个人单元。节能模式能节省制冷能源的使用。

连续模式操作为每天 24 h,每周 7 天。比如服务于医院病房和冷藏仓库的系统。在一个 24 h 工作循环中,一次或几次间歇操作的模式通常会关闭一次或几次。这样的系统服务于办公室、班级、零售店等。一天 24 h 的和夜间的间歇操作系统又可以分为：

1. 冷却或预热期。当空间未被占用,空气温度高于或低于预定值时,空气应在空间被占用前被冷却或加热。

2. 调整期。在所占用的时间内,空调系统的运行应保持所需的室内环境。

3. 夜间关闭期。空气系统或终端被关闭或仅部分运行以维持在一个设定的温度。

夏季、冬季、节能及连续操作模式都包括全负荷(设计荷载)运行和部分负荷运行。当系统负荷小于设计负荷时,部分负荷产生。选择设备的容量时应满足夏季和冬季系统的设计载荷,以及在所有工作模式下的系统负载。

制冷(4.3)

制冷与制冷系统

制冷是从较低温度的热源、物质或冷却介质中提取热量,并将其传送至更高的温度下散热,可能是大气和地表水,并维持周围环境中的热源温度的冷却效应。

制冷系统是组件、设备和管道的组合,它们在一个连续的顺序中连接,以产生制冷效果。空调的制冷系统主要分为以下几类：

1. 蒸汽压缩式系统。在这些系统中,压缩机将制冷剂从低压低温蒸发的蒸汽压缩到一个更高的压力和温度。压缩的制冷剂通过释放凝结水的潜热冷凝成液体的形式。液态制冷剂再节流成低压低温的蒸汽,在蒸发过程中产生了制冷效果。蒸汽压缩通常被称为机械式制冷,即通过机械压缩制冷。

2. 吸收式系统。吸收式系统通过热量输入的方式产生制冷效果。在蒸发过程中,液态制冷剂在非常低的压力下蒸发产生制冷效应,蒸汽被作为吸收剂的水吸收。通过直接燃气炉或余热加热,制冷剂再次蒸发,然后再凝聚成液态。液态制冷剂节流变为极低压状态,以准备再次产生制冷效应。

3. 气体膨胀式系统。在空气或其他气体膨胀的系统中,空气或气体被压缩到一个高压压缩机中,然后由地表水降温或在大气中冷却,并膨胀到低压状态。由于空气或气体在膨胀过程中温度降低了,便产生了制冷效应。

制冷剂、冷却介质和吸收剂

在制冷系统中使用的制冷剂是主要用于制冷的工作流体。所有的制冷剂都能在低温和低压下通过蒸发放出热量,在高温和高压下通过冷凝吸收热量。

冷却介质是冷媒在蒸发过程中冷却的工作流体,用在从中央工厂到远程冷却设备和终端的蒸发冷却过程中。在一个大型的集中空调系统中,将冷却介质送到较远的需要冷却的位置是更经济的一种方式。冷却水和盐水都是冷却介质,它们通常被称为二级制冷剂,以将它们与原制冷剂区分开来。

液体吸收剂是在吸收式制冷系统中蒸发后用来吸收汽化的制冷剂工质(水),它包含吸收蒸汽和再加热的过程。制冷剂蒸发后,为恢复到原来的浓度,应再吸收水蒸气。

现开发了一种用于烃和卤代烃类制冷剂编号的系统。根据 ANSI／ASHRAE 标准 34—1992,第一个数字是复合不饱和碳碳键的数量。如果这个数字为零,可以省略。第二位是碳原子数减 1。如果这个数字是零也可省略。第三个数字表示氢原子数加 1。最后一位数字表示氟原子的数目。例如,制冷剂 R-123 的化学公式是 $CHCl_2CF_3$,在这个化合物中:

无不饱和碳—碳键,第一位数字是 0;

有 2 个碳原子,第二位数字是 2-1 = 1;

有 1 个氢原子,第三位数字是 1 + 1 = 2;

有 3 个氟原子,最后一位数字是 3。

比较各种制冷剂相对臭氧耗竭的指数称为臭氧消耗潜能值(ODP)。ODP 定义为 1 磅任何卤代烃制冷剂对 1 磅 R-11 的臭氧损耗率。对于 R-11,ODP = 1。

电力公用事业电站燃用矿物燃料的锅炉(5.1)

蒸汽发生设备的选择

美国使用的绝大部分电力是由燃用矿物燃料的蒸汽锅炉和高速汽轮机生产的。

每台锅炉必须以最经济的方式满足设备用户的特定要求。要达到这一点,就要求设计人员和设备用户的工程技术人员或顾问人员的密切合作。

在制订锅炉规范之前,设备用户或者电站的设计人员必须对整个电站进行成本评价。在矿物燃料费用高的地区,对核装置和矿物燃料装置进行评价并加以比较,可能是必要的,以便决定哪种装置能更好地满足设备用户的需要。

火电站的发电成本主要包括以下三种费用:
1. 设备的投资费用;
2. 燃料费用;
3. 其他运行、维修费用。

设备投资费用的调查必须包括锅炉、汽轮机和发电机、凝汽器、给水加热器和水泵、输煤装置、厂房和实际产业的费用。燃料费用的调查必须包括可能使用的各种燃料的费用,以及在电站的运行寿命期内,这些燃料价格可能发生的变化。电站效率和所使用的燃料之间有直接的关系,电站的效率和设备的费用之间也有重要的相互关系。

其他重要的项目是按燃料供应和电力用户所在地区来考虑发电站的厂址位置。在某些情况下,输送电力比运输燃料更为经济。一些大型火电站正在煤矿坑口进行建设,而其发出的电力却是用在几百英里以外的地方。如果电站设备的用户是电网系统的一个发电单位的话,那么电网系统中其他发电单位的要求也可能就是一个重要的因素了。当然在评价中还必须包括运行和维修费用预算。

对工程的各项因素进行全面考虑,需对将来的扩建或规划的变更作出判断,对明确的或不明确的事项做出估计等,来确立足够精确的基本资料是需要花费相当长的时间和精力的,以便使锅炉制造厂家和其他供货厂家的经验和工艺能够完全适合电站设计人员和电站主人的利益。设备用户应该在一开始就决定下来由谁来准备这些资料。如果设备用户缺乏具有必要资格的人员,那么就应该借助于顾问工程师的帮助。与锅炉制造厂家详细进行讨论,将能提供有助于设备用户做出正确决定的很多详细情况。

在选择设备之前,必须规划出运行的依据和整个锅炉设备的布置。最后,取得的资料必编制成设备规范的形式,使各种部件的制造厂家能按设备用户的要求提供设备。在选择设备之后,必须准备基础、厂房、管道和通道的施工图纸。为了有效地经营和安装工作的完成,施工必须采用现代化的进行方式和管理技术进行配合。

对锅炉设计人员的要求

对锅炉设计人员来说,最重要的是所需要的蒸汽量和要使用的燃料,以及设备用户进行成本评价之后所规定的特定蒸汽条件。这些蒸汽条件包括主蒸汽和再热蒸汽的温度和压力。

锅炉的设计人员需要所有与蒸汽产生的有关资料,使他能够设计出最经济的蒸汽发生设备,以满足设备用户的需要。这就要求锅炉设计人员和设备用户、工程技术人员或顾问人员之间密切合作。

可作为设计人员选择设备的根据的要求和条件可以概括如下:

1. 燃料——目前可利用的资源,其成分的分析、价格和将来的趋势。
2. 蒸汽条件
(a)压力和温度——用汽地点和锅炉出口的压力和温度,允许的温度偏差。
(b)供热率(或蒸汽流量)——到终端用汽点的;到锅炉房辅助设备和给水加热器的;到排污点的;由锅炉出口的、最低、平均和最高的变化等的供热率,以及可预测的将来要求。
3. 锅炉给水——水源和水质分析,锅炉入口的给水温度。
4. 占用空间和地形的考虑——占地限制;新设备与现有老锅炉房设备之间的关系;环境要求和地方法律的限制;地震和风的要求;海拔高度;地基条件;气候以及运行和施工用的交通道路。
5. 辅助设备运转所消耗的能源种类和费用。
6. 运行人员——运行和维修人员的经验水平和人工费用。
7. 保证条件。

8. 评价基础——机组效率;所需厂用电量;厂房面积和各种固定费用。

有了这些资料,锅炉设计人员能够分析设备用户的特定要求,将设备投资与长期节省的费用进行平衡、协调组成整个锅炉的许多部件使之成为最经济的设计。

设计实践

锅炉设计人员一般按标准(即已设计好的)部件进行设计。这些部件的详细设计已经完成,因此加快了车间化生产的速度,而且操作经验证明是可靠的。这些标准设计的部件有燃烧器、磨煤机、炉膛组成部分、汽包和承压部件等。这些部件可以很容易地组成各种容量和尺寸的锅炉。这样使费用更低廉,交货期更迅速,而且也提高了设备运行的可利用率。

用于电力公用事业的整套设计几乎很少标准化。这主要是因为每个设备用户的条件特性不同。蒸汽容量、压力和温度的变化不像所燃用的燃料种类和设备用户在自己系统内采用什么蒸汽发生设备的方案变化那么大。这类方式的变化需要改变部件的设计和部件的总布置。这些因素连同不断变动的货币价值、燃料、材料和人工一起,使整个机组的标准化不可能实现。

过热器和再热器(5.3)

蒸汽机运行时,如果对蒸汽予以一定程度的过热,就会节约大量燃料,这一点早在 18 世纪就得到了证明。在 19 世纪后期,往复蒸汽机遇到了各种润滑问题,但一旦这些问题得到了解决,过热器又继续向前发展。

汽轮机的商业性发展加速了过热的普遍应用。到 1920 年,普遍同意蒸汽温度为 650 °F,即相当于 250 °F 的过热。在 20 世纪 20 年代初期,利用汽轮机抽汽加热给水的再生循环得到了发展,在没有进一步提高蒸汽温度的情况下改善了电站的经济性。同时,过热器的发展允许将蒸汽温度提高到 725 °F。那时,进一步提高温度以使在经济上获得更多的收益,受到了过热器管金属容许温度的限制。这导致了再热的商业应用,即是从汽轮机高压级出来的蒸汽在另外的再热器里再热,待其温度和焓提高后再返回低压级。

用于电站的第一台再热机组于 1922 年提出,1924 年 9 月便投入运行。其设计压力为 650 psi。但运行时为 550 psi 和 725 °F。汽轮机高压级的排汽在 135 psi 的压力下被再热至 725°F。

1924 年设计了压力更高的再热机组,主蒸汽压力为 1 200 psi,汽温为 700°F,再热蒸汽为 360 psi,700°F,于 1925 年 12 月投入运行。

过热和再热的优点

当饱和蒸汽用于汽轮机时,蒸汽在做功以后,即使压力有所下降,也有一部分蒸汽凝结成水造成一部分能量的损失。汽轮机能做的功量,受到汽轮机在其叶片不会过度磨损的情况下所能容许的水量的限制。正常情况下,水分在 10%~15% 的范围之内,可以采用将汽轮机各级间的水分离出来的办法来增大做功量,但这只在特殊情况下才是经济的。即使进行水分离,与将水从给水温度提高到饱和温度然后再蒸发所需的热量相比,汽轮机里能转换成功的总能量还是少的。因此,在汽轮机设计中,水分是主要限制。

因为汽轮机通常将过热的热量转换为功,不会形成水分,因此在汽轮机里,基本上能将过热的热量全部回收。理想的郎肯循环温-熵图对此做了解释。从图中可以看出,加到饱和蒸汽线右边的热量 100% 能回收。尽管这并非总是完全正确的,但从郎肯循环图中可以看出,在实际循环中,这基本上是正确的。

前面的讨论并不是特别适用于临界点附近的蒸汽压力。在给处于或高于临界点的工作流体温度下定义时,"过热"一词并不真正合适。然而,当温度高于 705°F 时,甚至压力超过 3 208 psia,所加入的热量基本上也能在汽轮机里全部得到回收。

图 5.1 用图表对过热的好处作了图解,从图中可以看出,当压力从 1 800 psi 增加到 3 500 psi 时,将蒸汽温度从 900°F 提高到 1 100°F,热循环的热耗就会降低。

过热器的型式

过热器和再热器的原型是对流装置,这多少也是它们的基本型式。这种型式适用于辐射传热很小的各种炉烟温度。在这种型式的装置里,从过热器出来的蒸汽温度随锅炉出力的升高而升高。这是因为炉膛吸收的热输入比例减少,过热器能吸收的热量就增多。由于对流传热率差不多是出力的直接函数,过热器每磅蒸汽吸收的总热量随锅炉出力的增长而增长(见图 5.2)。

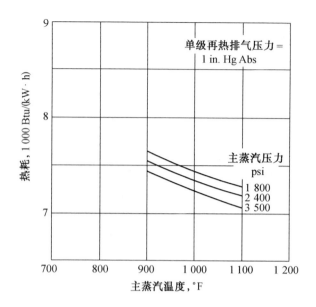

图 5.1　蒸汽温度和压力的变化对单级再热理想郎肯循环性能的影响

当过热器离炉膛较远,即进入过热器和炉烟温度较低,这一影响就更明显。

另一方面,辐射式过热器从辐射热中接收热量,实际上,它没有从对流热中接受热量。因为炉膛中的受热面吸收的热量不是与锅炉出力成正比例增长,而是以慢得多的速度增长,所以作为负荷函数的辐射过热曲线随着锅炉出力的增长而向下倾斜。

在某些情况下,两条相对倾斜的曲线由于辐射式和对流式过热器组合的调整,使得过热曲线在广阔的负荷范围里都很平坦。图 5.2 所示就是典型曲线。布置在单独炉膛内的过热器的特点为,运行所得的过热曲线较平坦。

过热器的发展

最初的对流式过热器设置在深度大的锅炉管束的上面或后面,以便为过热器挡住火焰或高温炉烟。为了提高蒸汽温度,过热器需要吸收较多的热量,因此有必要将过热器移得靠近火焰一些。这一新位置给过热器带来了一些问题,这些问题在过热器位于原来的低温烟气区时并不明显。通过对过热

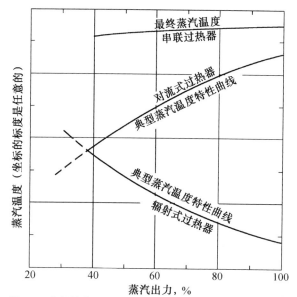

图5.2 将辐射式和对流式过热组件串联排列就能使整个出力范围内的最终蒸汽温度很均匀

器设计的改进,包括提高蒸汽质量流速,蒸汽和烟气分配的困难和管子金属普遍过热等问题终于得到了解决。这加大了蒸汽膜的热导,从而降低了管子金属温度。蒸汽的分配,也通过加大管子的压降得到了改善。

现代过热器的蒸汽质量流速范围从 100 000 lb/($ft^2 \cdot h$) 到 1 000 000 lb/($ft^2 \cdot h$) 或更高些,这根据压力、蒸汽和炉烟的温度,以及过热器里的允许压降而定。

过热器设计时考虑的一些基本问题也适用于再热器设计,然而,再热器里的压降是关键性的,因为再热器循环所得到的热耗降低的优点可能被再热系统太大的压降完全抵消而为零。因此,在再热器里,蒸汽质量流量常常比较小。

管子尺寸 在固定式锅炉上,过热器和再热器主要是外径为 2 in 或 $2\frac{1}{2}$ in 的圆筒形光管。船用装置使用直径较小(1 in 或 $1\frac{1}{4}$ in)的管子是为了节省重量和空间。管子直径较小,蒸汽压降则较大,管子调整中心线也更困难,管子直径越大,就会使压应力越大。

最近的设计要求卧式过热器管子吊架之间的间隔较大,每排管子的管距较宽或根数较少,以避免灰渣堆积。$2\frac{1}{2}$ in 管能够满足这些新条件,牺牲的细管好处也最少。在某些情况下,使用 3 in 管也很好。当蒸汽温度升高时,由于容许应力的原因。可能迫使重新使用小直径薄壁管。

现代过热器装置几乎毫无例外地都用光管。过热器管采用鳍片、环或销钉等形式扩展受热面,这不仅使得炉烟侧的清洗变得困难,而且厚度增加会使金属温度和热应力增大超过允许限值。

过热器设计中的各种关系

有效的过热器设计要求解决几个因素。突出要考虑的是:

1. 要求的蒸汽温度;
2. 达到这一蒸汽温度所需的过热器受热面面积;
3. 要放置受热面的炉烟温度区;
4. 最适于制造受热面和支吊架的钢、合金钢或其它材料的种类;
5. 流过管子的蒸汽流速(质量流速),这受到允许蒸汽压降的限制,但反过来,它又是控制管金属温度的主要因素;
6. 受热面的布置要满足指望使用的燃料特性的要求,特别是关于管距,要避免积灰和结渣,或者采取措施将这样的形成物在其形成的最初阶段除去;
7. 过热器作为一种构架本身的设计和型式。

前 6 项中的任何一项发生变化,都会使其它各项随之而变化。

先进电站设计所要求的蒸汽温度是过热器设计人员和制造厂可以生产的经济结构的最高温度。在这种情况下,经济要求对下述相互有关的两个因素要作出决定。这两个因素是:初始费用,也就是初投资和以后的维修费用(为使运行故障,停机和更换都减少到最少的程度)。如果维修费用能大量减少,并在一段合理的时间内抵补超出的那部分初始费用,则较大的初投资是有根据的。因此,要求的蒸汽温度这一因素是根据对其它五项因素组合的最佳值的计算和特定工程需要的现有的全部配合认识而定的。最近几年的运行经验使得购买来安装在美国的几乎全部的大型机组都采用 1 000 °F 左右的蒸汽温度作为主过热和再热的蒸汽温度。

在要求的蒸汽温度具体确定或规定下来以后,下一步需要考虑的就是达到这一过热度所需要的受热面面积。需要的过热器受热面面积决定于余下的四项因素,由于相互关系不是单一的,所以受热面面积必须通过试布置的方法来确定,即将它放置在看来令人满意的炉烟温度区。在所谓的标准锅炉里,通过实际布置和通过先占据的过热器受热面空间就能很好地确定这一区域。

在确定了试布置的和试规定管距的受热面面积以后,就可以计算蒸汽质量流速,蒸汽压降和过热器管金属温度。然后为管子、联箱和其它部件选择合适的材料,还可能需要对几种布置进行比较,以便获得最佳组合。它们应考虑到如下几点:

1. 需要成本较低的合金。
2. 在不危及管子温度的情况下,得到一个较为合理的蒸汽压降。
3. 使蒸汽质量流速较高,以便降低管子温度。
4. 采用不同的管距,在燃料种类不定的情况下,那将更好地防止积灰。
5. 在知道了供给的燃料较为有利时,允许采用更小的管距,以便使布置更为经济。
6. 在通风阻力值很紧要的地方,管子将布置成能减少装置的通风阻力。
7. 允许过热器受热面位于炉烟温度较高的区域,从而节约一些受热面,与标准布置之差就可以得到补偿。

采用最佳的经济和运行特性,采用比较满意的各种准则,就可能完成实际的设计。但是,还需要大量的经验,并使用正确的实际原则,才能获得令人满意的结果。

再热器设计中的各种关系

总的说来,过热器和再热器需要考虑的问题差不多。但是,再热器的设计强度受到了允许蒸汽压降的限制。再热器管里的蒸汽质量流速应足以使汽膜温度降保持在150°F以下。一般情况下,再热器管里的压降小于5%就可以做到这一点。这允许再热器管路和阀门的压降再下降5%而不会超过通常允许的10%总值。

管子用金属

抗氧化性,最大允许应力和经济性决定了过热器和再热器管材料的选择。只要这些考虑可行,就应扩大碳钢的使用。在此限度以外,应使用经认真选择的合金钢。

锅炉的技术经济指标(5.5)

锅炉的技术经济指标通常用经济性、可靠性和机动性三项指标来表示。
(1)经济性。
锅炉的经济性主要指热效率、成本、煤耗和厂用电量等。
锅炉的热效率是指送入锅炉的全部热量中被有效利用的百分数,即锅炉有效利用热 Q_1 与单位时间内所消耗燃料的输入热量 Q_r 百分比。

$$\eta = \frac{Q_1}{Q_r} \times 100\%$$

锅炉的有效利用热是指单位时间内工质在锅炉中所吸收的总热量,包括水和蒸汽吸收的热量,以及排污水和自用蒸汽所消耗的热量。而锅炉的输入热量是指随每千克或每立方米燃料输入锅炉的总热量,它包括燃料的收到基低位发热量和显热,以及用外来热源加热燃料或空气时所带入的热量。热效率 η 也称为锅炉的总效率。

实际中只用锅炉效率来说明锅炉运行的经济性是不够的,因为锅炉效率只反映了燃烧和传热过程的完善程度,但从火电厂锅炉的作用看,只有供出蒸汽和热量才是有效产品,自用蒸汽及排污水的吸热量并不向外供出,而是自身消耗或损失掉了。而且,要使锅炉能正常运行生产蒸汽,除使用燃料外,还要使其所有的辅助系统的附属设备正常运行,也都需要消耗电力。因此,锅炉运行的经济性指标,除锅炉效率外,还有一个锅炉净效率。

锅炉净效率是指考虑到锅炉机组运行时的自用能耗(热耗和电耗)以后的锅炉效率。锅炉净效率 η_j 可以表示为

$$\eta_j = \frac{Q_1}{Q_r + \Sigma Q_{zy} + \frac{b}{B} 29\ 300 \Sigma P} \times 100\%$$

式中 B ——锅炉燃料消耗量,kg/h;
         Q_{zy} ——锅炉自用热耗,kJ/kg;
         ΣP ——锅炉辅助设备实际消耗功率,kW;
         b ——电厂发电标准煤耗量,kg/(kW·h);

29 300——标准煤热值,kJ/kg。

现代电站锅炉的热效率都在90%以上。

在中国,强制性规定以水为工作流体的工业锅炉效率应不低于表5.6(见原表)中列出的值,生活锅炉的热效率应该不低于表5.7(见原表)中列出的值。

锅炉成本一般用成本中的重要经济指标钢材消耗率来表示。钢材消耗率定义为锅炉单位蒸发量所用的钢材质量,单位为t/(t·h)。锅炉参数、循环方式、燃料种类及锅炉部件结构对钢材消耗率均有影响。

由于钢材、耐火材料等价格经常变化,为了便于比较,往往用钢材消耗量来表示锅炉成本。增大单机容量和提高蒸汽参数是减少金属消耗量和投资费用的有效途径。一般来说,机组容量由300 MW提高到600 MW,每kW投资可降低10%~15%;由亚临界压力增加到超临界压力,每kW投资增加1%~5%。所以超临界与大容量相结合,机组的综合经济效益可大大提高。国外资料显示,一台600 MW机组与两台300 MW机组相比,电站单位造价可降低10%,运行人员和检修费用降低50%,金属耗量减少20%,基建劳动消耗减少30%。

锅炉钢架占大型锅炉金属耗量很大比重,20世纪70年代我国生产的300 MW机组就采用钢筋混凝土结构。用水泥主柱不仅可以节省钢材,而且可以现场浇灌,建设周期比钢结构缩短。

工业锅炉的钢材消耗率在5~6 t/(t·h)左右;电站锅炉的钢材消耗率一般在2.5~5 t/(t·h)范围内。在保证锅炉安全、可靠、经济运行的基础上应合理降低钢材消耗率,尤其是耐热合金钢材的消耗率。

电厂每发出(或供应)1 kw·h的电所消耗的煤量,称为发电(或供电)煤耗率。辅机设备用电量占机组发电量的比称为厂用电率。厂用电率与辅机设备的配置选型密切相关,尤其是燃料制备系统,另外还受燃料品种、燃烧方式的影响。煤耗还与机组参数有关,参数越高,供电煤耗越低。但是,燃料种类、负荷方式、厂房布置条件、单机容量及其他一些条件也影响供电煤耗。所以,只有在相同的条件下才能比较参数和煤耗的关系。例如,燃煤的变负荷的超临界压力机组的供电煤耗可能高于燃油的基本负荷的亚临界压力机组。在条件相同的前提下,超临界机组的供电煤耗比亚临界压力机组的低。

(2)锅炉可靠性。

锅炉可靠性常用下列三种指标来衡量。

①连续运行时间=两次检修之间的运行时间(用小时表示)
②事故率=事故停用时间/(运行总时间+事故停用时间)×100%
③可用率=(运行总时间+备用总时间)/统计时间总时间×100%

目前中国电站锅炉的较好指标是:连续运行时间在4 000 h 以上,可用率约为90%。

(3)机动性。

随着现代社会生活方式和用电负荷新的变化,用户对锅炉的运行方式提出了更多的新要求,也就是要求锅炉运行有更大的灵活性和可调性。在电站负荷方面,除基本负荷、调峰负荷和循环负荷外,还具有承担最低负荷的能力。从运行压力来看,存在定压、滑压等运行方式。如 300 MW 国产亚临界压力控制循环锅炉就可适应定压或滑压运行,带基本负荷,可二班制运行,也可用于峰调。负荷变化率为:定压运行,5% MCR/min;滑压运行,3% MCR/min;瞬间运行(在 50% MCR 以上)10% MCR/min。汽温调节方式:过热器为一级、二级喷水及燃烧器摆动;再热器为燃烧器摆动及过量空气系数调节。汽温保证范围:定压运行(70% ~ 100%)MCR;滑压运行(50% ~ 100%)MCR。锅炉最低无油稳定燃烧负荷:烟煤(30% ~ 40%)MCR;贫煤(55% ~ 65%)MCR。

因此,机动性的要求是:快速改变负荷,经常停运及随后快速启动的可能性和最低允许负荷下持久运行的可能性。这些要求已成为锅炉产品的重要性能指标。另外,燃煤锅炉在遇到煤质降低、燃用劣质燃料、燃料品种改变等都会降低机组的机动性。

锅炉的发展历史(5.6)

据考证,公元前 200 年左右,古希腊一位叫希罗的人发明了图 5.3(见原图)所示的一种可供宫廷欣赏之用的装置。由于下方容器中的水受热后转变成蒸汽,在反冲力的作用下会使得上方的圆球旋转。据认为,这是利用水蒸气产生动力最早的装置,也因此被认为是最早的锅炉。

但直到工业革命之前,所谓的锅炉几乎没有发展。工业革命在英国迅速发展后,由于矿井抽水的需要,对动力的需要增大,瓦特在纽卡门的发明基础上,完善了蒸汽机,分别如图 5.4,5.5(见原图)所示。但当时由于产生蒸汽的锅炉主要为圆筒形,采用筒外加热,如图 5.6(见原图)所示.

随着工业的发展,锅炉向两个方向发展:

(1)在圆筒内部增加受热面积。开始是在一个大圆筒内增加了一个火筒,然后两个,直到多个,最后发展为现代的火管锅炉。

圆筒锅炉有单火筒锅炉和双火筒锅炉。随着锅炉的进一步发展,在 1860 年左右出现了烟管锅炉。这种锅炉采用数目众多的细烟管代替直径大的火筒,增加了锅筒的受热面积。该种锅炉的炉膛在锅筒外部,由耐火砖砌筑而成。燃烧产生的烟气从烟管中流过。后来又出现了烟管-火管组合锅炉。

(2)增加筒外部受热面积,即增加水筒的数目,从而出现了水管锅炉。燃料在筒外燃烧,与水管锅炉的发展相似,水筒的数目不断增加,发展成为很多小直径的水管。由于水在管中流动,称为水管锅炉。

实践证明,减小水筒的直径,增加水筒的数目对改善传热、降低钢材消耗量、提高蒸发量和蒸汽压力极为有利。从 1840 年出现第一台水管锅炉后,相继出现了各种类型的水管锅炉。水管锅炉的发展为大容量、高参数现代大型动力锅炉奠定了基础。

水管锅炉的发展有两个分支:横水管锅炉和竖水管锅炉。横水管锅炉早期是整联箱锅炉,水管全部连接在两个大联箱上。由于联箱很大,故而耐压低。后来发展为横水管分联箱锅炉,由很多小联箱代替大联箱,使承压能力提高。横水管接近水平放置,其中水的流动不好,此外增加受热面积仍受到锅筒直径的限制,后逐渐被淘汰。

竖水管锅炉是现代锅炉的主要形式,它出现于 1900 年。初期采用直水管,后逐渐被弯水管所代替。为了布置更多的受热面,锅筒的数目也随之减少。随着传热学的发展,证实了炉膛中设置的水冷壁管吸收火焰的辐射换热,比一般对流管束的吸热强度高得多。因此,尽可能增加水冷壁的数量,减少对流管束的数量,锅筒的数目也随之减少。现在已出现了单锅筒的大容量锅炉和无锅筒的直流锅炉。

总之,锅炉的发展史就是为了增加蒸发量、提高蒸汽参数、减少煤耗、节省钢材和改进工艺过程的历史。

随着经济的发展,我国锅炉制造的技术水平和生产规模不断提高。锅炉制造企业的级别分为 A 级、B 级、C 级、D 级等。表 5.8(见原表)给出了截至 2006 年我国锅炉制造业的现状。

我国工业锅炉目前仍存在许多问题,主要有:

(1)锅炉效率低。我国工业锅炉煤几乎都是以未经洗选的原煤为主要燃料。

(2)单台容量小。生活及生产用工业锅炉平均单台容量仅2.28 t/h。

(3)污染严重。我国小型锅炉,尤其是2 t/h以下锅炉绝大多数消烟除尘设备不完善,或根本没有消烟除尘设备,同时又无脱硫装置。

(4)机械化和自动化水平低。我国小型工业燃煤锅炉多数还是人工填煤、人工除灰,并且司炉水平参差不齐。

(5)锅炉制造水平低。我国拥有相当比例的小型锅炉制造企业,但缺少专业技术人员,图纸不完整、不齐全,检验设备简陋。

以油(气)为燃料的燃油(气)锅炉具有高效、环境污染小甚至无污染等特点,因此倍受人们青睐。尤其在国外,燃油(气)锅炉目前已得到了普遍应用。据统计,国外一些发达国家供暖用锅炉中,燃油(气)锅炉中已占相当大的比例,俄罗斯占60%,美国占98%,日本占99%。

多年来,人们对环保要求日益强烈,燃油(气)锅炉也因此得到了空前发展。

我国第一台发电机组于1882年在上海投运,到1949年我国装机容量仅为43×10^8 kW·h,几乎没有锅炉制造工业。1953年创建了上海锅炉厂,1954年建立哈尔滨锅炉厂,以后又建立武汉锅炉厂等锅炉制造厂及有关科研单位。高等院校也先后设立相应的专业,形成了完整的教育、科研、设计、制造和安装体系。我国现在已能设计、制造各类锅炉,基本能满足国内的工业需要。我国大型电站锅炉已出口到很多国家,发电设备已成为我国主要出口产品之一。

目前电站锅炉向高效率(部分减少污染)、大容量、高参数、低污染、自动化、高可靠性、低成本(金属耗量)方向发展,工业锅炉更注重高效率、低污染、自动化、低成本(金属耗量),而生活锅炉则追求低污染、自动化、安全可靠。

汽轮机(6.1)

涡轮机是靠一股射向转子叶片的流体(液体或气体)来驱动的回转式发

动机。在汽轮机中这股流体是蒸汽。蒸汽通过驱动涡轮叶轮旋转而将部分热能和压力能转换成机械能。涡轮机是靠蒸汽直接作用在叶轮或转子上而产生旋转运动的。在水轮机中,流体的流速是由水位降而产生的。在汽轮机中,流体的流速是由锅炉蒸汽的压力降而产生的。蒸汽在喷嘴中或叶片上,由高压侧向低压侧逐渐膨胀,靠着耗用热和压力使其速度逐渐增大。然后,由于对运动叶片作功,蒸汽的速度便减慢下来。

涡轮机最大优点是没有振动和噪音,转动力平稳而均匀,并能处理大量的流体——在汽轮中就是蒸汽。汽轮机结构简单,运转可靠,使它成为一种适合于驱动泵、压轮机和其他设备的发动机。在这些情况下,汽轮机最有效的转速通常比它所驱动的机械的转速要高得多,因此通常必须利用减速箱,小型汽轮机的效率不是很高的。

大型汽轮机配上减速箱可用来驱动舰船。事实上,汽轮机是唯一适用于驱动舰船的发动机。在大型电站中,汽轮机得到了最大的发展,一些新电站正在安装每台功率超过 600 000 马力的汽轮机。

汽轮机由下列主要部件组成:

1. 涡轮壳——通常沿平面中心线剖分为二,用螺栓固定在一起,以便于装配和拆卸,壳体上带有定叶系统。
2. 转子——叶轮上装有动叶,转子两端装有轴颈。
3. 轴承箱——安装在气缸上,用来支承转子的轴。
4. 调速器和阀门系统——通过控制蒸汽流量来调节涡轮的速度和出力,同时还有轴承润滑系统以及一套安全装置。
5. 某种类型的联轴器——用来连接从动机械。
6. 管路接头——在进汽口接供汽管道,在涡轮壳出汽口接排汽系统。

图 6.1(见原文)所示为一种简单的冲动式汽轮机。在这种汽轮机里,蒸汽从一个固定的喷嘴(或若干喷嘴)中喷出,喷嘴的弯度正好使喷出的蒸汽能射向安装在转动叶轮或圆盘的一圈叶片上。这些叶片制造成一定的形状以便用来平稳地拦截从喷嘴喷出的蒸汽。叶片是弯曲的,以便改变蒸汽射流的方向,同时承受向前推进的冲力。

要是不使用固定的喷嘴和单独的叶轮而把喷嘴安装到轮子上,喷出的气流的反作用就会推动这个轮子朝向与冲击式叶片相反的方向转动。最早期的汽轮机就是这种纯反力式涡轮机,但是由于种种原因现在已不采用了。

另外还有一种涡轮机,(见原文中图 6.2)它综合了冲力和反作用力的原理。但通常简称做"反力式"涡轮机,其喷嘴的基本特征是从进汽口起,通道逐渐变窄,因此流体进入通道时速度较低,离开喷嘴时速度必然要高得多。速度的增加是由于压力降而产生的,因为流体进入喷嘴时的压力比离开喷嘴时的压力要高。图 6.2 中的涡轮壳带有一整圈喷嘴,这些喷嘴和冲动式涡轮机里的一样,也是弯曲的,并以最有效的角度引导蒸汽喷向转动的叶片。这些转动叶片与固定喷嘴类似,也是喷嘴,但朝着另一个方向,除拦截从固定的喷嘴喷出的蒸汽并使之偏转之外,它们还能使蒸汽加速,其驱动力一半来自冲力,一半来自反作用力。这类汽轮机的气流速度是叶片转速相同的冲动式汽轮机的气流速度的一半。不论是冲动式的或是反力式的,离开动叶片时的蒸汽流的方向都大致与叶片运动的方向成直角。

最简单的汽轮机只有一个级,即定叶和动叶各一排。这种汽轮机通常用于最多几百马力的功率输出,具有中等的进汽温度和中等的进汽压力,排汽压力为一个大气压或高于一个大气压。在这些条件下,单级涡轮就能达到相当高的蒸汽利用效率。

为了从锅炉燃烧的每磅煤中获得尽可能多的动力,蒸汽在进入汽轮机时必须具有很高的温度和压力,而在排出时,压力要尽可能低。利用大量的冷却水把废汽在单独的冷凝器里冷凝,就能保持很低的排气压力,然后再用泵把冷凝蒸汽抽回到锅炉里作为纯净的给水。假如让蒸汽在一级里从锅炉压力膨胀到冷凝器压力,从喷嘴喷出的气流速度就会高到无法制造一个转速快到足以有效地利用这么高的气流速度的汽轮机;实际上单级式汽轮机的效率通常是很低的。为了使冲动式汽轮机或反力式汽轮机具有很高的热效率,就需要很大的功率输出,很高的进汽压力和很高的进气温度以及很低的排汽压力,这时单级式是不适用的。在这样的条件下,蒸汽可以得到的能量很高,为了有效利用能量,必须采用多级涡轮。此外,在这样的条件下,排汽流量增大,排汽级也必须不止一个,例如,大型汽轮机可以有三个平行的排汽级。在这些多级汽轮机中,安装在涡轮壳内的一排排定叶片和安装在转子上的一排排动叶片是交替排列的,这样的布置可使蒸汽以适当的角度进入每排定叶片和动叶片。定叶片总是喷嘴,对反力式汽轮机来说,转子上的叶片也是喷嘴,但是对冲动式汽轮机来说转子上的叶子只是导槽。

各级叶片通常是沿着水平轴一套一套地并列安装的,从而构成了所谓的"轴流式"汽轮机。蒸汽从一头进入而从另一头排出;如果流量非常大,蒸汽也可以从中间进入,而从两头排出,这种装置就称为"双流式"。机壳是由上下两半组成,下半部通常安装有轴承以支承转子,当转子安装就位以后,再把上半部沿水平配合面用螺栓连接在下半部上。

当级数很多时,业已证明用两个或两个以上的汽轮机壳或气缸是最切实可行的,这些气缸通常排成一直线,所有的轴都连接在一起。

现代的汽轮机是用锅炉来提供高度过热蒸汽的。当蒸汽通过汽轮机时,压力和温度逐渐下降,直到在某一级过热已全部消失,此后,有些蒸汽就会冷凝成水滴。这些水滴会损害叶片并降低汽轮机的效率,这就是蒸汽在通过高压涡轮之后,和进入中压涡轮之前,有时要予以再过热的原因之一。

燃气轮机(6.2)

燃气轮机是一种内燃机。这种内燃机的空气由于燃料燃烧受热膨胀,从而直接驱动一个特殊形状的叶轮(涡轮),而不像往复式发动机那样推动活塞上下运动。

由于内部运转连续、平稳,燃气轮机跟蒸汽轮机一样几乎完全没有振动,再加上它最基本的特点——结构简单,这就使得它运动更加可靠而且更易于维护。燃气轮机比活塞发动机重量轻、体积小,因此能制成较大的尺寸,从而通过单机可以产生较高的功率。基于上述原因,燃气轮机在海、陆、空各种形式的运输工具中的使用正在日益增加。从上述这些优点来看,人们可能感到奇怪,为什么燃气轮机没有更早地被采用,特别是并不是什么新的概念。的确,利用热燃气的能量来直接转动叶轮的概念也许比活塞发动机中采用的比较复杂的系统更明显易懂。但事实上,要在实践中应用涡轮机的原理则更为困难。

早期的效率比较低的小型燃气轮机是利用活塞发动机的废气来工作的,并用它来驱动增压器。只是到了20世纪30年代才成功地制成了自动旋转的燃气轮机,并用作飞机推进器。差不多在制成航空涡轮机的同时,还研制成用于固定用途以及用作铁路机车发动机的燃气轮机。

燃气轮机主要由空气压缩机、燃烧室、涡轮叶轮组成。

压气机 燃气轮机用的压气机有两种基本类型:即轴流式和离心式压气机。在少数特殊情况下,也使用被称为混流式的压气机,这就是部分离心式部分轴流式的压气机。轴流式压气机用得最广泛,因为它能够高效率地处理大容积的空气。但是对于500马力或500马力以下的小型燃气轮机,则采用离心式压气机而不用轴流式压气机。

燃烧室 燃气轮机的燃烧器有时叫燃烧室。它有各种各样的形状和形式,例如环形、筒形或环管形。燃气轮机的燃烧室的部件有:燃烧喷嘴、燃烧段以及通向涡轮进口的过渡段。

燃烧室用的空气由压气机压入发动机。燃料同压缩空气混合,然后在燃烧室里燃烧。再由涡轮把释放出来的热能转换成旋转能。由于燃烧产物的初始温度很高,通常采用过量空气来冷却燃烧产物,使之降到涡轮进口的设计温度。

涡轮叶轮 燃气轮机使用的涡叶轮有两种,一种是向心式,另一种是轴流式。小型燃气轮机用径流式涡轮叶轮。对于大容积流量,几乎全采用轴流式涡轮叶轮。虽然某些小型燃气轮机使用的涡轮是纯冲动式,但大多数高性能的涡轮既不是纯冲动式,也不是纯反动式。高性能的涡轮通常是按不同大小的各种冲力的反力相配合设计而成,以便获得最佳性能。

压气机与涡轮叶轮都安装在同一根轴上一起转动,由燃烧室出来的高温燃气,冲击涡轮叶片,使轴转动,从而带动压气机。从大气中来的空气通过压气机的进口吸入,然后向前流经每一级叶片(轴流式压气机)。随着空气压力逐渐增大,其体积则逐渐减小,在末一级压缩到最大限度。然后,高压(同时也是高温)空气被排入通向燃烧室的导管。燃烧室有一个或多个燃料喷嘴,通过喷嘴使燃料雾化,以便和流动的空气混合。起动时,利用电火花塞将燃料喷雾点燃。燃料与空气的混合气一经点燃,便连续不断地燃烧,因此点火装置就可以关掉。

以筒形燃烧室或环管形燃烧室组成的若干分燃室常常用来代替单一的燃烧室(即环形燃烧室)。例如在标准的飞机用燃气轮机中,使用8~10个筒形燃烧室,每个燃烧室都有自己的燃料喷嘴。

从燃烧室出来的燃烧产物经过导管、固定导叶片或喷嘴进入涡轮。燃气在涡轮里沿轴向流动,由于燃气的大部分能量传给了涡轮叶轮,燃气的温度和压力都逐渐下降。

图6.3(见原文)为燃气轮发动机的基本原理示意图,从中可以清楚地看出推迟研制成功燃气轮机的种种技术方面的困难。(A)是进气口,空气由此进入压气机(B),由于被压缩,空气以很高的压力(至少为50磅/平方英寸)和比原来高的温度进入燃烧室(C)。在燃烧室里燃料被喷射进压缩空气里,

并以高效率燃烧。燃烧使温度升高到1 850℃,甚至更高,从而使空气膨胀。生成的高温、高压燃气连续不断地喷射到驱动压气机的涡轮(D)上。燃气离开涡轮(D)之后,其压力和温度还相当高并且继续膨胀,因此能够以两种方法来加以利用。在燃气轮机本身以及在涡轮螺桨飞机发动机中,排出的气体用来驱动固定在动力轴上的另一个涡轮(或多级涡轮)(E)。这根轴可以用来驱动螺旋桨(例如在涡轮螺桨发动机中),还可以用来驱动机车的齿轮箱(例如在燃气轮机机车中)。

反之,在单纯的喷气发动机中,喷出的燃气通过尾喷管直接排入大气,形成一股高速喷气流,根据反作用原则,像火箭一样,把发动机推向前进。在内外涵喷气式飞机发动机中,有一个低压压气机和一个高压压气机。从低压压气机出来的一部分空气绕过高压压气机和燃烧室,在尾喷管里形成一般温度较低、速度较慢、力量较强的空气喷气流,这种喷气流对速度较低的喷气式飞机是比较适用的。

涡轮的材料要连续不断地接触温度非常高的燃气,因此对用来制作燃气轮机叶片的金属的要求是非常之高的——甚至比对汽轮机叶片的要求还要高。另一个问题涉及压气机的效率,如果效率低的话,它本身就会消耗过多的功率,从而大量有用的燃气能量就被涡轮(D)用掉,结果成为推力的能量所剩无几,或第二涡轮(E)几乎产生不出多少有用的动力来。因此,一直到效率很高的压气机以及能耐高温的钢种或其他金属制造出来以前,燃气轮机的试制都没有成功。

对于某些用途来说,活塞式发动机仍然优于燃气轮机。对一定的输出功率来说,活塞式发动机的燃料消耗量一般明显地较低,但燃气轮机的重量则较轻。要制造出符合要求的低输出功率的燃气轮机(例如适用于公路车辆的),也还是不容易的,尽管现在正在努力解决这个问题。

燃气轮机由于重量轻、尺寸小,用作飞机推进器有许多独特的优点,所以首先在飞机制造业中得到重要的应用并大大促进了它的发展。燃气轮机作为航空发动机既可用作单纯的喷气推进装置,也可用来驱动普通的螺旋桨。

在高空飞行和空速很大时,喷气推进发动机的效率最高,因此它特别适用于高性能的军用飞机。现代军用喷气推进发动机能够产生惊人的动力。在紧急情况下,还能够借助一个加力燃烧室使动力进一步增大,因为这种燃烧室使即将进入排气喷管的燃气的温度增高。这样的加力燃烧可提高燃气的排气速度以及提高发动机的前进推力。

燃气轮机在飞机上另一应用是用作涡轮螺桨发动机。在这一应用中，燃气轮机具有两种用途：它驱动一个普通的螺旋桨，以及利用从发动机喷管排出的喷气的反作用力产生附加的推力。这样，就把螺桨式飞机所固有的起飞距离短的优点与普通喷气推进发动机飞机速度快、飞行高度高的能力结合起来。

介于普通喷气推进发动机和涡轮螺桨发动机之间的是后来研制成功的所谓涡轮风扇发动机。它与普通喷气推进发动机的区别在于：在进气口安装一个风扇，从而使进气口进入的空气量要比实际上流过发动机内涵的多得多。风扇把进入的空气稍稍压缩，然后将大部分空气引进环绕发动机的旁路空气导管，空气在导管里加速，并以比通过进气口时更高的速度排出来，从而增加了发动机的推力。余下的空气流过发动机的内涵，并且在那里如同在普通的喷气发动机中一样，通过涡轮和排气喷管被压缩、加热然后膨胀。

被分流流过环绕着发动机内涵旁路管道的空气同流过发动机内涵的空气之比称为双涵空气流量比（或涵道流量比）。双涵空气流量比根据不同的用途其比值大不相同。大型涡轮风扇发动机的双涵空气流量比通常高达 $8:1$。一般说来，高双涵空气流量比和高压缩比能够节省燃料。

涡轮风扇发动机有许多优点。发动机所增加的推力可以使飞机不必携带许多水（这是很重的附加载荷）；飞机在暖和的天气起飞时，有时就需喷注这些水以增加普通发动机的推力。当发动机在合适的速度和高度范围内工作时，可节省燃料 20% 左右。这些优点已经使得这类发动机成为在商业上应用于大型喷气式飞机的一种最受欢迎的发动机。

在发电领域中，同柴油机和蒸汽轮机相比，燃气轮机的容量受到限制，这是因为燃气轮机内的压力很低，因而需要空气的容积非常之大，所以必须使用大型涡轮和压气机。正是由于这一原因，在现代的中心电站中就没有做过什么认真的努力去设计一个燃气轮机电厂，来取代单机容量高达 1 200 000 kW 的蒸汽动力厂。

燃气轮机在发电领域中有三种用途值得特别提一提：
（1）与蒸汽发电站联合运动作为增加总效率的一种手段；
（2）用作备用机组和服务于峰值负荷；
（3）用于流动发电站。

另有一种很有前途的发电站是汽轮机-燃气轮机联合机组发电站。它利用从普通的燃气轮机排出的高温废气为蒸汽锅炉供氧，以代替预热的燃用空气。由于从燃气轮机排出的燃气中仍然含有输入压气机进气口的空气所含的大约80%的氧，所以这样的联合运行是切实可行的。这样的机组能够大大提高电站的总效率，它还可以缩减所需要的锅炉尺寸和重量，节省建筑体积，加快锅炉起动，并可以不用一般的锅炉所需要的强力鼓风机和抽风机。

利用燃气轮机来改进蒸汽电站效率的另一些办法是：通过利用废气来加热给水，或者用废热锅炉来产生蒸汽。

燃气轮机对于提供一个附加的峰值负荷及备用功率来说，是一种非常引人注意的手段。安装用于这一目的的燃气轮机造价比安装附加的蒸汽轮机或水力发电机机组要低。此外，燃气轮机还具有能够实现有效自动控制、结构简单、所需空间小、维修量最小等等优点。燃气轮机另一个类似的用途是用于线端升压器，为远距离输电线服务。第三是用于流动发电站。在这种情况下，燃气轮机可装在铁路车辆或驳船上供紧急情况之用。

除灰及灰的处理(7.1)

在燃用固体燃料情况下，除灰及其处理问题是很重要的。燃料油中的灰量往往很小，其问题主要是在炉膛内和炉墙上。电气除尘器有时也用于改善烟囱排出的视感。

早期煤的燃烧方法是在自然通风的炉排上燃烧，其大部分煤灰是留在炉排上而后排向灰斗再行处理。采用现代化的机械给煤机后，例如抛煤机炉中，部分燃料是在浮悬状态下完成燃烧的，这就使烟气中含有较大的颗粒物质。

采用煤粉燃烧时，煤的全部燃烧都在悬浮状态下完成。结果是在固态排渣的煤粉炉中大约有80%～90%的灰被烟气带走。在液态排渣的煤粉炉中，这个数字大约可减少到50%左右。

在旋风炉中燃烧时，烟气中飞灰量可以减少到煤的含灰量的20%～30%。与干态排渣煤粉炉相比较，旋风炉烟气中所携带的灰粒将降低2/3或3/4。从成本观点出发，这一点对能使在排烟中达到规定的含颗粒量的设备投资来说，是重要的。在有可能对旋风炉燃烧作出改进或发展一种经济的或可靠的烟气清洁系统以前，旋风炉仅用于经过很慎重选择的工程。它是为了达到高稳定的运行而采用的高度紊流和高燃烧率，同样也会使烟气中的成分不能满足现行的美国环境保护处理。

从炉膛中除灰 在机械加煤机炉和干态排渣煤炉设计中,灰是沉积在灰斗中然后再排除进行处理。这种炉渣的某些可能利用是填地、道路底层材料、屋顶颗粒填充材料、混凝土块骨料和混凝土预制件、柏油混合料、结冰路面覆盖料、保温和喷砂用的砂子。以干法取自机械加煤机炉和煤粉炉的灰渣也可用于上述大部分用途。

烟气中灰粒的清除 为了达到清洁排烟的目的,当燃料呈悬浮燃烧时,现在普遍需要某些型式的去除灰粒的设备去除掉机组烟气中的飞灰。现有好几种型式的灰粒去除设备,它们可以分为电气除尘器、机械除尘器、面袋式除尘器和湿式除尘等。对用这些型式的设备所除去的飞灰来讲,这些飞灰也可以用于上述的灰渣的大多数用途中。

电气除尘器 电气除尘器能在要收集的颗粒上产生一种电荷,由静电力将这些带电荷的颗粒推到集尘板上。这种除尘器在运行上包括四个基本步骤:

1. 在电晕电极和集尘板之间保持一个强的高电压电场;
2. 带飞灰的烟气被强力电场离子化,这些烟气离子又使携带的颗粒带电荷;
3. 处于静电场内的带负电荷的颗粒被吸引到带正电荷(接地的)的集尘板上;
4. 已收集的灰尘受到敲打后掉落到贮灰斗中。

电气除尘器的收集效率与灰粒暴露在静电场内的时间、电场强度以及灰粒的电阻有关。与其他形式设备比较,一般是在有利的投资条件下获得99%以上的效率。因此从1970年以来安装于商业用的锅炉房内的灰颗粒清除装置绝大部分是电气除尘器。

机械除尘器 机械除尘器的运行是使带有灰粒的烟气切向流入除尘器的本体,因而在要收集的灰粒上就产生一个离心力。灰粒甩在除尘器的壁上,在那里被排除掉。机械除尘器最有效的运动条件是灰颗粒尺寸在 10 μm以上,当灰粒在 10 μm 以下时,除尘效率大大下降,可能降到 90% 以下。由于对除尘效率要求日益增高,机械除尘器的采用率已经下降。

布袋除尘器 布袋除尘器的运动是将烟气碰撞在由织物构成的细密过滤器上将灰尘捕获,当将灰尘连续收集时,积累的灰粒粘住在织物的表面上。布袋除尘器获得最大效率是当灰尘积聚到堵塞织物前的这段时期,在固定运动周期以后布袋必须清理。紧接着布袋清理以后过滤效率将有所降低,直到灰尘又开始积聚起来。

布袋除尘器可以应用于任何需要干除尘的工艺流程和对要处理的气体中的温度和湿度并不对其产生限制的场合。在效率等于或低于99%时,布袋除尘器一般不能与电气除尘器在锅炉上的应用作竞争。可是,对于除颗粒物质,采用布袋除尘器可以获得99%以上的效率,在人口密集区的应用可能增加。

湿式除尘器　湿式除尘器是利用适当的液体来收集灰尘,从而将灰尘由烟气中除去(见原文),一种好的湿式除尘器可以使烟气流和液体之间形成密切的接触,从而达到由烟气中将浮悬颗粒物转移到液体中去的目的。在湿式除尘器运动中,其集尘效率、灰粒大小和压降三者是密切相关的。需要的运行压降是在给定效率下与灰粒大小成反比变化,或者是在给定的颗粒大小下,除尘效率由于运动压降的增加而增加。

和其他的颗粒物质收集设备不同之处是,湿式除尘器是利用一种液体去收集颗粒物质。为了这个缘故,往往除集尘外,常常还执行附加工艺过程的功能,如气体吸收、化学反应和热传导等,在湿式除尘器中采用合适的冲洗液体时可以同时完成除尘和除去气体污染物质。

油灰腐蚀(7.2)

高温腐蚀　当钠和钒的复合物熔化时是具有腐蚀性的,在油灰沉积物中经常有这种复合物。腐蚀的机理可能是由于金属的加速氧化作用,即由于熔融灰中的组成成分将氧传送到金属表面上去而引起的,还由于灰将金属表面正常的氧化保护层除去而引起的。

腐蚀也可能是由于硫酸盐的侵蚀而产生的,特别是当燃料油中也存在着氯化钠或其他氯化物时。这种腐蚀易于在燃用含低钒量但含有万分之几的氯化钠的燃油锅炉中产生。当围绕管子四周的气氛是还原气氛,或者是氧化和还原交替变化的气氛时,即使燃料油中所含有氯化物是少得可以忽略不计,但硫酸盐的腐蚀仍可能是严重的。

一个可以测量得出来的腐蚀率可以在较大的金属温度和烟温范围内观察出来,这取决于油灰沉积物的量及其成分。燃料油中含钒量的高低对腐蚀的影响不是十分明显的，因为燃烧条件或燃料油中氯化物的含量都可能在起主导作用。但是钠的含量对发生显著腐蚀的最低金属温度的影响则是肯定的。

在目前似乎没有任何一种合金不受油灰腐蚀的，一般说来，合金中的含铬量越高，则越能抗腐蚀。这就是在高温过热器管采用 18Cr–8Ni 合金的原因。含铬量大于 30% 的高铬合金可能增加抗腐蚀能力，但这是在牺牲了物理性能的条件下获得的。曾经用过 25Cr–20Ni 合金作为管子的包覆层，但是甚至这种合金也不能起完全保护的作用。在高温合金内加入锡是为了增加强度。高锡合金在氧化气氛条件下有相当抗油灰腐蚀的能力，但是易于受到由于局部还原性气氛或由于灰沉积物中存在氯化物而引起的硫化物侵蚀。要完全避免这种条件是有困难的，因此高锡合金的优点可能是有限的。无论如何，价格昂贵的材料要以长的使用寿命来证明是否合算，但这并不是经常可以预测准确的。

低温腐蚀 在燃油锅炉中的低温腐蚀问题，是由于炉烟中硫酸的形成和凝结而引起的，这与上述的燃煤锅炉的情况相似。

由于以下的两种原因，燃油锅炉比大多数燃煤锅炉易于受低温腐蚀：

(1) 油灰沉积物中的钒是将 SO_2 转换成 SO_3 的一个良好催化剂；

(2) 在烟气中的灰量较少。在烟气中的灰粒会减少烟气中的 SO_3 含量。由于油中的灰比煤中的灰少得多，所以这种显著的不同是在预料之中的。此外，煤灰比油灰的碱性大，这有助于中和任何淀积的酸，而油灰一般就缺少这种性能。

在某些情况下，燃油锅炉可能由烟囱排出酸性的灰粒，这种酸性灰粒会污染或腐蚀厂房附近有色彩物体的表面。酸性的沉积物或烟炱通常是由于金属表面(如空气预热器、烟道和烟囱)在低于烟气露点很多的情况下运动而引起的，或者由于流过锅炉通道中吸收了硫酸气的烟灰所引起的。有下列几种方法用来防止排出酸性的烟炱：

1. 在烟气中将 SO_3 的形成减到最小程度；
2. 将烟气中的 SO_3 中和；
3. 保持所有与烟气接触的金属表面温度高于 250 °F；
4. 燃料油完全燃烧，以消除烟炱颗粒。

控制方法 曾经采用或建议过控制燃油锅炉的沾污和腐蚀的一些方法，但是在每种情况下，这些方法的适用性都受到经济情况的支配。无疑地，减少进入炉膛的灰量和硫量是最有把握的控制手段,但是只要灰的组成成分已经沉积在管子上,要将其影响减到最小也是不可靠的。由于污染和腐蚀的严重性不仅取决于燃料油的特性,还取决于锅炉设计和运行中的变化,因此,对于这些问题,无法规定出一个笼统的解决办法。

燃料油的供应 虽然在美国,选择用油和用混合油的方式已实行到某种程度,但是这是为了在用户厂中的安全和可靠的运输和贮存而执行的,并不是为了解决污染的困难。由于对钠、硫和钒的极限限度不是为了避免沾污,也不是为了避免腐蚀而准确规定的,因此不能充分利用这些方法来作为控制的手段。

对燃料油的脱硫和除去灰分是两种可用的处理方法。对渣油用水冲洗的方法已经在少数船舶锅炉上应用得很成功。但是这一措施只能除去钠和以铁锈和沙子为主的沉淀物,因此,要广泛采用这种方法是有疑问的。燃用低含硫量,低灰分的原油和采用对燃料进行脱硫的方法预期会增加。

燃料油添加剂 在锅炉停役期间用冲洗的习惯做法以及在有限的范围内在锅炉运行时用水冲洗,这都能克服燃用现在的燃料油时有所遇到的困难。此外,对这种问题进行继续研究的结果,发现了在燃料油灰最令人麻烦的地方可以采用的一种其它方法。简单地说,这种方法是向燃料油中或向炉膛中加入少量能足够改变油灰特性的材料,就可以用蒸汽吹灰器或空气吹灰器或空气枪将灰除去。

添加剂对减轻与过热器沾污、高温灰的腐蚀和低温硫酸腐蚀等有关的困难是有效的。最有效的添加剂是氧化铝、白云石和氧化镁。高岭土也是氧化铝的一种原料。

沾污和高温腐蚀的减轻主要是靠生成了呈粉状或脆性而且易于用吹灰器或吹灰枪吹去的高熔点的灰沉积物。当灰呈干态时,腐蚀会大大地减轻。

形成的耐熔硫酸盐与烟气中的 SO_3 气体发生反应后,可以减少低温硫酸腐蚀,这样就除去了 SO_3 气体,烟气的露点能降低到足以保护金属表面的温度,这样形成的硫酸盐化合物是比较干燥的,易于用一般标准的清理设备来清除。

一般说来,所用添加剂的量约等于燃料油中的含灰量。在某些情况下,为了能获得最好的效果,需用稍为不同的比例,特别是为了减低高温腐蚀,一般公认的是以油中的含钒量为依据,所用添加剂,按重量的比例与含钒量之比应为 2∶1 或 3∶1。

曾经成功地用过几种方法将添加剂加入炉膛中去。其中普遍采用的一种方法是将规定剂量的添加剂溶液,有控制地加入燃烧器的供油管道中去。为了添加剂能很好地弥散和对油雾化器的磨损减少到最小的程度,要将添加剂粉碎到能100%通过325目的筛子,也就是44 μm的筛子。

对用高压回流油系统的燃油锅炉,有利的是在所需要的位置,将添加剂粉末吹入炉膛内。为了很好地弥散,添加剂粉末一定要能100%通过325目的筛子。

第三种方法,也就是最近采用的那一种方法,是将添加剂调成水浆的形式,通过专门的吹灰器或吹灰枪喷入锅炉。这种方法的优点是添加剂能正确地用在所需要的地点,这就有可能减少需用的添加剂量。用这个系统,一定要小心观察,以避免造成对管子的热冲击,也就是冷淬裂纹。在添加剂水浆中有氯化物时,就有可能对奥氏体钢产生应力腐蚀裂纹,这是应该注意的。氯化物或者于水中,或者来自于添加剂。

对各种添加剂的选用,取决于各个厂是否能获得这些添加剂及其价格是否合适,还取决于所选用的方法。例如,在用添加剂浆的方法时,用氧化铝就比用其他材料对喷雾板的磨损要快些。

从清理问题方面来讲,对每一台设备所生成的沉积物的量是要考虑的一个重要问题。采用不同的添加剂时,对其所生成沉积物的量进行比较,表明白云石生成的沉积物量最多,这是由于白云石与硫酸盐化合的能力强;氧化铝和高岭土生成的沉积物最少;氧化镁所生成的沉积物在这两者之间。但是,在有合适的清理设施时,沉积物是易于清除的,因此所生成的量应该不成为一个问题。

用过剩空气量控制 如上所述,在燃烧渣油时所遇到的高温沉积物(沾污)、高温腐蚀和低温硫酸腐蚀等问题,都是由于有呈最高氧化状态的钒和硫的存在而引起的。如果将过剩空气量由7%减少到1%或2%,就有可能避免完全氧化的钒化合物和硫化合物的形成,因此,也就减轻了锅炉的沾污和腐蚀的问题。

在一台试验锅炉上进行的一系列试验中发现,当过剩空气量由7%的平均值减到1%~2%的水平时,则304型不锈钢过热器合金管在2 100 ℉温度烟气中维持在1 250 ℉的温度时,其最大腐蚀率可减低75%以上。此外,与在过剩空气量约为7%时生成的紧紧粘在管子上的硬而且密集的灰沉积物相对照,在过剩空气量为1%~2%时,在过热器管束上所形成的灰沉积物是软的,并且是粉状的,其灰的聚集率也只有硬的密集的灰聚集率的一半那么大。在1%~2%的过剩空气量下运行,并保持所有的金属温度高于烟气中水的露点,实际上清除了碳钢的低温腐蚀。但是,假若在燃烧器处过剩空气量有波动,即使在短时间波动量仅达到5%的水平,则部分在低过剩空气量燃烧所得到的有益的效果也都损失了。低过剩空气量下的碳损失约为0.5%,这个数值一般来说,是能为电力公用事业和工业所接受的。

在美国和欧洲的大型工业锅炉曾有好几年都在低的过剩空气量下运行,其结果证明这对减轻低温腐蚀是有好处的。但是,它对减轻高温结渣和高温腐蚀是否有好处,还没有得出结论。无论如何,必须对各个燃烧器的燃料和空气的平均分配给以极大的注意,必须连续不断地监视燃烧情况,以保证燃烧气体在进入对流通道的管束以前,燃料已完全燃烧。

压力测量(7.11)

测量压力、温度、流量、蒸汽的干度和蒸汽的纯度所用的仪表和测量的方法,是在蒸汽发生设备的运行中必不可少的。为了确保设备安全、经济、可靠的运行,所用的仪表和测量方法所涉及范围是由最简单的手动装置到用于对锅炉和其有关设备实行完全自动控制的测量设备。

试验监测仪表往往是便携式的。它用于设备的性能试验中,以确定所要求的流量、压力和温度是否已经符合设计和运行的条件,使用户和设备供应者都感到满意。对这些仪表的要求在 ASME 性能试验法规中作了概述。这些仪表需要技术熟练的操作者小心地管理和经常地校验。这种仪表不适宜用于长期连续的商业运行。

商业所用的仪表是那些永久固定安装的仪表,并且预期在持久的时期内会有满意的准确度。要强调仪表的可靠性和复现性。这往往要求对绝对的准确度作些让步。但是,商用仪表的准确度正在逐步改进,现在用于试验目的的商用仪表也正在增加。

压力测量

压力表可能是最早用于锅炉运行的仪表。在第一台"水管安全式"锅炉问世一百多年以后的今天,虽然采用了现代化控制设备和联锁装置使锅炉超压在实际上是不可能的,但是用压力表来测定汽包的压力仍是需要的。图7.9(见原文)示出了已经多年采用作为指示压力的波登管式压力表。虽然这种仪表在结构上和准确度方面已经作了许多改进,但是其基本原理还是没有什么变化。

压力测量仪表根据压力的大小、所需要的准确度和其他条件,有各种不同的型式。

流体压力计是根据压力的大小在表内装有各种不同的流体。这种表在仔细运用时,可以有高的准确度。装用的流体是不同的,由测量低压时采用的比水为轻的流体,到测量比较高的压力时采用的水银,图7.10(见原文)示出一个用于测量低压力时能读出小压差的倾斜式差压计。磁力作用的膜片式差压计现已用于低压测量。图7.11(见原文)示出高压水银压力计。这些压力计是用于压力测量或压差测量的准确工具,符合于 ASME 性能试验法规的要求。在测量小压差而精确度又较高的测量中,例如要读出流量孔板的压差的准确读数时,就可以用管压力表(或者叫做微压计)来测量。图7.12(见原文)所示为一种管压力计。

波登压力表可用于各种不同程度的精确度和准确度的范围大的静压测量。必需的精确度和准确度是由应用的要求来决定的。作为运行指导用的压力表不需要高的精确度,一般表计的分刻度约为表盘的全刻度范围的1%就可以了。在某些试验过程中,如承压部件的静水压试验和锅炉效率试验,就需要较高的精确度。分刻度为表盘的全刻度范围的0.1%的仪表是合用的,并且是为了这些目的所必须采用的。在要求得到高精确度的温度和压力,以便能准确地确定蒸汽和水的焓的锅炉效率试验中,这时对压力的测量采用自重压力计比采用波登压力计更好些。

膜片式压力表可以作测量压差之用。图7.13(见原文)所示为一种典型的能读出小压差的挠性膜片压力表,用在总压力不超过1 psig 的地方,读出的压差单位为英寸水柱。用对称安装的两个波纹管式的压力表(见原文图7.14),可以读出范围大的压差。这种压力表适合于读出流过锅炉回路的流体压降。在压力高达6 000 psi 时,可以用来测量从2到1 000 psi 的压差。

目前市场上有许多测量压力和压差用的技术先进的装置。这些装置一般称为变换器,它是根据不同的原理工作的。例如,有装在薄膜上的应变计式的变换器,或者是晶体变换器,当元件变形时,晶体的电阻就发生变化。由于这些元件需要精密的和经常的较验,因此一般不作为运行指导或设备试验用的基本仪表。但是这种仪表的可靠性正在提高，并且它易于应用，因此压力变换器的应用愈来愈广泛。

压力读数

在记录和报告压力读数时，如果表计有连接的水柱的情况，则对表计的读数一定要作对水柱的修正。如果有需要时，将压力表的读数加上大气压，换算成绝对压力值。水柱仅仅是添加在表计的额外压力，而不是实际压力所起的作用，它不过是在表计上面的凝结水柱或水柱的实际压力。图7.15（见原文）说明对压力表读数作水柱修正的应用。在实际使用中，在系统中没有压力时，将仪表水柱充满水，然后将表计重新校正到零，这种作法是完全可以的。

在各种形式测量装置两端的压降可作为测量流量的一种手段，诸如孔板、喷嘴或皮托管等的压差。这将在本章末叙述。

压力测量仪表的连接

确定测量装置连接到压力源的位置的指导原则，不管测量压力的大小、测量设施的形式或被测量的流体的类型是怎样的，一般都是一样的。

在管道、烟道或导管的压力连接管或取压接头一定要放在能避免由于流体冲击或涡流而会引起误差的位置。这样就可以保证所测得的是真正的静压。连接管线要尽可能短和尽可能直接连接，而且没有泄漏。为了得到压差数值时，宁可用一个压差测量装置而不用在两个仪表上取得读数后，再求出其差值。

7.12 洁净煤技术

众所周知，煤是一种"脏"燃料，因此，必须开发洁净煤技术，以满足严格的环境法要求。

第一个方法是开发除污染设备，以减少现有煤粉炉的排放污染物。这一设备处理过程包括炉内燃烧处理（一次过程）和/或炉膛出口烟道气的处理（二次过程）。

第二个方法是在锅炉设计中完全采用流化床燃烧这一新技术，它可以保证炉内煤燃烧的状态,以同时消除 NO_x 和 SO_x。除此之外,煤气化技术也包括在内。

本文所考虑的洁净煤技术包括:
1. 对已有锅炉,一次和二次除污染系统;
2. 装有烟气净化设备的煤粉炉;
3. 常压循环流化床燃烧;
4. 增压鼓泡流化床燃烧;
5. 增压循环流化床燃烧;
6. 整体煤气化(蒸汽-燃气)联合循环;
7. 混合循环应用于循环流化床。

对已有电厂的洁净煤技术改造

·一次过程

脱氮装置。燃烧器的设计越来越注重控制燃烧过程中氮氧化物的生成量。这些燃烧器被称作"低 NO_x 燃烧器",其方法是空气分段送入并改变燃料分配(以分段燃烧)。其原理是避免过高的火焰温度,以减少炉内的过量氧气,从而降低氮氧化物的生成量。另一种一次过程是将炉膛燃烧用的空气分段,称为"过燃风"。还有一种方法是将燃料分段送入炉膛,称为"再燃料"。

脱硫装置。一次除硫工艺是向炉内喷入细粉状石灰或石灰石,以吸收燃料过程中产生的二氧化硫。如有必要,可向烟气中喷入熟石灰和水,以提高脱硫效率。这一工艺的效率适中,约为 40%~70%,但花费较低。

·二次过程

脱氮装置。可使用有催化或无催化化学过程,以减少 NO_x 排放量。最常用的二次过程(95%的已安装系统)选用选择性催化氧化过程。氨气与烟气在炉膛出口空气预热器之前混合,然后混合气体通过附有催化剂的反应器(反应)生成 N_2 和水。运行时温度控制在 350~430℃。

脱硫装置。新近安装的机组中,一般使用以湿石灰/石膏作原料的烟道气除硫系统,以减少 SO_2 的排放量。SO_2 是以 $CaSO_4$ 的形式从烟气中清除掉的。该工艺必须通过一个湿式过程生成悬浮的钙的碳酸盐、亚硫酸盐、硫酸盐产物。

常压循环流化床燃烧

常压循环流化床燃烧的电厂的工作原理是,煤在流化床炉体内完全燃烧发出热量,(加热水)以产生高温高压的水蒸气。炉内压力大致为常压,流化速度很高。被带出炉膛的固体颗粒被搜集并重新送回炉内。这种固体物质的炉内循环可保证煤在约850℃的炉温下充分燃烧(这一温度有利于二氧化硫与石灰石合并使氮氧化物生成量最少)。蒸汽膨胀冲动汽轮机,汽轮机带动交流发电机发电。

增压鼓泡流化床燃烧

在增压鼓泡流化床燃烧的电厂中,锅炉工作在 $1.0 \times 10^6 \sim 1.6 \times 10^6$ Pa 的压力下,炉床的流化速度很低。这样,流化床上的固体颗粒与上部的气化层完全分开。在这样的流化速度下,气化鼓泡可通过炉床到达其表面,因此被称作"鼓泡床"。电力由两台发电机发出,一台连接蒸汽轮机,它通过蒸汽扩容过程带动发电,另一台连接燃气轮机,它通过燃气的膨胀做功带动发电。增压鼓泡流化床燃烧技术是一个联合循环。

增压循环流化床燃烧

在增压循环流化床燃烧的电厂中,锅炉工作在 $1.0 \times 10^6 \sim 1.6 \times 10^6$ Pa 的压力下,炉床的流化速度很高,近似于常压循环流化床燃烧。增压循环流化床燃烧,其循环流化床上的特点与常压循环流化床燃烧相同。惟一不同的是,增压循环流化床燃烧,其炉膛是在增压的条件下运行。

整体煤气化(蒸汽-燃气)联合循环

在整体煤气化联合循环中,首先将煤气化产生的煤气净化,特别是除尘、除硫化物,再燃烧,(燃气)一般进入燃气轮机以带动发电。余热锅炉利用燃气的部分显热产生蒸汽。这些蒸汽也被用来驱动蒸汽轮机发电。

今天,残煤或残油的气化新技术为高效率的联合循环发电提供可能。整体煤气化联合循环技术分多种类型。它们既可以按气化床的种类(固定床、流化床)划分,也可以按所用的氧化剂(空气或氧气)种类和按燃气净化系统不同来划分。

附 录 I

常用缩写词

a absolute 绝对的
　　ampere 安培
A angstrom 埃(10^{-8}厘米)
AAEC Australian Atomic Energy Commission 澳大利亚原子能委员会
ABAI American Boiler & Affiliated Industries 美国锅炉及附属设备制造商协会
abbr abbreviation 缩写
ABC automatic boiler control 锅炉自动控制
ABMA American Boiler Manufactures Association 美国锅炉制造商协会
abr abridged 节略
　　abridgement 节略
abs absolute 绝对的
ABS American Bureau of Standards 美国标准局
Abs E absolute error 绝对误差
abstr abstract 提要,简解
abs visc absolute viscosity 绝对粘度
abt about 大约
AC air-coal 风-煤,空气-煤[粉]
　　alternating current 交流电
acc acceleration 加速度
　　according to 按照

ACC　　automatic combustion control 自动燃烧调节
ACE　　automatic computing equipment 自动计算设备
ACM　　Association for computing machine 计算机协会(美)
　　　　automatic computing machine 自动计算机
ACRS　　Advisory Committee on Reactor Safeguards 反应堆安全监察咨询委员会
ACS　　American Ceramic Society 美国陶瓷学会
　　　　American Chemical Society 美国化学学会
ADC　　analog digital converter 模拟数字变换器
add　　addenda 补遗
ADI　　American Documentation Institute 美国文献资料工作研究学会
adj　　adjustment 调节,调整
ADP　　automatic data processing 自动数据处理
AE　　acoustic emission 声发射
AEA　　Atomic Energy Authority 原子能局(英)
AEC　　Atomic Energy Commission 原子能委员会(美)
AEEW　　Atomic Energy Establishment Winfirth 原子能中心(英)
AEI　　Associated Electric Industries Ltd. 联合电气制造公司(英)
AERE　　Atomic Energy Research Establishment 原子能研究所(英)
AESC　　American Engineering Standards Committee 美国工业标准委员会
AF　　audio frequency 声频
　　　　automatic following 自动跟踪
AFC　　automatic frequency control 自动频率调整
AFWC　　automatic feed water control 给水自动调节
AGA　　American Gas Association 美国煤气协会
AGC　　automatic gain control 自动增益控制
agg　　aggregate 总计,总数
AICE,AIChE　　American Institute of Chemical Engineers 美国化学工程师学会

AIEE　　American Institute of Electrical Engineers 美国电气工程师学会
AIME　　American Institute of Mining, Metallurgical & Petroleum Engineers 美国采矿、冶金与石油工程师学会
AIMME　　American Institute of Mining & Metallurgical Engineers 美国采矿及冶金工程师学会
AISC　　American Institute of Steel Construction 美国钢结构研究所
AISE　　American of Iron & Steel Engineers 钢铁工程师学会
AISI　　American Iron and Steel Institute 美国钢铁学会
ALGOL　　algorithmic language 算法语言（电子计算机用的一种自动化语言）
alk　　alkali 石
　　　　alkaline 碱性
alt　　alternating 交变,交替
　　　　alteration 改变,变化
　　　　altitude 高度
AM　　amplitude modulation 调幅
amb　　ambient 周围的
amp　　ampere 安培
amt　　amount 数量,合计
amu　　atomic mass unit 原子质量单位
ANACOM　　analog computer 模拟计算机
ANGA　　American Natural Gas Association 美国天然气协会
ANL　　Argonne National Laboratory 阿贡国家实验所（美）
ANSI　　American National Standards Institute 美国全国标准学会
Anth　　anthracite 无烟煤
AOV　　automatically operated valve 自动阀
APC　　American Power Conference 美国动力会议
APCA　　Air Pollution Control Association 空气污染控制协会
API　　American Petroleum Institute 美国石油学会

app　　apparatus　仪表,工具,装置,设备
appl　　applied　应用的,实用的,外加的
appr, approx　　approximate　近似的
appx　　appendix　附录
ap　　aqueous　水的
ARC　　automatic remote control　自动遥控
ASA　　American Society of Acoustics　美国声学学会
　　　　American Standards Association　美国标准协会
asb　　asbestos　石棉
ASC　　automatic sequence control　自动顺序控制
ASCE　　American Society of Civil Engineers　美国土木工程师学会
ASHAE　　American Society of Heating & Air-condition Engineers　美国采暖与空气调节工程师学会
ASHRAE　　American Society of Heating Refrigerating & Air Conditioning Engineers　美国采暖、制冷及空气调节工程师学会
ASHVE　　American Society of Heating & Ventilating Engineers　美国采暖及通风工程师学会
ASM　　American Society for Metals　美国金属学会
ASME　　American Society of Mechanical Engineers　美国机械工程师学会
ASME PTC　　ASME Power Test Codes　美国机械工程师学会动力试验规程
ASNT　　American Society for Nondestructive Testing　美国无损检验学会
ASQC　　American Society for Quality Control　美国质量检验学会
Assn　　Association　协会,学会
assoc　　association　协会,学会
ASST　　American Society for Steel Treating　美国钢材处理学会
ASTC　　automatic steam temperature control　蒸汽温度自动控制
ASTM　　American Society for Testing Materials　美国试验与材料学会

at atmosphere 大气压
at atomic heat 原子热容量
atm atmosphere 大气压
att attached 附件
at wt atomic weight 原子量
aut automatic 自动的
aux auxiliary 辅助的
av ,avg average 平均的
AWS American Welding Society 美国焊接学会
BAEA British Atomic Energy Authority 英国原子能管理局
BAERE British Atomic Energy Research Establishment 英国原子能研究中心
BBC Brown Boveri & Company Ltd 勃朗·鲍维利公司(瑞士)
bbl barrel 桶(美制=159公升,英制=163.7公升)
BBS British Standard Sieve 英国标准筛
BCS British Computer Society 英国计算机协会
BCURA British Coal Utilization Research Association 英国煤炭利用研究协会
BE boiler extration valve 炉膛排水阀
BEAMA British Electrical & Allied Manufacturers Association 英国电气制造商协会
BES burner executive system 喷燃器执行系统
BESA British Engineering Standard Association 英国工程标准协会
BEV billion electron volts 十亿电子伏
BFP boiler feed pump 锅炉给水泵
BFPT boiler feed pump turbine 带动锅炉给水泵的汽轮机
BH Brinell hardness 布氏硬度
BHP boiler horsepower 锅炉马力
　　　　brake horsepower 制动[有效]马力(轴功率)

BHRA　British Hydromechanics Research Association 英国流体力学研究学会

BISRA　British Iron & Steel Research Association 英国钢铁研究协会

Bit　bituminous 烟煤

BIW　British Institute of Welding 英国焊接研究所

BM　Bailey Meter Co. 倍莱仪表公司
　　　bill of material 材料清单

BMN　Beckman Instruments Inc. 贝克曼仪器公司

BNES　British Nuclear Energy Society 英国核能学会

BNL　Brookhaven National Laboratory 布鲁克海文国家实验所(美)

bp　boiler pressure 锅炉压力
　　　boiling point 沸点

BP, Br Pat　British Patent 英国专利

BR　breeding ratio 再生系数

Brit　British 英国的

BRRA　Basic Refractory Raw-materials Association 碱性耐火材料原料协会

BS　British Standard 英国标准
　　　Bureau of Standards 标准局(美)

bsh　bushel 蒲式耳(等于8加仑)

BSI　British Standards Institution 英国标准协会

BSS　British Standard Sieve 英国标准筛
　　　British Standard Specification 英国标准规范

BSWG　British Standard Wire Gauge 英国标准线规

BT　boiler throttle valve 锅炉节流阀

BTB　boiler throttle by-pass valve 锅炉节流旁路阀

BTU　British thermal unit 英热单位(等于252卡)

Bull　Bulletin 会报,公报

B & W　Babcock & Wilcox Co. 拔柏葛[-威尔考克斯]公司

BWC boiler water concentration 炉水浓度
BWR boiling water reactor 沸水[反应]堆
BWRA British Welding Research Association 英国焊接研究学会
c centi 百分之一
  constant 常数,恒定的
  cubic 立方的
  cycle 周,循环
C carbon 碳
  centigrade 摄氏温标,百分度,摄氏
  current 电流
CAD computer aided design 用计算机设计
cal calorie 卡
CBL Common Business Oriented Language 通用商业性语言(电子计算机用的一种自动化语言)
CC cubic centimeter 立方厘米
CCT continuous cooling transformation 连续冷却相变
CE Combustion Engineering Co. 燃烧工程公司(英)
  Consolidated Edison Company 联合爱迪生公司
CEA Central Electricity Authority 电力总局(英)
  Combustion Engineering Association 燃烧工程协会
CEGB Central Electricity Generating Board 中央电力局(英)
CERL Central Electricity Research Laboratories 中央电力研究试验所
cf compare 比较
  confer 参看
CFM cubic feet per minute 英尺^3/分
CFS cubic feet per second 英尺^3/秒
cg center of gravity 重心
CG chain grate 链条炉排
CGE Canadian General Electric Co Ltd. 加拿大通用电气公司

CGS　centimeter-gram-second 厘米-克-秒制
chap, ch　chapter 章
chem　chemical 化学的
CHU　caloric heat unit 测热单位
　　　centigrade heat unit 百度热量单位
cit　cited 引用
CM　centimeter 厘米
CMER　continuous maximum and most economical rating 连续最大和最经济的功率
CMIA　Coal Mining Institute of America 美国采煤研究所
CMR　continuous maximum rating 最大连续功率
CNC　Computer Numerical Control 群控,计算机数值控制
Co　company 公司
COD　crack opening displacement 裂纹张开位移
coef, coeff　coefficient 系数
const　constant 常数
Corp　corporation 公司
cp　centipoise 厘泊
　　　chemically pure 化学纯
CPC　card programmed electronic calculator 卡片程序电子计算机
cpm　counts per minute 每分钟次数
　　　cycles per minute 次/分
cps　cycles per second 周/(秒·赫兹),每秒循环次数
crit　critical 临界的
CRT　cathode ray tube 阴极射线显像管
CRV　convection recirculating valve 对流段再循环阀
CS　centistoke 厘沲(运动粘度单位)
CSIR　Council for Scientific & Industrial Research 科学与工业研究委员会

CT current transformer 电流互感器
ct cent 百分之一
CTU centigrade thermal unit 百分度热单位,磅-卡(454 卡)
cu cubic 立方的
CUC Coal Utilization Council 煤炭利用委员会(英)
cu ft cubic foot 立方英尺
cu in cubic inch 立方英寸
cu m cubic metre 立方米
cu mm cubic millimeter 立方毫米
CWT hundred weight 英担(英制=112 磅,美制=100 磅)
d depth 深度
D diameter 直径
DAC digital analog converter 数[字]模[拟]转换器
      digital-to-analog convertion 数[字]模[拟]转换
db decibel 分贝
     dry bulb 干球
DC digital computer 数字计算机
    direct current 直流电
DDC direct digital control 直接数字控制
def definition 定义
deg degree 度,级
Dept department 局,科,部门,车间,处,系
dev deviation 偏差
dia diameter 直径
diag diagram 图,图解
diff difference 差,不同
dil dilute 稀释,冲淡
dim dimension 尺寸,量纲
dist distance 距离

dm decimeter 分米
DNB departure from nucleate boiling 偏离核态沸腾
DNC Direct Numerical Control 群控,直接数值控制
do ditto 同前,同上,如前所述
doz dozen 一打,十二个
dp differential pressure 压差,压力降
DP data processing 数据处理
DSH desuperheater 减温器
DSIR Department of Scientific & Industrial Research 科学与工业研究总署
DVM digital voltmeter 数字电压表
Dwg drawing 图,图纸
EBR Experimental Breeder Reactor 实验性增殖反应堆
ECMB European Committee of Manufacturers of Burners 欧洲燃烧器制造商协会
Eco economizer 省煤器
ed edition 版,版次
EDP electronic data processing 电子数据处理
EEC English Electric Co Ltd 英国电气公司
　　European Economic Community 欧洲经济共同体
EEI Edison Electric Institute 爱迪生电气研究所
eff efficiency 效率
eg exempli gratia 例如
EGD Electro Gas Dynamics 电气体动力学
EI Engineering Index 工程[技术文献]索引
elec electrical 电的
el, elev elevation 高度
EMF electromotive force 电动势
enc, encl enclosure 附件

encyc　encyclop(a)edia 百科全书

Engng, Engg　engineering 工程

eq　equation 方程[式]

equip　equipment 设备,装置

equiv　equivalent 相等的,相当的,等效的,当量

ERE　Esso Research & Engineering Co 埃索工程研究公司

ERW　electric resistance welding 电阻焊

esp　especially 特别,尤其

ESSA　Environmental Science Services Administration 环境科学服务管理局(美)

est　estimated 估计的

et al　et alibi 等等

etc　et cetera 等等

et seq　et sequentia 及以下等等,参看以下等句或等项

Eu　Euler number 欧拉数

EURATOM　European Atomic Energy Community 欧洲原子能联营

EV　electron volt 电子伏特

EX　example 例,实例

excl　excluding 除去,不包括

exp　experiment 实验,试验
　　　exponent 指数

ext　external 外部的

f　foot 英尺
　　force 力
　　frequency 频率

F　Fahrenheit 华氏[温标]
　　force 力
　　function 函数

FBB　fluidized bed boiler 沸腾床锅炉

FBI Federation of British Industries 英国工业联合会
FBR Fast-Breeder Reactor 快中子增殖反应堆
FC fixed carbon 固定碳,结合碳
FCB fast cut back 快速切断
FD forced-draft-fan 送风机
fig figure 图
fl fluid 流体,液体
fl pt flash point 闪点,闪火点
FM frequency modulation 调频
Fortran formula translation 程序设计语言(电子计算机用的一种自动化语言)
FP feed pump 给水泵
　　 flash point 闪点
FPC Federal Power Commission 联邦电力委员会(美)
fph feet per hour 英尺/时
fpm feet per minute 英尺/分
fps feet per second 英尺/秒
FPS unit foot-pound-seconds unit 英尺-磅-秒单位,英制单位
Fr Froude number 弗鲁德数
FrP French Patent 法国专利
FPV furnace recirculating valve 炉膛再循环阀
FSH final superheater 末级过热器
FSS fuel safety system 燃料保护系统
ft foot 英尺
ft hd feet head 以英尺表示的压头
FW Foster Wheeler Corporation 福斯特·惠勒公司
FWB feedwater by-pass valve 给水旁路阀
FW-JB Foster Wheeler Ltd-John Brown Land Boilers Ltd 福斯特·惠勒-约翰·布朗陆用锅炉公司

FWPCA　Federal Water Pollution Control Administration 联邦水质污染管制局(美)
g　gauge 表计
　　gram(me) 克
gad　general assembly drawing 总装配图,总图
G　generator 发电机,发生器
　　giga 千兆,十亿(10^9)
gal　gallon 加仑
GB　Great Britain 英国
GCFBR　gas-cooled fast breeder reactor 气体冷却快中子增殖反应堆
GCR　Gas-Cooled Reactor 气冷反应堆
GEC　General Electric Co Ltd 通用电气公司(英)
　　General Electric Company 通用电气公司(美)
GGA　Gulf General Atomic, Inc 海湾通用原子能公司
GL　ground level 地平面
gm　gram(me) 克
g-mol　gram-molecule 克分子
GMR　Graphite-Moderated Reactor 石墨减速反应堆
gph　gallons per hour 加仑/时
gpm　gallons per minute 加仑/分
gps　gallons per second 加仑/秒
gr　grain 格令(等于 0.064 克)
Gr　Grashof number 格拉晓夫数
grad　gradient 梯度
GrBrit　Great Britain 英国
gr w　gross weight 毛重
h　hecto 百(10^2)
　　height 高度
　　hour 时,小时

HAZ heat affected zone 热影响区
HCV high calorific value 高热值
Hd head 扬程,压头
HEI Heat Exchange Institute 热交换学会
HF high frequency 高频
Hg abs inches mercury absolute 真空度,绝对英寸水银柱
HHV high(er)heat(ing) value 高热值
hon horizontal 水平的,水平线
HP high pressure 高压
　　　horse power 马力
hp -hr horsepower-hour 马力-小时
hr hour 小时
HRT horizontal return tubular boiler 卧式回火管锅炉
hs heating surface 受热面
ht height 高度
HTC heat transfer coefficient 传热系数
HTGR High Temperature Gas (Cooled) Reactor 高温气冷堆
HTR heater 加热器
HWR heavy water reactor 重水反应堆
Hz hertz 赫[兹]
IAE integral of absolute error 偏差绝对值积分[准则]
LATM International Association for Testing Materiasl 国际材料试验协会
ib ,ibid ibidem 在同书,在同章,在同处
IBM International Business Machines Corporation 国际商业计算机公司
IBWM The International Bureau of Weight & Measures 国家度量衡局
IBR Institute of Boiler and Radiator Manufacturers 锅炉及散热器制造商协会
IC integrated circuit 集成电路

International Combustion Engineering Co 国际燃烧工程公司(英)
ICE　Institute of Chemical Engineers 化学工程师学会
　　　internal combustion engine 内燃机
ICL　International Combustion Engineering Ltd 国际燃烧工程公司(英)
id　idem 同样,同前,同上
ID　induced draft 引风
　　　inside diameter 内径
IDF　induced-draft-fan 引风机
IDP　integrated date processing 综合数据处理
i e　id est 换言之,就是,即
IEC　International Electrotechnical Commission 国际电工委员会
IEE　Institute of Electrical Engineers 电气工程师学会(英)
IFAC　International Federation of Automatic Control 国际自[动]控[制]联合会
IFRF　International Flame Research Foundation 国际火焰研究中心(荷)
IG　Imperial Gallon 英加仑
ihp　indicated horse-power 指示马力
IIW　International Institute of Welding 国际焊接学会
illus　illustrated 附插图[的],插图[的]
　　　illustration 附插图,插图
IME,I Mech E　Institution of Mechanical Engineers 机械工程师学会(英)
in　inch 英寸
IN　inlet 入口,进口
Inc　incorporated 股份[公司]
incl　included 包括
　　　inclusive 包括
　　　index 指数,索引
ind　index 指数,索引
inf　infinity 无穷大

inHg inches of mercury 吋汞柱
inH$_2$O inches of water 吋水柱
inst institute 学会,协会,研究所,学院
institution 学会,协会
IP intermediate pressure 中压
iq idem quod 如同
IR infrared 红外线,红外[线]的
reheater injection valve 再热减温器进水控制阀
IS superheater injection valve 过热减温器进水控制阀
ISA Instrument Society of America 美国测量仪表学会
International Standardization Association 国际标准化协会
ISE integral of squared error 偏差平方积分[准则]
ISO International Standardization Organization 国际标准化组织
isoth isothermal 等温的
ISPR superheater injection pressure reducing valve 过热减温器进水压控制阀
ISU International Standard Unit 国际[标准]单位
ITV industrial television 工业电视
IU International Unit 国际单位
IV intercepter valve 遮断阀
j joule 焦耳
JAERI Japan Atomic Energy Research Institute 日本原子能研究所
JICRT Japan Information Center of Science & Technology 日本科技情报中心
JIS Japanese Industrial Standard 日本工业标准
jour journal 杂志期刊
JT John Thompson Group 约翰-汤姆逊公司,约翰-汤姆逊集团
K kelvin 开氏(绝对温标)
kilo 千

Kcal　kilocalorie 大卡
KE　kinetic energy 动能
kev　kilo electron-volt 千电子伏
Kg　kilogram 公斤,千克
Km　kilometre 公里
kv　kilovolt 千伏
KVA　kilovolt-ampere 千伏安
KW　kilowatt
kw-hr　kilowatt-hr 千瓦小时,度
l　left 左
　length 长度
　liter 升
lab　laboratory 实验室,试验所,实验所
LASL　Los Alamos Scientific Laboratory 洛斯·阿拉摩斯科学实验所（美）
lat ht　latent heat 潜热
lb　libra(pound) 磅(等于0.454千克)
lb per sq in　pound per square inch 磅/平方英寸
LCV　low calorific value 低热值
LEFM　linear elastic fracture mechanics 线弹性断裂力学
LF　low frequency 低频
LH　left hand 左的
LHV　low(er) heat(ing) value 低热值
lg　logarithm 对数
lib　library 图书馆
lim, lm　limit 限度,极限
liq　liquid 液体,液体的
LMBR　liquid-metal breeder reactor 液态金属增殖反应堆
LMFBR　Liquid-Metal Fast-Breeder Reactor 液态金属快中子增殖反

应堆
LMFR liquid-metal fuel reactor 液态金属燃料反应堆
LMTD logarithmic mean temperature difference 对数平均温差
L &N Leeds & Northrup Company 李兹、诺思拉普公司
LNG liquefied natural gas 液化天然气
LO Lox liquid oxygen 液态氧
log logarithm [常用]对数
long longitude 经度,经线
LP low pressure 低压
LPG liquefied petroleum gas 液化石油气
Ltd Limited 有限[公司]
l tn long ton 长吨
lu lumen 流明(光通量单位)
lub lubricant 润滑剂
LWBR Light-Water Breeder Reactor 轻水增殖反应堆
LWR light-water reactor 轻水[反应]堆
m mass 质量
mean 平均,平均值
metre 米
millki 毫(10^{-3})
minute 分
M Mach 马赫[数]
Mega 兆(10^6)
moment 力矩
ma milliampere 毫安
Ma Mach number 马赫数
mae mean absolute error 平均绝对误差
math mathematics 数学
matl material 材料

max maximum 最大的,最大值
mb millibar 毫巴
mc machine 机器,机械
 megacycle 兆周,兆赫
 millicurie 毫居里
MC manual control 手控
 master controller 主控制器
MCP master control program 主控程序
MCR maximum continuous rating 最大连续出力
ME Mechanical Engineering 机械工程
mech mechanical 机械的
mehp mean effective horse power 平均有效马力
meq milli-equivalent 毫克当量
MEV million electron-volts 百万电子伏特,兆电子伏特
MF medium frequency 中频
mfg manufacturing 制造,生产
mg milligram 毫克
MHD magnetohydrodynamics 磁流体动力学
MHF medium-high frequency 中高频
MIG metal inert gas welding 金属极惰性气体保护焊
min minimum 最小的,最小值
 minute 分
mip mean indicated pressure 平均指示压力
MISC miscellaneous 混杂的,各种各样的,多方面的
mixt mixture 混合物
mk mark 标记,符号
MKS meter-kilogram-second 米-公斤-秒制
ml milliliter 毫升
mm millimeter 毫米

mm Hg　millimeters of mercury 毫米汞柱
MMSA　Mining and Metallurgical Society of America 美国采矿冶金学会
mo　manually operated 用手操作的，手控的，手动的
mol　molecular 分子的
　　　molecule 分子
mol wt　molecular weight 分子量
MP　medium pressure 中压
　　　melting point 熔点
MPD　magnetoplasmodynamic 磁等离子动力学的
mph　miles per hour 哩/英寸
mps　meters per second 米/秒
MS, ms　main steam 主蒸汽
　　　manuscript 原稿
　　　mild steel 低碳钢
MSBR　Molten Salt Breeder Reactor 熔盐增殖反应堆
MSR　Molten Salt Reactor 熔盐反应堆
MT　metric ton 公吨
MTD　mean temperature difference 平均温差
mtl　material 材料
mv　millivolt 毫伏
MW　megawatt 兆瓦，千
MWh　megawatt-hour 兆瓦小时
na　non available 没有
NACA　National Advisory Committee for Aeronautics 国家航空咨询委员会(美)
NAM　National Association of Manufacturers 全国制造商协会(美)
NAPCA　National Air Pollution Control Administration 国家大气污染管制局
NAS　National Academy of Science 国家科学院(美)

NASA National Aeronautics and Space Administration 国家航空和宇宙航行局(美)
NB nota bene 注意
NBBPVI National Board of Boiler and Pressure Vessel Inspectors 国家锅炉及压力容器监察局
NBS National Bureau of Standards 国家标准局(美)
New British Standard 新英国标准
NC numerical control 数[字]控[制]
NCB National Coal Board 国家煤炭委员会(英)
NCR normal continuous rating 额定连续出力
NDI non-destructive inspection 无损探伤,无损检验
NDT non-destructive test 无损探伤,无损试验
neg negative 负的,负极,底片
NEMA National Electrical Manufactures Association 全国电气制造商协会(美)
National Electronic Manufacturing Association 全国电子制造协会
NERC National Electric Reliability council 全国电力安全委员会(美)
Nuclear Engineering Society 核工程学会(英)
nom nominal 额定的,名义的,铭牌的
NPA National Petroleum Association 国家石油协会(美)
NPI National Petroleum Institute 国家石油研究所(美)
NPSH net positive suction head 净吸入压头(泵)
npt normal pressure and temperature 标准压力及温度
NRC National Research Council 全国研究委员会(属美国科学院)
NRCC National Research Council (of Canada) 国家研究院(加拿大)
NRL Naval Research Laboratory 海军研究实验所(美)
NRV Non Return Valve 止回阀
NSA Nuclear Science Abstracts 核子科学文摘

NSS Nuclear Steam System 核蒸汽系统
NSSS Nuclear Steam Supply System 核蒸汽供应系统
ntp normal temperature and pressure 标准温度及压力
Nu Nusselt number 努赛尔特数
n(t)wt net weight 净重
o ohm 欧[姆]
OD outside diameter 外径
OF oil fuel 石油燃料
OFA over fire air 二次风(炉排上的),上部引入的助燃空气
OPEC Organization of Petroleum Exporting Countries 石油输出国组织
oper operation 运用,工作,运算
operator 操纵员,运行人员
opp opposed 对面,相反的
opt optimum 最佳值
ORNL Oak Ridge National Laboratory 橡树岭国家试验所(属美国原子能委员会)
OSRD Office of Scientific Research and Development 科学研究与发展部(美)
O T Boiler once through boiler 直流锅炉
oz ounce 盎司,(等于1/16磅)
p pitch 节距,齿距,螺距,间隔,行距
power 功率
P page 页
pico 微微(10^{-12})
poise 泊(黏度单位)
positive 正的,阳的
pressure 压力
par paragraph 段
pat patent 专利

PAW plasma arc welding 等离子弧焊
PB Publication Board (Report)(U. S. Dept. of Commerce) PB 报告书(美商务部技术服务处发行的政府研究报的总称)
PCC programme controlled computer 程序控制计算机
PCRV Prestressed-Concrete Reactor Vessel 预应力混凝土反应堆壳体
pcs pieces 个,件,片
pct percent 百分数
PCV pressure controlling valve 压力控制阀
PD pitch diameter 节径
pdl poundal 磅达(力的单位)
Pe Peclet number 贝古列数
PE potential energy 位能,势能
PF power factor 功率因数
      pulverized fuel 煤粉,粉状燃料
pkg package 包装,整装
PL program language 程序语言
pos positive 正的,阳的,阳极
pp pages 页(复数)
ppb parts per billion 十亿分之一(10^{-12})
ppm parts per million 百万分之一(10^{-6})
PPS purge and prelight system [炉膛]吹扫及点火准备系统
Pr Prandtl number 普朗特数
pri primary 初级,第一的
proc proceedings 论文集,学报,会议录
PS post scriptum 后记,附言,附录
psf pounds per square foot 磅/英尺^2
psi pounds per square inch 磅/英寸^2
psia pounds per square inch, absolute 磅/英寸^2,绝对
psig pounds per square inch, gauge 磅/英寸^2,表计

pt　pint 品脱
　　　point 点
PT　potential transformer ［测量用］变压器
pub　publisher 出版者
PVC　polyvinylchloride 聚氯乙烯
PVRC　Pressure Vessel Research Committee 压力容器研究委员会
PWR,pwr　power 功率,动力
　　　　　pressurized water preactor 压水［反应］堆
Q,qt　quart 夸脱(1/4 加仑)
ques　question 问题
quot　quotation 引语
R　radius 半径
　　　resistance 电阻,阻力
　　　right 右,右方
rad　radian 弧度
RAND　Research and Development Corporation 兰德［研究与发展］公司
R C　reinforced concrete 钢筋混凝土
rd　round 圆的
R &D　Research &Development 研究与发展
Re　Reynolds number 雷诺数
ref　reference 参考,引证,参照
reg　register 记录,指示；记录器,寄存器,调风器
rem　remark 备注
rep,rept　report 报告
req　required 所需要的
res　research 研究
resp　respectively 分别地,各自地
rev　review 评论
　　　　revolution 旋转

RH reheat 再热
   reheater 再热器
   relative humidity 相对湿度
   right hand 右侧,右的
RHN Rockwell hardness number 洛氏硬度值
R & M reports and memorandum 报告及备忘录
RMS root mean square 均方根
rpm revolutions per minute 转/分
rps revolutions per second 转/秒
RR research report 研究报告(特种文献)
RS Riley Stoker Corp 莱雷层燃炉公司
rs rolled steel 轧制钢
RSV reheat stop valve 再热截止阀
SA steam admission valve 进汽阀
sat,satd saturated 饱和的
satn saturation 饱和
sc scale 标度
SC standard conditions 标准状态
SCF standard cubic foot 标准立方英尺
SCFBR Steam-Cooled Fast-Breeder Reactor 蒸汽冷却快速中子增殖反应堆
scfm standard cubic feet per minute 标英尺^3/分
SCR silicon controlled rectifier 硅可控整流器,可控硅
SD standard deviation 标准偏差
   steam lead drain valve 主蒸汽疏水阀
sec second 秒
   secondary 二次的,第二的
sect section 截面,区域,部分
ser serial 连续的,顺次的

series 级数,系列
SESA Society for Experimental Stress Analysis 试验应力分析学会
sfc specific fuel consumption 单位燃料耗量
Sh Strouhal number 斯特劳哈尔数
SH superheater 过热器
sh tn short ton 短吨(=907公斤)
SGR sodium graphite reactor 钠石墨反应堆
SIC semiconductor intergrated circuit 半导体集成电路
sig signal 信号,信号的
SIGMA shielded inert-gas metal arc welding 惰性气体保护金属电弧焊
SMA Stoker Manufacturers Association 层燃炉制造商协会(美)
SM -steel Siemens-Martion steel 平炉钢
soc society 学会,社团
sol solution 溶液
SP specific 比[的],单位的
　　spillover valve 启动蒸汽溢放阀
　　standard pressure 标准气压
spec special 特殊的
　　specification 规格,说明书
sp ht specific heat 比热
sq vol specific volume 比容
sq square 平方
sq ft square foot 平方英尺
sq in square inch 平方英寸
sq yd square yard 平方码
ss superheated steam 过热蒸汽
SSFF Solid Smokeless Fuels Federation 固体无烟燃料联合会(英)
s t(n) short ton 短吨(等于907公斤)

St　Stanton number 史坦顿数
ST　standard temperature 标准温度
std　standard 标准,标准的
STP　standard temperature and pressure 标准温度与压力
suppl　supplement 补遗
supr　superheater 过热器
sym　symbol 符号,标志
　　　symmetric(al) 对称的
sys　system 系统
T　tee 三通
　　temperature 温度
　　time 时间
　　ton 吨
tab　table 表[格]
TC　thermocouple 热电偶
TDS　total dissolved solids 总固形物
tech　technical 技术的
temp　temperature 温度
term　terminology 术语,专门词汇
th　thermal 热的
TIG　tungsten inert-gas arc welding 钨极惰性气体保护[电弧]焊
TM　technical manual 技术手册
　　　technical memorandum 技术备忘录
tn　ton 吨
Torr　Torricellian unit 压力单位(=毫米汞柱)
TR　technical report 技术报告
trans　transactions 会报,学报
TS　tensile strength 抗拉强度
　　　tool steel 工具钢

TS diagram　temperature-entropy diagram 温-熵图
TU　thermal unit 热单位
TV　television 电视
　　throttle valve 节流阀
U　uranium 铀
UHV　ultrahigh vacuum 超高真空
UKAEA　United Kingdom Atomic Energy Authority 英国原子能委员会
ULF　ultralow frequency 超低频
ult　ultimate 极限的,最后的
UP　universal pressure 通用压力
USG　United States gallon 美制加仑
USP　United States Patent 美国专利
USPO　United States Patent Office 美国专利局
USS　United Stantes Standard 美国标准
UTS　ultimate tensile strength 抗拉强度极限
UV　ultraviolet 紫外线
v　valve 阀
　　variable 变数
V　velocity 速度
　　volt 伏[特]
　　volume 容积,卷
VA　volt-ampere 伏安
Vac　vacuum 真空,负压
val　value 数值
vap　vapo(u)r 蒸汽
var　variables 变数,变量
　　variety 变化,变种,多种多样
vel　velocity 速度
vers,vs　versus 对,与……比较

VHN Vickers hardness number 维氏硬度值
VI viscosity index 黏度指数
viscosity indicator 黏度指示器
visc viscosity 黏性
viscous 黏性的
VM volatile matter 挥发物,挥发分
vol volume 体积,卷
VTR video tape recorder 磁带录像机
vv vice versa 反之亦然
W watt 瓦特
weight 重量
width 宽度
work 功
WB wet bulb 湿球
WD water drain valve 分离器疏水阀
We Weber number 韦伯数
WE Westinghouse Electric Co 威斯汀毫斯电气公司
WG water gauge 水位表
wire gauge 线规
WH Watt-hour 瓦特小时
WI wrought iron 锻钢,熟铁
WP working pressure 工作压力
WPC World Power Conference 世界动力会议
WPC Welding Research Council 焊接研究委员会(英)
WT weight 重量
yd yard 码

附 录 Ⅱ

常用计量单位换算

(凡有 * 者为国际单位制规定的基本单位及导出单位)

1. 长 度

*米 (m)	英尺 (ft)(′)	英寸 (in)(′)	码 (yd)
1	3.281	39.37	1.094
0.304 8	1	12	0.333 3
0.025 4	0.083 3	1	0.027 8
0.914 4	3	36	1

1 米 = 100 厘米(cm) = 1 000 毫米(mm)

2. 面 积

*米^2 (m^2)	英尺^2 (ft^2)(′)	英寸^2 (in^2)(′)
1	10.76	1 550
0.092 9	1	144
0.064 52	0.694 4	100

1 米^2 = 10^4 厘米^2 = 10^6 毫米^2

3. 体积、容积

*米^3 (m^3)	英尺^3 (ft^3)(′)	英寸^3 (in^3)(′)	升 (l)	美加仑 (U.S. gal)	英加仑 (Imp. gal)
1	35.31	61 024	1	0.264 2	0.220
0.028 32	1	1 728	3.785	1	0.832 7
1.639×10^{-5}	5.787×10^{-4}	1	4.546	1.201	1

1 米^3 = 1 000 升
1 桶 = 315 加仑(美) = 36 加仑(英)

4. 质量

*公斤 (kg)	磅 (lb)	公斤力·秒^2/米 (kgf·s^2/m)
1	2.205	0.102 0
0.453 6	1	0.046 23
9.807	21.62	1

1 吨(t) = 1 000 公斤
1 公斤 = 1 000 克
1 磅 = 16 盎司(OZ)
1 长吨(英) = 1 016.6 公斤
1 短吨(美) = 907.2 公斤

5. 重量、力

*牛顿 (N)	公斤力 (kgf)	吨力 (tf)	磅力 (lbf)
1	0.102 0	1.020×10^{-4}	0.224 8
9.807	1	0.001	2.205
4.448	0.453 6	4.536×10^{-4}	1
9.807×10^3	1 000	1	2 205

1 牛顿 = 10^5 达因

6. 密度

*公斤/米^3 (kg/m^3)	公斤力·秒^2/米^4 (kgf·s^2/m^4)	磅/英尺^3 (lb/ft^3)
1	0.102 0	0.062 43
9.807	1	0.612 2
16.018	1.633	1

1 公斤/米^3 = 1 克/升

7. 重度(比重)

*牛顿/米^3 (N/m^3)	公斤力/米^3 (kgf/m^3)	磅力/项尺^3 (lbf/ft^3)
1	0.102 0	0.062 43
9.807	1	0.612 2
16.018	1.633	1

1 公斤力/米^3 = 1 克力/升

8. 压力

*牛顿/米^2 (N/m^2)	公斤力/厘米^2 (kgf/cm^2)	磅力/英寸^2 (lbf/in^2)
1	1.020×10^{-4}	1.449×10^{-4}
9.807×10^4	1	14.22
6.894×10^3	0.070 3	1

公斤力/厘米^2 (kgf/cm^2)	巴 (bar)	标准大气压 (atm)	公斤力/米^2 (kgf/m^2)	毫米汞柱 (mmHg)	毫米水柱 (mmH$_2$O)
1	0.980 7	0.968 1	1	0.073 53	1
1.020	1	0.987 2			
1.033	1.013	1	13.6	1	13.6

1 工程大气压(at) = 1 公斤力/厘米^2 1 公斤力/米^2 = 10^{-4} 公斤力/厘米^2

9. 动力黏度

*牛顿·秒/米^2 (N·s/m^2)	公斤力·秒/米^2 (kgf·s/m^2)	磅力·秒/英尺^2 (lbf·s/ft^2)	泊 (p)
1	0.102 0	2.089×10^{-2}	10
9.807	1	0.204 8	98.07
47.88	4.888	1	478.8
0.1	1.020×10^{-2}	2.088×10^{-3}	1

1 泊 = 100 厘泊

10. 运动黏度

*米²/秒 (m²/s)	英尺²/秒 (ft²/s)	泡 (St)
1	10.76	10^4
0.0929	1	929.3
10^{-4}	1.076×10^{-3}	1

1 泡 = 100 厘泡

11. 温度

*开氏温度 (K)	摄氏温度 (℃)	华氏温度 (℉)	列氏温度 (°R)

$K = ℃ + 273.15$

$℃ = \dfrac{5}{9}(℉ - 32)$

$°R = 460 + ℉$

12. 功、能

*焦耳 (J)	公斤力·米 (kgf·m)	磅力·英尺 (lbf·ft)
1	0.102	0.7359
9.807	1	7.215
1.356	0.1386	1

*焦耳 (J)	千卡 (kcal)	英热单位 (Btu)
1	2.388×10^{-4}	9.48×10^{-4}
4187	1	3.968
1055	0.252	1

1 千瓦·时(kW·h) = 367.1×10^3 公斤力·米 = 860 kcal

1 焦耳 = 1 牛顿·米

13. 功率

*瓦 (W)	公斤力·米/秒 (kgf·m/s)	公制马力 (ps)	英制马力 (Hp)
1	0.1020	1.36×10^{-3}	1.341×10^{-3}
9.807	1	1.333×10^{-2}	1.315×10^{-2}
735.5	75	1	0.9865
745.1	76	1.013	1

1 千卡/时 = 0.1186 公斤力·米/秒 = 1.163 瓦

1 英热单位/时 = 0.252 千卡/时 = 0.293 瓦

14. 热值、发热量

*焦耳/公斤 (J/kg)	千卡/公斤 (kcal/kg)	英热单位/磅 (Btu/lb)
1	2.388×10^{-4}	4.298×10^{-4}
4.187×10^{3}	1	1.80
2.326×10^{3}	0.555 6	1

*焦耳/米^3 (J/m^3)	千卡/米^3 (kcal/m^3)	英热单位/英尺^3 (Btu/ft^3)
1	2.388×10^{-4}	2.682×10^{-5}
4.187×10^{3}	1	0.112 4
3.725×10^{4}	8.896	1

15. 导热系数

*瓦/米·度 (W/m·℃)	千卡/米·时·度 (kcal/m·h·℃)	英热单位/英尺·时·℉ (Btu/ft·h·℉)
1	0.859 8	0.577 8
1.163	1	0.672 0
1.731	1.488	1

16. 传热系数

*瓦/米^2·度 (W/m^2·℃)	千卡/米^2·时·度 (kcal/m^2·h·℃)	英热单位/英尺^2·时·℉ (Btu/ft^2·h·℉)
1	0.859 8	0.176 2
1.163	1	0.204 9
5.678	4.882	1

17. 面积热强度

*瓦/米^2 (W/m^2)	千卡/米^2·时 (kcal/m^2·h)	英热单位/英尺^2·时 (Btu/ft^2·h)
1	0.859 8	0.317 0
1.163	1	0.368 8
3.154	2.712	1

18. 容积热强度

*瓦/米^3 (W/m^3)	千卡/米^3·时 (kcal/m^3·h)	英热单位/英尺^3·时 (Btu/ft^3·h)
1	0.859 8	9.664×10^{-2}
1.163	1	0.1124
10.35	8.898	1

19. 原子能

原子能量单位 (amu)	兆电伏特 (MeV)	尔 格 (erg)	卡 (cal)
1	9.31×10^2	1.492×10^{-3}	3.564×10^{-11}
1.074×10^2	1	1.602×10^{-6}	3.827×10^{-14}
6.705×10^2	6.242×10^3	1	2.389×10^{-8}
2.807×10^{10}	2.613×10^{13}	4.187×10^7	

1 焦耳 = 10^7 尔格

1 兆电子伏特 = 4.450×10^{-20} 千瓦·时 = 1.519×10^{-16} 英热单位